BARBARA S[illegible]

Beginning Bridge

BARBARA SEAGRAM • LINDA LEE

Master Point Press
331 Douglas Ave.
Toronto, Ontario, Canada
M5M 1H2
(416) 781-0351
Website: http://www.masterpointpress.com
Email: info@masterpointpress.com

Library and Archives Canada Cataloguing in Publication

Seagram, Barbara
Barbara Seagram's beginning bridge / written by Barbara Seagram and Linda Lee.

ISBN 978-1-897106-33-4

1. Contract bridge. I. Lee, Linda (Linda Marcia), 1947- II. Title. I. Title: Beginning bridge.

GV1282.3.S418 2008 795.41'5 C2008-902053-7

We acknowledge the financial support of the Government of Canada through the Book Publishing Industry Development Program (BPIDP) for our publishing activities.

Editor	Ray Lee
Copy editing	Suzanne Hocking
Interior format	Sarah Howden
Cover and interior design	Olena S. Sullivan/New Mediatrix
Cover photo	Olena S. Sullivan

Printed in Canada

1 2 3 4 5 6 7 12 11 10 09 08

TABLE OF CONTENTS

To my wonderful kids, Heather & Christopher Seagram, who had more freedom than most children due to our obsessive preoccupation with the greatest game on earth: bridge. They are now delightful adults. One day, they'll even take up bridge!

— *Barbara Seagram*

For my elegant mother, Toby Waldman, who loves bridge almost as much as I do.

— *Linda Lee*

Introduction

Contract bridge is now almost one hundred years old. It has maintained its popularity over all these years because it is a game of unending fascination. It has something for everyone. It is a social game played by four people, so you have a partner to work with and support. It is a game of problem solving. It is a game that you can play for love or for money.

Even if you have never played any card game before, by the time you finish this book you will be ready to sit down and play a friendly game. You will also be able to play bridge online at one of several online bridge-playing communities. Most online sites have teachers who will be happy to work with you to develop your skills. Or you can go to your local bridge club, which may have games every day or be a once-a-week club located in a golf club or recreation center.

Playing bridge does not require much equipment. There are just a few items that you will need: a deck of playing cards, some comfortable chairs and a table. While this book can be used with a teacher in a classroom setting, it is specifically designed to allow you to learn the game at home by yourself or together with friends. If you are going to work through the lessons with some friends, it is best if each of you has a deck of cards to set up the practice deals.

Some readers will be familiar with card games or may even have played some bridge before. If you are among them, you will find Chapter 1 a bit redundant. It contains some information you will already know and moves along quite slowly. Bear with us. Read Chapter 1 anyway — at the very least, read the end-of-chapter summary and make sure you know everything it contains. If the concepts are familiar, then move through them quickly. We will soon arrive at material that is new to you.

A final word: don't try to finish the book in a weekend. Take each chapter slowly and carefully. Make sure you understand everything in it before you move on. If you are like us, learning to play bridge will be the start of a lifetime of happy experiences — no need to rush!

Good luck!

Barbara Seagram
Linda Lee

1 Getting the Idea

DID YOU KNOW?

The earliest known deck of playing cards is from China, and dates from more than 1000 years ago . However, there is some suggestion that playing cards actually originated in India. Ardhanari, a goddess in Hindu mythology, was represented holding in her four hands a wand, a cup, a sword and a ring (for wealth), symbols that appeared almost unchanged on medieval cards. Eventually, these 'suits' morphed into the familiar clubs, hearts, spades and diamonds.

WHAT YOU'RE GOING TO LEARN

This chapter will introduce you to the basic concepts of the game of bridge. By the end of the chapter, although you will not yet be ready to join a game at your local bridge club, you will understand how the game works. If you have already played similar card games, such as euchre or whist, you may find that this chapter moves slowly. We suggest that you skip over any parts that you find boring and advance to the sections that are new to you.

We will start at the very beginning — how to deal out the cards. You are then going to progress through all of the major aspects of the game. You will find out about the auction where players bid to decide the goal for each deal. You will then learn about the different roles players take on during the play of the cards — defender, declarer and dummy (don't worry, the name isn't personal!). You will be guided through the play of a bridge deal. You will discover the concept of trumps and have a chance to try your hand at the two types of bridge contracts, trump and notrump.

You will also learn a little about scoring, because it will factor into some of your decisions during the auction. Scoring will be explained in more detail in later chapters.

How to Play Bridge

Welcome to the wonderful world of bridge! Bridge is a social game played among four people sitting around a table. If there are four of you starting out together, introduce yourself to the person sitting across from you. Bridge is a partnership game and the person across the table is your partner, someone to be respected and nurtured. The people on either side of you are your worthy opponents.

In bridge, it is usual to use the compass directions to talk about the four players around the table. We're going to do that in this book. It might be helpful to create a guide card. Draw this diagram on a piece of paper:

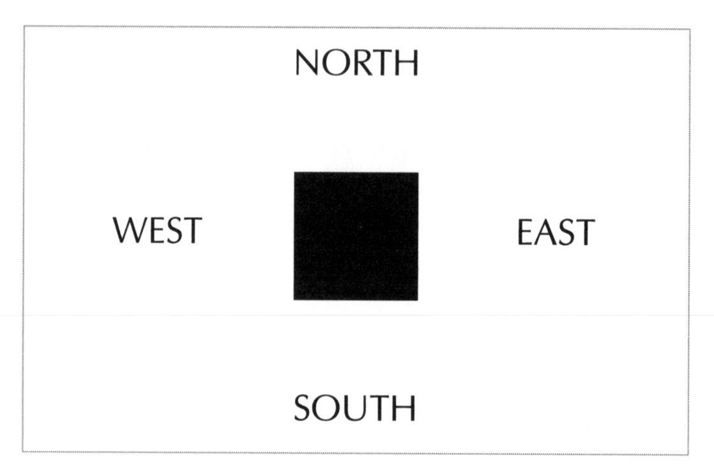

Don't worry about placing the guide card so that North faces the real North pole. (The actual geography doesn't matter.) If you are following this chapter in a group of four, then you should be sitting at one of the four compass points. That means that North and South are partners, and East and West are partners. If you are reading this by yourself, then we are going to suggest that you arbitrarily consider yourself to be South. From now on, when we show hand diagrams, we are going to refer to each player by their direction.

Pull four cards from the deck and place one face down in front of each player. Starting with East (for now) and going clockwise, each player should put their card face up on the table in front of them. You have just played a **trick**.

> ***"Trick"***
> **During the play, each player in turn, going clockwise, places a card face up on the table until four cards have been played.**

Dealing the Cards

Whoever is designated South should pick up the whole deck and shuffle it. Now deal out all fifty-two cards, face down, one at a time to each player, starting on your left (West) and going clockwise. You will end up placing the last card in front of yourself. All players can now pick up their cards. The collection of cards you are holding is called your **hand**. Notice that you have thirteen cards in your hand (fifty-two divided by four). Thirteen is an important number in bridge, as we'll see over and over again. All four hands taken together (all fifty-two cards) are called a **deal**.

The player who dealt the cards is called the **dealer** — this may seem a redundant statement, but knowing which player is the dealer is important for another reason, as we shall see shortly.

Sort your thirteen cards into suits. Group all of the hearts together, all of the diamonds together, all of the spades together and all of the clubs together. Then sort the cards in each suit from highest to lowest ranking. In bridge, the ace is the highest card in a suit and the deuce is the lowest. Keeping track of your cards is easier if you alternate the red suits and the black suits. This is an example of the kind of pattern you should see in front of you:

"Dealer"
The player who distributes the cards at the start of a deal.

"Hand"
The thirteen cards a bridge player is dealt.

"Deal"
The distribution of fifty-two cards dealt around the table to all four players.

You can put your hand down again for now. Let's move on to some new concepts. You are going to have a chance to play in a moment.

How to Play the Cards

We saw earlier that when each player has contributed one card, the resulting package of four cards is called a **trick**. Since each player has thirteen cards, the entire deal is going to consist of thirteen tricks. When no one has any cards left, it will be time for a new deal. The person who plays the first card to a trick is said to **lead** to the trick. The very first card played in a deal is called the **opening lead**. For the sake of example, let's suppose that West is the opening leader and he has led the ◊2.

Going clockwise (to the left), each player in turn plays a card to the trick. After West leads, North plays a card, followed by East and then South — but there is a catch: everyone must play a card of the suit led to the trick if they have one. This is called **following suit**. In this case, where the ◇2 was led, everyone must play a diamond if they can. If a player has no diamonds at all, then he can play any card he chooses; this is called a **discard**. Whoever plays the highest card in the suit led is the winner of the trick. In our example, where the ◇2 was led, the highest diamond played to the trick will be the winner.

◇ 8

N

W E

S

◇ 2 ◇ A

◇ 5

Imagine that after West leads the ◇2, the play continues with North playing the ◇8, East the ◇A, and South playing the ◇5. Who has won the trick?

East has won the trick, since East played the highest diamond, the ace. In fact, since we are playing in partnerships, East and West are both winners. It is the total number of tricks taken by East and West together that counts. Let's look at another trick. This time the trick starts with West playing the ♠4 and continues clockwise like the deal shown below.

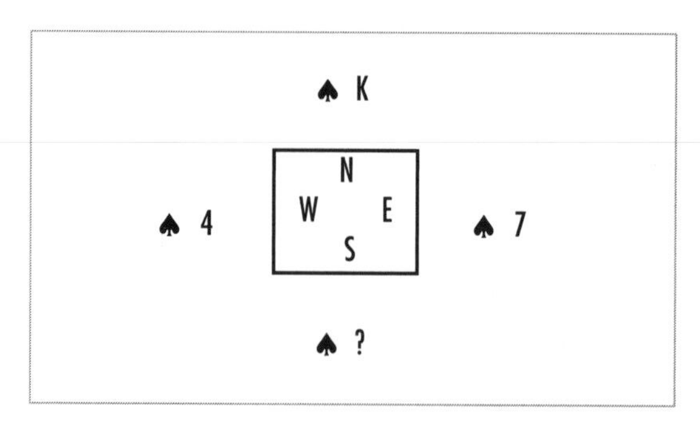

Suppose that South has the ♠A. There is no need to play that card. Do you see why? *Because South's partner has already won the trick for their side.* There is no need to win the trick twice, so South will play his lowest spade.

The player who wins the trick leads to the next trick. In our first example, East's ◇A won the trick. Now East can pick any card he wants and lead it to the next trick. In the second case, North won the trick and it is up to him to start the next trick off. Each time, all of the other players must follow suit if they can. If they can't follow suit, then they must discard. The player making the discard knows he won't win the trick, since only the highest card of the suit led matters, so he will usually choose a small card.

Keeping Track of Tricks

There are two ways to keep track of who won each trick. Usually, when you play at home, each card is tossed into the middle of the table as it is played. At the end of the trick, one player from the side that won the trick will gather the four cards together and place the packet face down in front of them. At the end of the deal, you can count the number of packets in front of your side to check how many tricks you have won. It is best to designate one player from each partnership to collect the tricks.

In a lesson, or when you play competitive bridge, you may want to keep track of exactly what happened during the deal. For this reason, you should not mush the trick together. Instead, you should place each of your cards face down in front of you in order as it is played. If your side has won a trick, position the card so it is lying vertically, as if standing tall in celebration. If you lost the trick, then lay the trick down on its side in defeat. At the end of the deal, you and your partner will each have a row of cards in front of you that looks something like this:

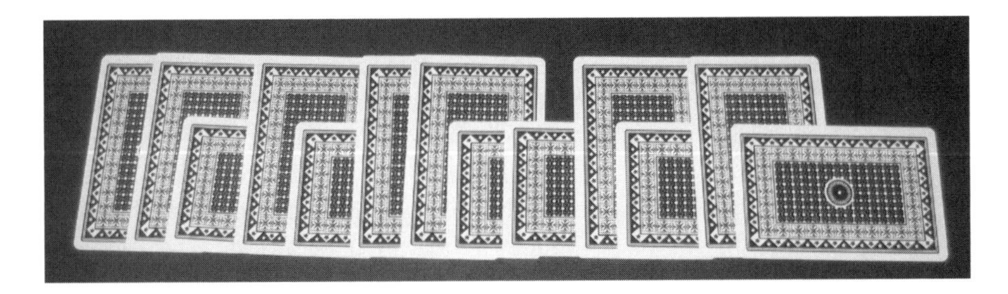

In this example, seven tricks point up and six tricks are lying down, adding up to the thirteen tricks in a bridge deal. Your side has won seven tricks. The row of tricks in front of you should look identical to the row in front of your partner across the table. If you keep track of the play in this fashion, at the end of the deal you will know exactly what happened on each trick and each player's hand will be kept separate for discussion purposes.

Playing Your First Deal

Pick up the hand that was dealt to you a few minutes ago. Hold it in one hand and fan it out so that you can see all of the cards. Remember to hold your cards in such a way that only you can see them. Bridge is a game of hidden cards and partial information. If your opponents see your hand, they will have an advantage.

If there are four of you, have West lead a card and then play out the deal, keeping your cards concealed at all times. Try to take as many tricks as you can for your side. If you are alone, place each hand face up in the correct compass position around the table. You are going to get to play all four of the hands.

In either case, start with West who leads a card, and then follow suit around the table. The player who wins a trick leads to the next trick. When you complete a trick, turn the card face down pointing vertically or horizontally as appropriate. Keep going until you have played all of the cards. When you have played all thirteen tricks, the deal is over. There should be no more cards in anyone's hand. You can count up your tricks and see how you did.

You have just played your first bridge deal!

Trump Contracts

Now things get a little more interesting: we are going to introduce the concept of a **trump suit**. Up until now, the highest card played in the suit led always won the trick. When there is a trump suit, matters become more complicated. A trump suit is a special suit that has magical powers. Well, not really — but a card played in the trump suit will beat any card played in an ordinary suit. If more than one trump is played, then the highest trump played will win the trick. However, you must still follow suit if possible, so you may only choose to play a trump if you are out of cards in the suit led.

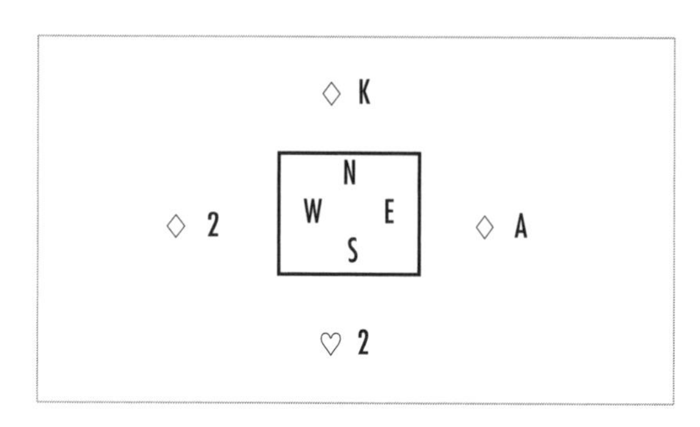

For now, let's suppose the trump suit is hearts. West leads the ♢2. If this is the trick, who wins?

South wins the trick because he played a trump. Yes, that ♡2 beats East's ♢A, because it is a trump. Of course, South still has to follow suit if possible. Therefore, if South had a diamond, he would not have been able to play the trump. So, in our example, South has no diamonds.

Playing a trump when a different suit has been led is called **trumping** or **ruffing**. You may have heard someone say, 'I can't believe partner trumped my ace.' That's because he had already won the trick with the ace and didn't want his partner to waste a trump winning the trick for their side a second time.

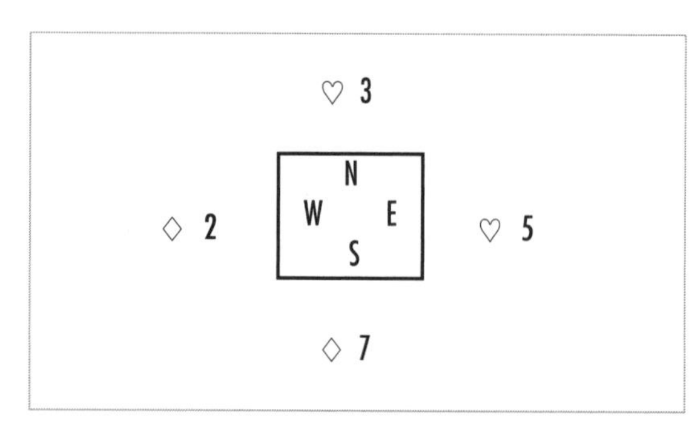

What about this trick? Hearts are still trumps and again West leads the ♢2.

East wins the trick because he played the highest trump. If you like, you can deal out the cards and play through an entire deal with hearts as the trump suit and see how it goes. Bridge deals can be played with or without trumps. When you play without a trump suit, you are said to be playing the deal in **notrump**. The very first deal you played was in notrump.

The Auction

Now look at this deal (top of next page). Lay it out on the table and leave it there. You are going to play this deal a little later on.

If you were North-South, what suit would you like to pick as the trump suit? You should pick spades (although clubs is also a possibility). Why? Because you would have many more trumps than your opponents and would be able to win a lot of tricks with your cards in the trump suit. When the defenders tried to play their high cards in other suits, you would be able to trump them. What if you were East-West? In that case, you would pick hearts or diamonds as the trump suit.

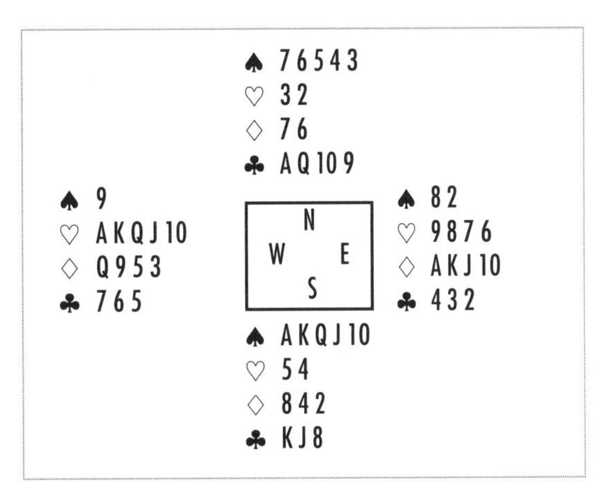

As it turns out, if you are North-South your side can make nine tricks with either spades or clubs as trumps. If you are East-West, you can make nine tricks with either hearts or diamonds as trumps. As you can see, being the side to select the trump suit is a considerable advantage.

In bridge, the players select the trump suit by means of an **auction**. A bridge auction is very much like an auction where you might buy some furniture or an antique. During the auction, each side bids for the right to choose the trump suit. However, in a bridge auction, you don't bid dollars, you bid tricks. The final bid made in the auction is called the **contract**. The side that makes the winning bid has set the trump suit and contracted to make a specific number of tricks.

In a bridge deal, there are thirteen tricks available, so (pardon the pun) it is no trick at all to take six of them when you get to name the trump suit, since that is less than half of the total. So we simplify. When you make a bid in the auction, the first six tricks are taken for granted — they are just added in. Therefore when you bid 1♠, you are in fact promising that your side will take *seven* tricks with spades as trumps — the first six *and* the one you bid. The first six tricks are called **book**. (Don't ask us where the name came from!) 'Making book' means that you have won six tricks. The number of additional tricks over book that are needed to make your contract depends on the amount of your winning bid: one more trick if you bid one; two more if you bid two, and so on.

"Contract"

The final bid of the auction. It identifies the trump suit and the number of tricks that must be taken by the partnership that won the auction.

When we talk about scoring, you'll see that you get points for making your contract, and lose points if you bid too much and don't make it.

The minimum bid you can make in a suit is one, promising to take seven tricks. The maximum bid you can make is '7' (7 + 6 = 13, which is the maximum number of tricks it is possible to take on any deal), so a bid of seven of anything is a contract to take all of the tricks. That is called a **grand slam**. It is very exciting, but it doesn't happen very often. If you bid to the six-level, i.e. you make a bid of 6♣, 6♢, 6♡, 6♠ or 6NT, you are bidding a **small slam**. Bidding at the six-level means that your side is promising to take twelve tricks — that is all of the tricks but one. When we complete our discussion of the scoring later in the book, you will find out that you get a big bonus if you bid and make a slam.

"Slam"

A contract at the six- or seven-level.

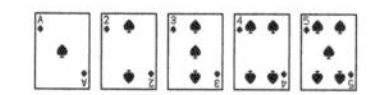

LET'S TRY IT!

How many tricks are you committing your partnership to take when you make each of the following bids? What will be the trump suit in each case?

a) 3♣
b) 5♢
c) 6♡
d) 7NT

Answers:

a) You promise to take nine tricks (six plus three) with clubs as trumps.
b) You promise to take eleven tricks (six plus five) with diamonds as trumps.
c) You promise to take twelve tricks (six plus six) with hearts as trumps. This is all of the tricks but one and is called a small slam
d) You promise to take thirteen tricks (six plus seven) in notrump — there will not be a trump suit when the deal is played. A seven-level contract is all of the tricks. It is called a grand slam. Making one is one of the great moments in bridge.

Bidding and the Auction... Climbing the Stairs

Starting with the dealer and going clockwise, each player in turn has a chance to bid. If you don't want to bid, you can say 'pass' and the turn passes to the next player on your left. The auction continues with each player either passing or making a higher bid. The auction ends when three players in turn say 'pass' to indicate that they do not want to make another bid. To recap, players keep making higher bids or passing until three passes in a row finalize the last bid.

REMEMBER THIS! ☑
You must bid up the ladder.

As in any auction, your bid must be higher than the previous bid. Obviously, if your bid promises to take more tricks, it is higher. What if you want to offer to take the same number of tricks, but in a different suit? To handle this situation, the suits themselves are ranked. The lowest suit is clubs and the next up is diamonds: these suits are called **minor suits**. Next in rank is hearts and, after that, spades: these are called the **major suits**. Did you notice that the higher the suit, the higher up in the alphabet it is? That may help you remember the order. So a bid of 1♠ is a higher bid than a bid of 1♡, but a bid of 1♢ is a lower bid than 1♡. Last and highest is notrump, so a bid of 1NT is higher than any of the suit bids at the one-level. Notrump is highest because it is generally considered the most challenging contract to play; later you will see why.

Let's see how this works in practice. Suppose you are South; East, your right-hand opponent, deals and bids 1♡. Now it is your turn. If you want to bid 1♠, you can do so, because spades rank higher than hearts. You could also bid 1NT, as that too is a higher bid than 1♡. You cannot bid 1♣, however, because clubs are a lower-ranking suit and that bid is therefore lower than East's 1♡ bid. If you want to bid clubs, you must bid at least 2♣ — any bid at the two-level is higher than any bid at the one-level. Even though clubs are lower ranking than hearts, your 2♣ bid is higher than 1♡, since you are committing to take more tricks.

Think about an apartment building with seven floors. In this apartment building, there are five steps between the floors. The lowest step on each floor is clubs, then diamonds, followed by hearts, spades and notrump. You can go *up* the steps, but never *down*. (Fortunately, there are never any fire alarms in this building!)

So if one player bids 1♡, he is on the third step of the first floor. If the next player wants to bid diamonds, he can't bid 1♢, since that would involve walking down a step. He must keep going higher and bid at least 2♢.

Bidding in bridge is a language. It has only twelve basic words: the numbers from one to seven, the four suits and notrump. There are also three other words, the most important of these being the word 'pass'. As you have seen, 'pass' says that you do not want to make a bid — you are passing your turn in the auction. The remaining two words are 'double' and 'redouble'. These are not words you will use just yet in your bridge career, so we aren't going to spend any more time on them in this chapter.

7NT	**Floor 7**
7♠	
7♡	
7♢	
7♣	
6NT	**Floor 6**
6♠	
6♡	
6♢	
6♣	
5NT	**Floor 5**
5♠	
5♡	
5♢	
5♣	
4NT	**Floor 4**
4♠	
4♡	
4♢	
4♣	
3NT	**Floor 3**
3♠	
3♡	
3♢	
3♣	
2NT	**Floor 2**
2♠	
2♡	
2♢	
2♣	
1NT	**Floor 1**
1♠	
1♡	
1♢	
1♣	

LET'S TRY IT!

1. You hold a good hand with lots of hearts and you want to suggest them as trumps. What is the lowest possible bid you can make in hearts if the previous bid was:

a) 1♠
b) 1♢

2. South, your partner, opens the bidding with 1♡. West, the opponent on your right, now bids 2♣. You want to show your partner that you like hearts too and are prepared to outbid West. What is the lowest possible heart bid you can make?

3. South, your partner, deals and opens the bidding with 1♡. Your right-hand opponent (West) now bids 2♢. You want to outbid West and suggest clubs as a trump suit. What is the lowest bid with which you could do this? How many tricks does your bid commit your side to take with clubs as trumps?

Answers

1. **a)** 2♡. Since hearts are lower ranking than spades, you must go up one level.
   b) 1♡. You don't need to go to 'the second floor', since hearts are higher ranking than diamonds.

2. 2♡ is the lowest possible heart bid, since hearts are higher ranking than clubs.

3. You have to go to the third floor and bid 3♣, since clubs are lower ranking than diamonds. You are committing your side to take nine tricks (six plus three) with clubs as trumps.

A Little About Scoring

We will talk more about scoring later, but for now we will simply talk about the points you get for making a contract or defeating one. If you bid and make a contract, you score a little more for playing in a major suit than in a minor suit. A major suit scores 30 points for each trick you bid (as usual, not counting book, the first six), but only if you make your contract. So if you bid 2♡ or 2♠ and make your eight tricks, you will get a trick score of 30 multiplied by 2, or 60 points. If you do not make eight tricks, then you have failed to make your contract and your opponents will get points instead of you. They will get at least 50 points a trick for each one you were short by (you will see later exactly how many points they get). You can see that it is important not to bid too much, since you want to be reasonably sure you can make your contract.

If you play in a minor suit, you will get 20 points per trick, assuming you have fulfilled your contract. So 3♣ making nine tricks gives you the same 60 points as 2♡ or 2♠ making eight tricks. In notrump, you get 30 points a trick, except for the first trick, which is worth 40 — so 1NT making seven tricks is worth 40 points, while 3NT making nine tricks is worth 100.

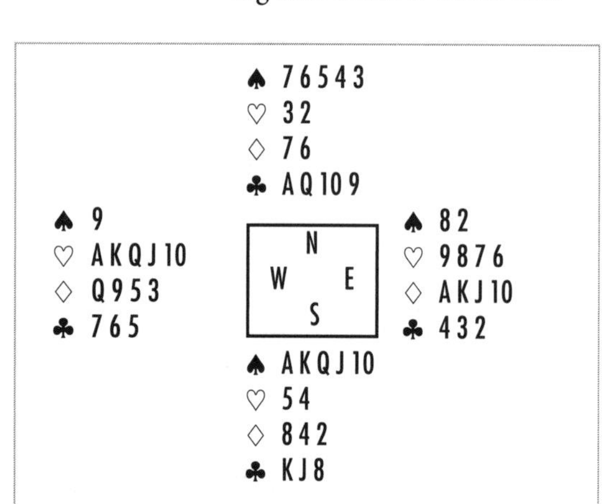

The Language of Bidding

Since bridge is a partnership game, you need to use the language of bidding to tell partner about your hand so that the partnership as a whole can decide the best place to play.

Back to the deal on the table (left). South is the dealer and the dealer always has the first chance to bid (a reward for the extra work of dealing the cards!). As South, you have a good hand with lots of spades, so suppose you bid 1♠. West has a bunch of hearts and wants to tell his partner about them. What does he bid? It has to be 2♡ — he can't bid 1♡, because he has to go up the steps and never down. Next, it's North's turn and he likes spades. He is able to bid 2♠, because it is a step up from 2♡. East likes hearts, but he has to keep going up from 2♠, so he must bid 3♡. South and West pass and North bids 3♠, since he still wants to compete in the auction. At this point, the next three players pass and the auction is over. Remember, the auction always ends with three passes, giving everyone one last chance to bid. Now spades have been chosen as trumps and North-South together must take nine tricks to make their contract.

Don't worry for now about knowing how high to bid: we'll talk about that later. For now, we just want to show you how the auction works.

Declarer and the Dummy

The player who initially bids the suit that becomes his side's final contract gets to play the deal. He is called the **declarer**. Note that his partner may make the final bid in the auction, but that does not influence who becomes declarer.

> ***"Declarer"***
> **The player who first named the trump suit for the side that won the auction. Declarer decides what to play to each trick from both his hand and dummy.**

Being declarer is a special privilege, as you will see. The person on declarer's left is the **opening leader** and starts the play by leading to the first trick. Once the opening lead is made, declarer's partner puts all of his cards face up on the table. His hand is known as the **dummy**. (Calling it the dummy is not a comment on your partner, who usually has been nice enough to let your suit be trumps. It is simply the name of the hand on the table.) When it is your turn to lay down a dummy, make sure to put the trump suit on your right — declarer's left. This is something that bridge players use as a memory aid. If you are ever unsure about which suit is trumps, you can check in dummy.

For the duration of the play, bridge becomes a three-person game. On each trick, the declarer decides which card to play from both his hand *and* the dummy at their respective turns. His goal is to take enough tricks to meet the commitment made by his side during the bidding.

> ***"Dummy"***
> **Partner's hand, which is laid face up on the table after the opening lead.**

The opening leader and his partner are called **defenders**. Their goal is to prevent declarer from taking all of the tricks he needs to make his contract. In this case (the contract is 3♠, remember), South needs to take at least nine tricks to make his contract. If East-West can take five tricks, South will not be able to take more than eight, and he will **go down** in his contract.

When you play at home, the player who has put down the dummy is allowed to step away from the bridge table for the duration of the deal. Meanwhile declarer may reach across the table to play dummy's cards himself and gather the tricks that he has won into a pile in front of him. When you play competitively or in lessons, however, you have a lot of work to do as dummy. Declarer does not physically play the cards from dummy, but calls out the card he wants played; your job is to detach the card from dummy and place it on the table in front of you. This is to indicate that the card has been played. When the trick is over, you must lay the card face down behind the unplayed cards, either pointing up (you won the trick) or lying down (you lost the trick).

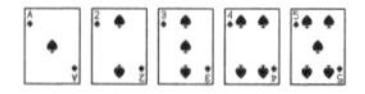

LET'S TRY IT!

South bids 1♡, West passes, North bids 2♡ and everyone else now passes.

1. What is the contract?
2. What are trumps and how many tricks do North-South have to take?
3. Who is declarer?
4. Who leads to the first trick?
5. Who puts their hand down on the table?
6. Who plays second and third to the first trick?

Answers

1. The contract is 2♡.
2. Hearts are trumps and North-South must take eight tricks.
3. South is declarer because he bid hearts first, even though North's 2♡ bid named the final contract.
4. West makes the opening lead since he is sitting on declarer's left.
5. Declarer's partner's hand becomes the dummy. North puts his hand down on the table face up after the opening lead.
6. Dummy plays second, which means declarer calls the card from dummy. East plays third.

A Bidding Diagram

In this book, we will show auctions by using a bidding diagram. Here is an example:

West	North	East	South
	pass	1♡	1♠
2♡	2♠	all pass	

Our diagrams always show West on the left. However, West will not always bid first, since the position of dealer will change with each deal. In the example diagram, North is the dealer and makes the first bid. He starts the auction with a pass and East then opens the bidding with 1♡. South bids 1♠. West bids 2♡ and North bids 2♠. Now all three players pass, ending the auction. In our diagrams, the final three passes will always be represented as 'all pass'.

LET'S TRY IT!

West	North	East	South
	1♡	2♣	2♡
3♣	all pass		

In the example shown:

1. What is the contract?
2. Who is declarer?
3. What suit is trumps, and how many tricks does declarer have to take?
4. Who is the opening leader?

Answers

1. The contract is 3♣, since it was the last bid of the auction before all three remaining players passed.
2. East is declarer, since he was the first one to bid clubs on his side.
3. Clubs are trumps, and declarer must take nine tricks (6 + 3).
4. Since East is declarer, South makes the opening lead before dummy comes down.

THE PLAY OF THE HAND

Drawing Trumps

Before you finally get to play the deal we showed you on page 7, we are going to talk about one very important idea that applies to trump contracts. Usually when you play a trump contract, your side has many more trumps than your opponents. Look at the spade suit in the deal still on the table. (You can temporarily turn the other cards face down if they are distracting you.)

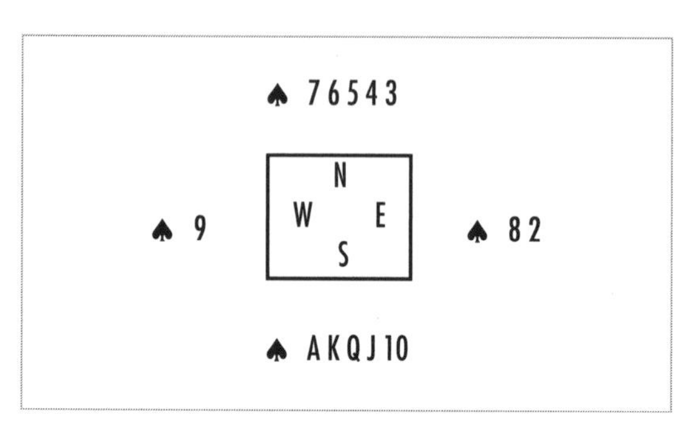

Assume spades are trumps. You have ten trumps including all of the high ones and the opponents have only three. You do not want the opponents to win any tricks with their little trumps. Can you see how you can prevent them from doing so? *As soon as you can, lead a high trump.* After you win this trick, you will lead another high trump. Since the opponents are forced to follow suit, by the end of these two spade tricks, all of their trumps will be gone. If one of the opponents had three trumps and the other had none, then you would have to play three rounds of trumps to remove all of your opponents' small trumps. The act of leading high trumps to remove the opponents trumps is called **drawing trumps**. Some people call it 'pulling' trumps or, facetiously, 'getting the kiddies off the street'.

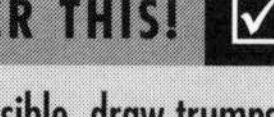

Whenever possible, draw trumps so that the defenders cannot trump your winners with their little trumps.

We suggest that you keep count of the trump suit so that you know how many trumps your opponents have and how many rounds of trumps you will need to play in order to draw them. The best way to count trumps is to count trump tricks. If everyone follows suit, then four trumps have been played on a trick. You must also remember to count any trumps that may have been played when a different suit was led.

After you have drawn the opponents' trumps, it is usually right not to lead trumps any more. You should save these extra trumps as you will often need them later.

Deal 1

Okay, it is finally time to play the deal you laid out earlier. The contract is 3♠ by South (i.e. South is declarer). If you are playing with four people, everyone should pick up their hands. On this deal, we are going to suggest that West, the opening leader, leads the ♡A, since it is likely to win the trick. Also, West has all of the high hearts. As you'll see, leading from a sequence of top cards is usually a good idea. North should now put down the dummy.

North: ♠ 7 6 5 4 3 ♡ 3 2 ◇ 7 6 ♣ A Q 10 9
West: ♠ 9 ♡ A K Q J 10 ◇ Q 9 5 3 ♣ 7 6 5
East: ♠ 8 2 ♡ 9 8 7 6 ◇ A K J 10 ♣ 4 3 2
South: ♠ A K Q J 10 ♡ 5 4 ◇ 8 4 2 ♣ K J 8

Before you read on, play out the deal with each side trying to take as many tricks as possible.

South: did you take nine tricks and make your contract? Nine tricks are always available to South in spades, so the defenders shouldn't feel too bad if they could not prevent declarer from making his contract.

Quite likely West will play another heart after his ace wins the first trick, so he will win the second trick too. Seeing that there are no more hearts in dummy, West will probably switch to either a club or a diamond at Trick 3. If West switches to a diamond, East can take two diamond tricks. After this, whatever East leads, declarer can win the trick with either a high card or a trump. Let's say that East leads back a third diamond. Since dummy has no more diamonds, declarer can trump this third round of diamonds in dummy. Now declarer should draw trumps. To do this, he leads a spade from dummy and plays the ace of spades. Since everyone follows to this trick, four trumps are now accounted for; declarer also trumped the third diamond in dummy, so that is five trumps gone. Declarer can see seven more spades between his hand and dummy, for a total of twelve. That means there is still a lurker in one of the defenders' hands. Declarer should play one more high trump. After that, declarer can safely take his club and spade tricks.

Deal 2

On this deal, you are going to have an opportunity to make a slam! Remember, a slam is when you bid to the six- or seven-level. West is declarer in 6◇ (South doesn't play *all* of the hands!). The opening lead is the ♡K, by North, after which East puts down his hand as dummy. See if you (West) can make the contract.

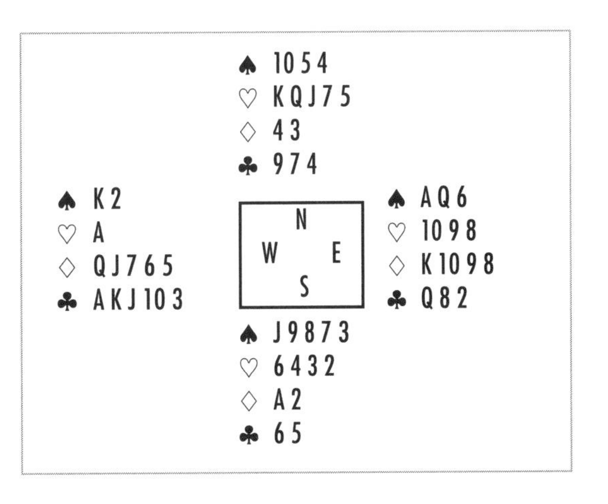

Play out the deal first and then read on.

First, West wins the ♡A in hand perforce. (It's his only heart!) Declarer has lots of tricks, but he does have to draw trumps. Unfortunately, he doesn't have the ace of trumps, but there is no need to despair — he should lead a trump anyway, playing a high diamond from one of the two hands (any of the king, queen, jack, ten or nine will do, since they are all equals). This will force South to use his ace to win the trick. South will likely return a heart, which West will ruff. In any case, declarer will be able to win the trick. West will then lead another trump, pulling all of the remaining trumps from the North-South hands. At this point, declarer can cash his club and spade winners and then his good trumps. Making six!

CHAPTER SUMMARY

A Bridge is a four-person game played by two partnerships. Each player begins with thirteen cards; the ace is the highest card in each suit.

B To begin the deal, each player in turn, starting with the dealer, may bid for the final contract. Bids begin at '1', which represents a commitment to take seven tricks with the named suit as trumps. Each successive bid must be higher than the previous bid. Any bid that commits to more tricks is automatically a higher bid. The suits are also ranked (from low to high) within each numerical level: clubs, diamonds, hearts, spades. A bid of notrump ranks higher than spades. A player may pass at his turn, rather than making a bid. The auction ends after there has been a bid and then three successive players pass. If no one opens the bidding, the hand is "passed out" and is not played.

C The player who first named the final denomination (a suit or notrump) is declarer, and the player on his left makes the opening lead. Declarer's partner then places his hand face up as the dummy. Declarer controls the play of dummy's cards at its turn.

D Play goes clockwise, each player in turn contributing one card to make up a trick (a complete deal is thirteen tricks).

E Each player must follow suit if possible. If he cannot follow suit, he may play anything he wishes, usually discarding an unimportant small card. The highest card of the suit led wins the trick. The player who wins the trick leads to the next trick.

F If a suit has been designated as trumps, then the highest trump played wins the trick. A trump may be played when a player cannot follow suit to a trick; a trump may also be led.

G In a trump contract, it is usually a good idea for declarer to draw the opponents' trumps early in the deal to prevent the defense from making tricks with their small trumps.

H If declarer makes his contract, his side gains points; the number of points scored depends on the denomination and the level of the contract. If he fails, the opponents score points instead.

2 Opening the Bidding

DID YOU KNOW?

It's very unlikely that you will encounter the same hand twice in your bridge career: there are 635,013,559,600 possible hands you can be dealt. The number of ways that all 52 cards can be dealt to four players is truly staggering: it contains 29 digits!

WHAT YOU'RE GOING TO LEARN

One of the challenges when playing bridge is to decide just how good a hand you have. In this chapter, we will introduce a points system to help you evaluate your hand. You will learn the requirements for opening the bidding and how to decide on your opening bid, since your choice gives important information to partner. We will also get you started on important concepts for both defending and playing the hand. We will demonstrate a method for making extra tricks that works for both declarer and the defenders, and you will learn how to throw away a losing card on a winner in another suit. For the defenders, we will discuss how to select the opening lead and what it tells the opening leader's partner. We will also reveal our own favorite opening lead.

Counting Your High Card Points

As you have seen, it is an advantage to be able to name the trump suit. You bid in the auction to get that privilege. But how do you determine the number of tricks you and your partner can win? How can you tell if you have a good enough hand to bid at all? Bidding is such a simple language with so few words — how much can you tell partner about your hand?

In the 1950s, Charles Goren codified a system of bidding that is still commonly used in North America. It is called Standard American. Goren found a way to make evaluating hands very simple: his method is called Point Count.

REMEMBER THIS!

Card	Points
Ace	4
King	3
Queen	2
Jack	1

In this method, all bridge hands are assigned a point value. To figure out how many points your hand is worth, you look at the honor cards — the aces, kings, queens and jacks. It's very easy to remember the point values because the lowest honor card, the jack, is worth 1 point. You add one more point each time as you walk up the ladder of honors, so that a queen is worth 2 points, a king 3 and the ace gets 4 points. As you probably noticed when you played deals in Chapter 1, aces almost always take tricks, so you can see why they have such a high value. Here is one shortcut that may make it easier for you to count your hand: if you have an ace, a king, a queen and a jack (a royal family), together they add up to 10 points.

The first thing you do when you look at your hand is count your high card points (referred to as HCP from now on). Pretty well everyone who plays bridge, from novice to expert, counts their high card points this very same way, and they do it on every hand when they first examine their cards.

LET'S TRY IT!

For each of the following example hands, add up your high card points.

1. ♠ A K Q J ♡ Q 3 2 ♢ 10 9 8 ♣ A 3 2
2. ♠ 10 5 ♡ A K 9 2 ♢ Q J 7 6 5 ♣ K 2
3. ♠ J 10 9 8 7 6 ♡ 7 2 ♢ J 10 3 2 ♣ 9
4. ♠ 9 8 7 6 5 ♡ 9 3 2 ♢ 9 8 2 ♣ 8 3

Answers

1. You have 16 high card points.
2. You have 13 high card points.
3. You have 2 high card points.
4. You have no high card points at all. A hand this bad, lacking even a ten, has a special name — it is called a yarborough.

Counting Your Distribution

You still have one more task ahead of you. Which of these hands do you think will take more tricks?

Hand A

♠ A K Q J 5 ♡ 3 ◇ 4 3 ♣ K Q J 10 3

or

Hand B

♠ A K Q J ♡ 5 4 ◇ 7 6 5 ♣ K Q J 10

If you guessed the first one, you are right. It is an advantage to have long suits and short suits rather than to hold a hand with fairly even distribution. In fact, long suits are to die for! With a long suit, once the honors have been played, you will be able to take some tricks with the spot cards too. You will see in the play part of the chapter why having short suits can be helpful — you will be able to trump your opponents' kings, queens, jacks and sometimes even their aces.

There are two ways to count distribution points when you pick up your cards:

1. Counting short suits
   or
2. Counting long suits

Use one of these methods to count distribution points, but not both. Which method should you choose? Both methods work well and give similar, although not always identical, results. If you are in a class, your teacher will make a recommendation for you. If your bridge friends have a favorite method, then you will probably do it the same way. Otherwise, just use the method that seems most natural to you.

Method 1 - Counting Short Suits

Using short suit counting, you add distribution points for having short suits, which will deprive your opponents of tricks with their aces and kings. Your opponents will not be able to take all of their high card tricks in that suit because when you run out of that suit, you will be able to trump them. Let's say you have no cards in a suit at all (that's called a void). The opening leader proudly leads his ace and you can trump it right away. It is a big advantage to have a void in a suit in which the opponents hold a lot of high cards. When you have a void, you can count 3 distribution points. If you have one card in a suit, that card is called a singleton and you can count 2 distribution points. With two cards in a suit, you have a doubleton and can count 1 distribution point.

Method 1 - Counting Short Suits

Count your HCP and then add to them the following distribution points:
Distribution Points: Add points for any short suits (2 cards or shorter) as follows:

Void (no cards in a suit)	Add 3 points
Singleton (one card in a suit)	Add 2 points
Doubleton (two cards in a suit)	Add 1 point

Method 2 - Counting Long Suits

Count your HCP and then add to them the following distribution points:
Distribution Points: Add points for any long suits (5 cards or longer) as follows:

1 point for the fifth card in any long suit you have
1 point for the sixth card
1 point for the seventh card
etc.

Method 2 - Counting Long Suits

As we said earlier, long suits are wonderful. When you have long suits, you can take tricks even with little cards like twos and threes. If you have a six-card suit like this

A K Q J 3 2

you are likely to be able to take six tricks in this suit. Not only can you win tricks with your high cards, but after you play them, your opponents will have no cards in the suit and your 2 and 3 will each be worth a trick as well.

You always have at least one four-card suit, so a four-card suit is nothing special. If you have one or more suits that are five cards or longer, you have something worth celebrating. You add 1 point for the fifth card in a suit and another point for each extra card. Therefore, a six-card suit is worth 2 distribution points, a seven-card suit is worth 3 distribibition points, etc. If you have two five-card suits, then you get an extra point for each of them.

Once you have counted your high card points and your distribution points, add the two numbers together. The combined total will give you a value for your hand. If you have 13 HCP and 3 distribution points, your hand is worth 16 high card points. Let's look at an example:

♠ A K 7 ♡ A J 8 6 5 3 2 ◇ 5 ♣ 9 2

Using either method, start by adding your high cards. You have 12 HCP. Now, using Method 1, add your distribution points: a singleton (1 point) and a doubleton (2 points) for 3 distribution points. That makes a total of 15 points. Using Method 2, adding your HCP and your long-suit points, you also get a total of 15 points.

Most of the time, both methods come to approximately the same total. It is a matter of personal preference which style you use. You will be guided by your teacher or your friends. *Both methods are right.* It is even perfectly fine for you to be counting one way and your partner counting the other way. Don't try to convert your partner to counting points your way. It is unnecessary and ends up being frustrating!

LET'S TRY IT!

Count these example hands, this time adding distribution points. Use whichever method you prefer.

1. ♠ A K Q J ♡ Q 3 2 ◇ 10 9 8 ♣ A 3 2
2. ♠ 10 5 ♡ A K 9 ◇ Q J 7 6 5 ♣ K Q 2
3. ♠ J 10 9 8 7 6 ♡ 7 2 ◇ J 10 3 ♣ 9 2
4. ♠ 9 8 7 6 5 ♡ 9 3 2 ◇ 9 8 2 ♣ 8 3

Answers

1. You have 0 distribution points, since you have no long or short suits. Total: 16.
2. You have 1 distribution point. Total: 16.
3. You have 2 distribution points. Total: 4.
4. You have 1 distribution point. Total: 1.

Putting It All Together — Evaluating Your Hand

You have now counted both high card points and distribution. When you pick up your hand, you should count both kinds of points and add them together to provide a picture of the value of your hand. For example, suppose you have:

♠ A Q J 7 3 2 ♡ K J 2 ◇ A 3 ♣ 5 2

Add up the points. Did you get 17? This hand has 15 HCP and 2 distribution points. Here are a few more examples.

	HCP	Distribution	Total
♠ Q 7 6 ♡ A Q 10 9 8 7 ◇ 4 ♣ K J 2	12	2	14
♠ A K 5 4 ♡ Q J 10 ◇ 9 5 2 ♣ A 4 2	14	0	14
♠ K 5 ♡ 9 2 ◇ A K Q 10 9 8 ♣ A K 8	19	2	21

REMEMBER THIS! ☑

Each suit contains 10 HCP (the sum of the ace, king, queen and jack). That means that among all four players there is a total of 40 HCP. On average, each player will receive only a quarter of these points, or 10 HCP. That means that 10 HCP is an average hand. Of course, there will probably be some distribution points assigned as well, so an average hand will have a bit more than 10 points in total.

LET'S TRY IT!

For each of the following hands, count up your total points, including both HCP and distribution points.

1. ♠ A K Q ♡ A K Q 10 9 6 ◇ 7 2 ♣ K 3
2. ♠ 4 2 ♡ A Q J 7 6 ◇ A J 10 ♣ K Q 9
3. ♠ K J 9 7 5 3 2 ♡ — ◇ K Q J ♣ 7 6 3
4. ♠ 7 ♡ 10 ◇ K Q 10 9 8 7 5 4 ♣ A 8 7

Answers

1. This hand has 23 points. It has 21 HCP and 2 for distribution.
2. This hand has 18 points, 17 HCP and 1 for distribution.
3. This hand has 13 points, 10 HCP and 3 for distribution.
4. This hand has 13 points, 9 HCP and 4 for distribution.

Opening the Bidding

Okay, so you pick up your hand and count your points, both HCP and distribution. Assume for now that you are the dealer. You have the first chance to bid. How do you decide if you should open the bidding? In Standard American, we require a minimum of 13 total points (the bridge 'magic number') to open the bidding with one of a suit. This means that when you open, you will have a hand that is at least a little bit better than an average hand. With 13 points, you should always open the bidding. With 12 points or less, you should pass.

The Rule of 20

If you are counting short suits, then skip over this section. When you are counting long suits, you sometimes have a hand that has 11 or 12 points after counting both length and distribution. You theoretically do not have enough to open the bidding. You might have no long suits:

♠ A 8 6 5 ♡ A 7 4 3 ◇ A 6 5 4 ♣ 4

You have 12 HCP and no long-suit points. Take it from us, you will want to open the bidding on this hand. To make your final decision about whether to pass or open the bidding, use the Rule of 20 to evaluate your hand. Here's how it works.

Count up your HCP and then add in the lengths of your two longest suits. If the total comes to 20 or more, you have permission to open the bidding.
In the example above, your hand now adds to 20 (12 + 4 + 4).

Similarly:

♠ A K 8 6 3 ♡ K 7 4 3 2 ◇ 7 2 ♣ 4

You have 10 HCP. Using the rule of 20 you have:

REMEMBER THIS! 

If your hand measures up to the Rule of 20, you can now consider it an opening bid or the equivalent of 13 points.

10 HCP + 5 + 5 = 20 Open the bidding

If you are using the Rule of 20, don't get confused. You do not suddenly have a hand worth 20 points! The Rule of 20 is used only to decide on marginal hands whether you should or should not open the bidding.

Bidding or Passing

Remember that bidding is a language and everything you say or don't say carries a message. When you open one of a suit, you are telling your partner that you have a hand that meets the standards for an opening bid with at least 13 points (or it meets the Rule of 20 if you are using long-suit counting). By the same token, when you pass instead of opening, you are telling partner that you have fewer than 13 points.

With this hand, you should open the bidding:

♠ K Q J 8 3 ♡ A 5 4 2 ◇ Q 3 2 ♣ 5

But not with this hand:

♠ K Q 9 8 3 ♡ K 5 4 2 ◇ Q 3 2 ♣ 5

Opening the Bidding with 1NT

Now that you have decided to open the bidding, the next question is what bid to make. Let's look first at a very special opening bid: 1NT. It is special because it gives partner a very precise picture of your hand. An opening bid of 1NT promises exactly 15, 16 or 17 high card points. You are suggesting playing the deal in notrump because although you have a lot of high card points, you don't have any particular suit you want to play in. Your cards are evenly distributed between the suits. In fact, opening 1NT promises that you have no voids, no singletons and at most one doubleton. Hands like this are called **balanced** hands. If your hand has more distribution than this, you should be opening one of a suit instead.

> ***"Balanced Hand"***
> A hand with even distribution and no short suits — at most one doubleton.

Here is an example of a hand that is suitable for an opening 1NT bid.

♠ A Q 2 ♡ Q J 8 7 ◇ 10 7 6 ♣ A K 3

This is as balanced as you can be. We call this distribution 4-3-3-3 since you have one four-card suit and three three-card suits. You don't need to memorize this, but there are only a few specific distributions that qualify as balanced. They are 4-3-3-3, 5-3-3-2 or 4-4-3-2. Here are some other examples of hands suitable for opening 1NT.

> **REMEMBER THIS! ☑**
> With a balanced hand and exactly 15, 16 or 17 HCP, open 1NT. Do not count distributional points when bidding notrump.

a) ♠ J 6 ♡ Q 10 3 ◇ A Q 7 6 5 ♣ A K 2 — 16 HCP
b) ♠ A 10 9 3 ♡ A J 3 2 ◇ K 3 2 ♣ A J — 17 HCP

Hand (a) has 16 HCP and only one doubleton (it is 5-3-3-2 distribution). Hand (b) has 17 HCP and only one doubleton (it is 4-4-3-2 distribution).

Here are some hands that should not be opened 1NT:

c) ♠ J 6 ♡ Q 10 3 2 ◇ A Q 7 6 5 ♣ A K — 16 HCP
d) ♠ A 10 9 3 ♡ A Q 3 2 ◇ K 3 2 ♣ A J — 18 HCP

Hand (c) has two doubletons (it is 5-4-2-2 distribution). It is not balanced.
Hand (d) has 18 HCP — too many to open 1NT.

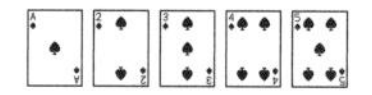

LET'S TRY IT
OPENING 1NT

Should these hands be opened 1NT? If not, explain why not.

1. ♠ A J 9 3 ♡ A J ◇ K Q 10 3 2 ♣ 3 2
2. ♠ A 10 9 3 2 ♡ Q J 2 ◇ K 3 ♣ K J 3
3. ♠ K Q 3 ♡ A J 3 ◇ K 3 ♣ A J 10 7 6
4. ♠ K J 3 ♡ A J 3 2 ◇ Q 10 3 2 ♣ A 2

Answers

1. No. Although this hand does have 15 HCP, it has two doubletons and is therefore not balanced.
2. No. This hand is balanced, but has only 14 HCP. We do not count distribution points for notrump.
3. No. This hand is balanced, but it has 18 HCP. That is too much to open 1NT.
4. Yes. This hand is perfect. It has 15 HCP and only one doubleton.

Opening with One of a Suit

STEP 1

If your longest suit is at least five cards in length, always open the longest suit.

Most of the time you will not have a hand that meets the very specific requirements for a 1NT opening and you will open the bidding with one of a suit instead. If your longest suit is at least five cards in length, you will open the bidding with one of that suit. You want to advertise the suit you have the most of. This will help you and your partner pick the most appropriate trump suit. Look at these hands:

a) ♠ A Q 7 6 5 4 ♡ K Q J 8 7 ◇ 3 ♣ 6
b) ♠ A K 6 5 2 ♡ K Q J 8 7 3 ◇ 3 ♣ 6
c) ♡ A Q 7 ♡ 8 7 ◇ K Q 10 4 3 2 ♣ 6 2

All three hands include a suit that is five cards or more in length. In each case, you should open your longest suit. With (a), you open 1♠; although you have two very good suits, the spades are longer. You plan to advertise hearts later. Hand (b) is similar. You open with 1♡ and bid spades later. With hand (c), you have only one suit to advertise: diamonds. Open with 1◇.

If you are lucky enough to have two suits that are five cards or longer, then you want to tell partner about both suits. You plan to bid one and then the other. *Bid the higher-ranking suit first.* Why? It is easiest to show you with an example. Suppose you are South. You are dealer and your hand is:

STEP 2

With two five- or six-card suits, open the higher-ranking one.

♠ A Q 7 6 5 ♡ A Q 7 6 5 ◇ 7 6 ♣ 3

If you open 1♠, then the auction might go like this (don't worry for now about the meaning of partner's 1NT bid — you will learn about that in the next chapter):

West	North	East	South
			1♠
pass	1NT	pass	2♡
pass	?		

If your partner has a poor hand and a preference for hearts, he can now pass. With a poor hand and a preference for spades, he can bid 2♠. In either case, you are only committing to eight tricks. Suppose you had opened with 1♡, your lower-ranking suit, instead:

West	North	East	South
			1♡
pass	1NT	pass	2♠
pass	?		

Now if partner likes hearts better, he must bid all the way to the three-level. Do you see how opening the higher-ranking suit keeps the bidding more economical? If partner likes your first suit better, he can go back to it without raising the level of bidding.

You may think that you should open the *stronger* of the two suits. For example, if you held

♠ 6 5 4 3 2 ♡ A K 10 9 8 ♢ A K ♣ 3

you might be tempted to open 1♡ instead of 1♠. Stifle that impulse. It is length that matters, not strength in the suit — quantity, not quality.

As we said earlier, we are playing 'Standard American'. We will now add 'with five-card majors' to our system description. That means that with a five-card major suit and 13 or more points, you can happily open one of that major (1♠ or 1♡). For instance, with

> **STEP 3**
>
> **With no five-card suit, open your longer minor, even if you have only three cards in it.**

♠ A K 9 6 4 ♡ K J ♢ A 10 7 5 ♣ 3 2

you would open 1♠ — spades are your longest suit and you have at least five of them.

However, what do you do if your longest suit is only four cards in length? You cannot open the bidding with one of a major unless you have five cards in that suit. If your hand is

♠ A K 9 6 ♡ K 3 2 ♢ Q J 6 2 ♣ 7 5

you cannot open 1♠, since you only have four spades. What do you think you should open? If you said 1♢, you got it right. You can open a four-card minor.

Suppose you hold this hand:

♠ A K Q 6 ♡ K 3 2 ◊ 6 5 3 2 ♣ J 2

You would still open 1◊. Remember, it is the length of the suit that matters, not the strength.

STEP 4

With no five-card suit and two four-card minors, open 1◊ (the higher-ranking suit).

With two four-card minors, open 1◊, the higher-ranking suit. You handle a decision between two four-card minors exactly the same way as you would handle two five-card majors — rank before strength.

Sometimes you will have to open a three-card minor. Don't worry — you will never open a two-card minor! Suppose your hand is:

♠ A J 9 6 ♡ K J 9 3 ◊ J 10 7 ♣ K 2

You have two attractive major suits, but you can't open either of them. You also can't open 1NT, although your hand is balanced, because you don't have 15-17 HCP. Remember, with 13 points, you must open, so your only choice is to open a minor suit. Partner is aware that when you open one of a minor, you may have only three cards in the suit. You open with 1◊ on the hand above.

STEP 5

With no five-card suit and two three-card minors, open 1♣.

Now let's consider what to open with two three-card minors and no five-card or longer major. For example, your hand is:

♠ A K 7 3 ♡ 5 3 2 ◊ A 3 2 ♣ Q 4 3

You would really like to open 1NT with this very balanced hand, but you do not have the necessary 15-17 points. You can't open 1♠ because you have only four spades. You have to open one of a minor. On this type of hand, you must open 1♣. If you start with 1♣, partner will be able to show his best suit at the one-level, unless it is clubs.

Here is a convenient table that contains all of the steps.

REMEMBER THIS! ☑

Never open a major that is fewer than five cards long.	
Never open a minor that is fewer than three cards long.	
With only one long suit of five cards or more	Open that suit
With two equal-length five- or six-card suits	Open the higher-ranking suit
With no five-card or longer suit	Open your longer minor
With no five-card or longer suit and two four-card minors	Open 1◊
With no five-card or longer suit and two three-card minors	Open 1♣

LET'S TRY IT 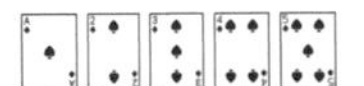

OPENING BIDS OF ONE OF A SUIT

For each of the following hands, fill in the columns (HCP, distribution and total points) and then indicate your opening bid.

Hand	HCP	Distribution	Total	Opening Bid
1. ♠ J 10 7 6 5 ♡ 3 2 ◇ A K Q J 3 ♣ 5				
2. ♠ A J 3 2 ♡ K Q 10 4 ◇ K 3 2 ♣ 5 2				
3. ♠ 7 ♡ K J 7 6 5 4 ◇ A Q 8 7 2 3 ♣ —				
4. ♠ Q J 9 ♡ A 2 ◇ Q 10 5 4 ♣ A 10 3 2				
5. ♠ A J 10 9 8 ♡ 4 ◇ 3 ♣ K Q 7 6 5 4				
6. ♠ A J 9 4 ♡ K J 4 ◇ K 3 2 ♣ A Q J				
7. ♠ A 10 9 8 7 ♡ K Q 10 3 2 ◇ 4 3 ♣ 2				

Answers

1. 1♠. Open the higher of two five-card suits.

2. 1◇. This hand pattern is the only time you will open 1◇ on three cards.

3. 1♡. Open the higher of two six-card suits when you are lucky enough to hold them!

4. 1◇. A balanced hand but not strong enough for 1NT. Open 1◇ with 4-4 in the minors.

5. 1♣. Open your longest suit.

6. 1♣. Again balanced, but this time too strong for 1NT. With no five-card major and 3-3 in the minors, open 1♣.

7. Pass. Not enough points, even using the Rule of 20.

THE PLAY OF THE HAND

The Opening Lead

Lay out this hand:

♠ 10 3 2 ♡ Q J 10 9 ◇ K 4 3 2 ♣ 4 2

Here is the bidding:

West	North	East	South
			1♣
pass	1♠	pass	2♣
all pass			

You are sitting West and South is the declarer in 2♣. It is your opening lead. What is your choice? Did you pick a high heart? We like to lead from an honor sequence of three or more cards if we have one. Why do we like this lead? Because it is safe and there is a good chance of setting up a trick. A lead from a **perfect sequence** like QJ109 is safe because all of the cards are of equal value. The only cards in that suit that can beat any of them are the ace and king. Even after you use the queen, your jack, ten and nine have the same potential to take a trick. Once the ace and king are gone, you will be able to win tricks with the other two if they aren't trumped.

Since all your hearts are of equal value, technically you could lead any of them. However, we always lead the top card from a sequence. This tells partner that it is your highest card in the suit and that you have the neighboring cards underneath it. Suppose partner leads a king — you can expect him to have the queen and probably the jack as well. He does not have the ace. What if partner leads a jack? He has the ten and probably the nine as well, but not the queen. Note that we only use this method with honor cards — leading an eight does not suggest holding the seven.

Okay, let's change the hand a little bit. Take away the ♡10 and replace it with a little heart. You should see this in front of you:

♠ 10 3 2 ♡ Q J 9 2 ◇ K 4 3 2 ♣ 4 2

You can still lead the ♡Q, even though you don't have the ♡10. It is still a sequence as long as the top two cards are touching. If there is a one-card hole between the second and third card, we call it a **broken sequence**.

We lead the top card from a broken sequence as well. Why? While it is a little more likely that you will give up a trick, you still have two cards backing up the top card.

Our favorite opening lead against a trump-suit contract is from the ace and king of a side suit (any suit except the trump suit) When you lead from an ace-king combination, you are unlikely to give up a trick, because leading the ace still leaves you with the king in reserve. Furthermore, leading the ace is probably going to win the trick, which is something you always like to do on defense. Winning the first trick means you retain the lead to the second one, so you will be able to decide what to do next after you see the dummy.

REMEMBER THIS!

Lead the top card from any type of honor sequence.

REMEMBER THIS! 

Lead the ace from an ace-king combination.

♠ 10 3 2 ♡ A K 9 2 ◇ K 4 3 2 ♣ 4 2

If you held this hand and were making the opening lead against 2♣ after the same auction, you would be very happy to lead a high heart. Here, the ace and king are equals. You should lead the ace, which is the equivalent of the top of a sequence. If you lead the king from this holding, partner will assume you hold a sequence headed by the king-queen.

What if you want to lead a suit, but do not have a sequence in it? Let's change the hand slightly and replace the ace of hearts with a little heart.

♠ 10 3 2 ♡ K 9 3 2 ◇ K 4 3 2 ♣ 4 2

The rule is that if you want to lead a heart, you should lead the bottom heart — in this case, the ♡2. When leading from a suit that contains a high card, we recommend that you lead the bottom card. When leading from a suit without any high cards, lead the top card. Suppose we remove the ♡K, so now your heart holding is 9-3-2. What do you lead? Lead the top card, the ♡9. Here is a simple mnemonic to help you remember: BOSTON. BOSTON stands for **B**ottom **O**f **S**omething and **T**op **O**f **N**othing. Just remember the Northeast American city with the chowder and the beans!

To be 'something', a card must be an honor — a ten does not count. Here is a table that summarizes the opening leads.

REMEMBER THIS!

OPENING LEADS	
With **AK**x	Ace
With an honor sequence	Top card
With no sequence, lead B.O.S.T.O.N.	Bottom of something and top of nothing

By the way, most players lead the bottom card if they have a three- or four-card suit headed by an honor. However, if they have a longer suit, they lead the fourth-highest card. We will discuss this idea further in Chapter 6; for now, just lead the bottom card.

Establishing Winners By Forcing Out Honors

Suppose you hold ♠KQJ10. With the ♠A in one of your opponents' hands, you have no tricks in the suit when you start. However, if you can eliminate the ♠A, then your remaining high cards in the suit will be winners. You will have the opportunity to take up to three more tricks in the suit. Look for opportunities to establish winners throughout the play. This method works whether you are declarer or a defender.

For each of the practice deals in the following section, look at your hand and decide whether you would open the bidding if you had the opportunity. We will identify the declarer and tell you the contract. Starting in the next chapter, you will have a chance to participate in a proper auction.

Discarding a Loser

One great use for winners is to throw away losers on them. It doesn't matter whether they are winners you have established or simply the top winners in a suit. Suppose you have a suit in your hand that is A-3-2 and dummy has 7-6-5 of the same suit. You are in danger of losing two tricks in this suit. After the ace is gone, the opponents will be able to take their king and queen. You won't be able to trump them, because you must follow suit. However, if you have winners in another suit, you may be able to throw one or more of your losers on them. Now one of your hands will be able to trump the defenders' high cards. Try it on this first practice deal:

Deal 1 — Dealer South

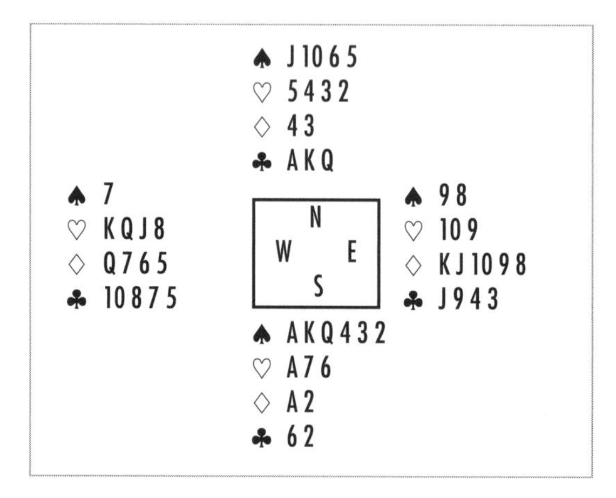

Look at the South hand and decide whether you would open the bidding. If so, what would you open?

South has enough to open the bidding. He would open with 1♠, his longest suit. Let's make South declarer in 4♠. Play out the deal first and then read on.

What opening lead should West choose? The ♡K. It is the top of an honor sequence. South should win the opening lead in his hand with the ♡A. Next, South should draw trumps. It will take two rounds of spades to eliminate the defenders' trumps. Now it is time to take the top club winners. When declarer cashes the third club, he can throw away a heart or a diamond from his hand. If he does so, he can make eleven tricks.

Deal 2 — Dealer West

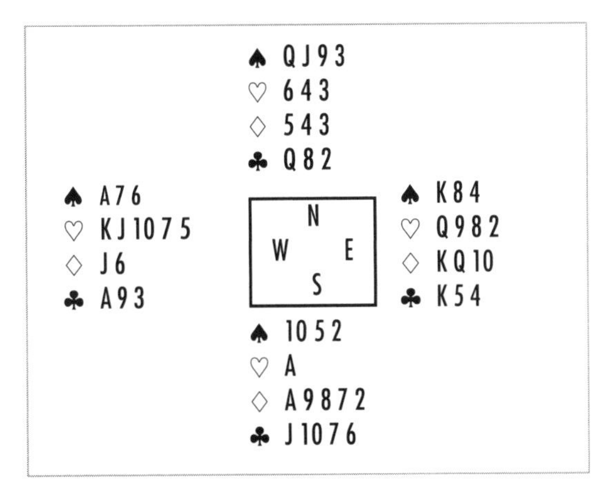

This time look at the West hand and decide if West should open the bidding. If so, what should he open? He would open 1♡. West becomes declarer in 4♡. Play out the deal and then read on.

North will probably lead the ♠Q, the top of a broken sequence. This is a very good lead, but West should still make his ten tricks. He should win the opening lead with either the ♠K in dummy or the ♠A in his hand — this time it doesn't matter which. West should now draw trumps. Since he is missing the ♡A, he will have to force it out before doing anything else. (This establishes the rest of the trump suit.) West should play a heart at Trick 2. South will have to win the heart and should lead back a spade. Now West draws trumps and establishes his diamond winners by leading out top diamonds. At this point, if North and South have led spades twice, when South gets in on the ♢A, he will be able to play a spade winner for his side. In effect, the defense will have established a spade winner by forcing out the ace and king. West will make only ten tricks.

Deal 3 — Dealer North

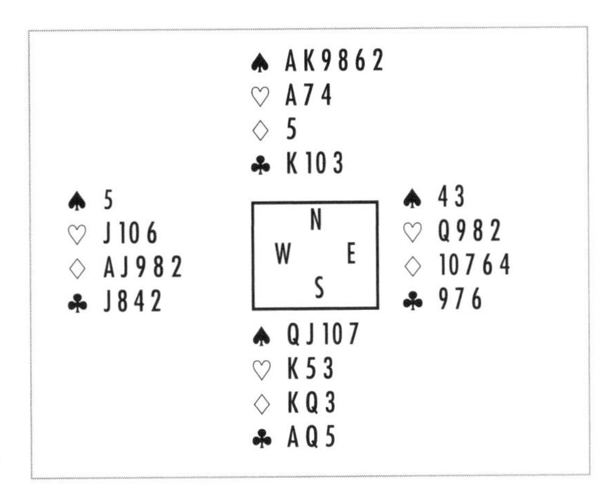

This time, start with the North hand and decide whether you would open the bidding. If so, what you would open? The North hand would open 1♠. North is declarer in 6♠ — yes, a small slam! Play out the hand first and then read on.

East is on lead and, with no really attractive choice, he could choose any suit at all. If East leads a heart, he should lead the ♡2 (bottom of something). If he leads a club or a diamond, he should lead a high one (top of nothing). North should draw trumps and then lead a diamond towards dummy's K-Q. West will win, but later North will be able to throw the heart loser in his hand on dummy's established diamond. North will make twelve tricks.

Deal 4 — Dealer East

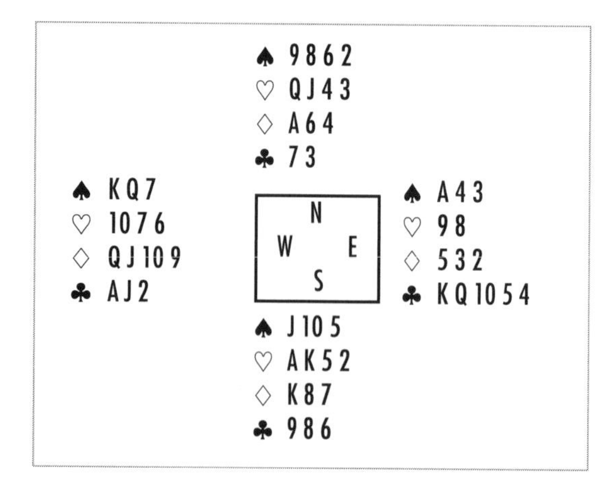

This time start with the East hand. Looking at each hand in turn, decide whether you would open the bidding and if so what you would open.

East and South should both pass, but West has enough to open. He would open 1◇, his longer minor. East becomes declarer in 3♣. Play out the deal first and then read on.

South would probably lead the ace of hearts, one of our favourite leads, ace from ace-king. North-South may attempt to cash three rounds of hearts. East will trump the third round of hearts in his hand and then draw trumps. After that, East will force out the ◇A and ◇K to establish two diamond winners. In order to "force out" the ace and king of diamonds, East must lead diamonds twice. After the opponents have won the ace and king of diamonds, two of the diamonds in the West hand (dummy) will now be high. East will make nine tricks on this deal.

CHAPTER**SUMMARY**

A Evaluate your hand by counting points as follows:
For high cards:
Ace = 4 King = 3 Queen = 2 Jack = 1
For distribution, use Method 1 or Method 2, but not both:
Method 1: Void = 3 Singleton = 2 Doubleton =1.
Method 2: count 1 point for the fifth and each subsequent card in a suit.

B You need 13 total points to open the bidding.

C If you count distribution points for long suits, use the Rule of 20 to decide whether to open marginal hands. Add the lengths of your two longest suits to your HCP, and open the bidding if this total is 20 or more.

D With 15-17 high card points and a balanced hand (no void or singleton and no more than one doubleton), you should open 1NT. Otherwise, open one of a suit.

E Open your longest suit if you have a suit of five or more cards. With two five- or six-card suits, open the higher ranking. If you do not have a five-card suit, open your longer minor. Playing five-card majors, you cannot open a four-card major. With two four-card minors, open 1♢; with two three-card minors, open 1♣.

F Leading from a perfect honor sequence of three or more cards is always a good idea. A broken sequence, which has two honors at the top, a one-card gap and then the next highest card (e.g. K-Q-10) is also a good lead. If you lead from any kind of honor sequence, lead the top card.

G Lead the ace from A-K — another very attractive lead.

H Lead BOSTON (Bottom of Something and Top of Nothing) when you are leading from a suit that does not include a sequence or two top honors.

I If you have a good suit missing some of the top honors, you may be able to force out the top honors to establish tricks in that suit.

J If you have winners or can establish winners in one suit, you may be able to throw losers in another suit on those winners.

3 More About Bidding

DID YOU KNOW?

In the days of whist, in the 19th century, the second Earl of Yarborough would offer to bet anyone 1000-1 that they would not be dealt a hand in which all the cards were lower than a 10. The Earl knew what he was doing — the true odds are about 1827 to 1! To this day, a bridge hand containing no card above a 9 is known as a yarborough.

WHAT YOU'RE GOING TO LEARN

In the previous lesson, you learned about opening the bidding, so you know how to make the first bid in an auction. What happens after that? In this chapter, we will begin to look at the rest of the story. Before we continue talking about the auction, we will have our first look at bridge scoring and in particular the concept of making a game, which is a way to score a lot of extra points. This will help you to set your objective when you bid. After that, we will focus on responder, the partner of the opening bidder. It is responder's job to keep the partnership momentum alive in the search for the right contract and to answer the two fundamental questions of bidding at bridge: 'Where?' and 'How high?' Can responder support his partner's suit or should the partnership look elsewhere in the search for a trump suit? What is his point range and what level of contract does that suggest?

Finally, we will spend some time planning the play of the hand. You will see how to count losers and then to identify your best chance of reducing them so that you can fulfill your contract.

Scoring

> **"Game"**
> A contract that is worth at least 100 points: 3NT, 4♡, 4♠, 5♣ and 5◇ are all game contracts.

Before we go any further, we need to talk about scoring. Your primary goal on any bridge deal is to bid and make a **game**. If you succeed, you will get a nice big bonus (several hundred points). In order to make a game, you have to succeed in a contract that scores at least 100 points. Recall that you get 20 points for each level in a minor suit (clubs or diamonds). Therefore, bidding and making 1♣ is worth 20 points; 2♣ is worth 40, etc. With a very simple calculation, you can see that you need to bid five of a minor to score 100 points and make game. In a major suit (hearts or spades), you get 30 points for each level you bid. That means that four of a major is 120 points, more than enough for game. Notrump is special, however. We said earlier that each notrump level is worth 30 points, except for the first level, which is worth 40. Conveniently, this means that 3NT is game (40+30+30).

The result of all this is that we have a strong preference for playing in a major suit if we are going to choose a trump suit. We need fewer tricks to make game. Notrump offers an even lower target and is often preferred on hands where the alternative is to play in a minor suit.

> **"Partscore"**
> A contract worth less than 100 points.

Contract needed for game	Tricks	Score
3NT	9	100
4♡ or 4♠	10	120
5♣ or 5◇	11	100

Note: you must both bid and make a game contract to get the bonus. If you bid 2♡ and then take ten tricks, you will still earn 120 points for your tricks, but you won't get the big game bonus. If you play a contract below game, such as 2♡ or 2NT, it is called a **partscore** and making it is worth only a small bonus (50 points).

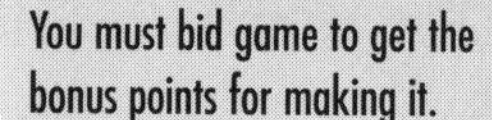

> You must bid game to get the bonus points for making it.

Opening Bid Review

The language of bridge is very concise. A combination of just two words can tell us quite a bit. Suppose partner has opened the bidding with 1♠. What do we know so far? We know he has at least five spades and at least 13 points. Do we know anything else? Yes! Partner does not have a suit that is longer than spades. With a longer suit, partner would have opened that one — always bid your longest suit first.

An opening bid of one of a minor isn't quite as helpful. Remember that an opening bidder who starts with 1♣ or 1◇ will occasionally have as few as three cards in the suit they have named, so it may not even be their longest suit.

Responding To Partner's Opening Bid — Can You Support Partner?

The partner of the player who opens the bidding is called the **responder**, since he is 'responding' to the opening bid. Let's look at the auction from that point of view.

Your partner has opened 1♠. What do you think he most wants to hear? He wants to know that you 'like' spades too. How can you tell if you 'like' partner's suit? If you have only one or two cards in partner's suit, then you want to suggest a different spot. What if you have three cards in partner's suit? Now do you like it? Well, that depends on how many trumps you know partner has. You obviously want to have more trumps than the opponents, so while seven between you, a bare majority, is more or less okay, eight is the magic number. *You are trying to find an eight-card fit or better.* If partner is known to have five trumps, then any three trumps is **adequate trump support**, since you have found an eight-card fit. However, if partner may have only four trumps, then you need at least three cards including an honor (ace, king, queen or jack) before you can claim to have adequate trump support.

Holding any four cards or more in partner's suit, you have **excellent trump support**. You are in trump heaven. You have found at least an eight-card fit, even if partner may have only four trumps.

"Adequate Trump Support"

Three cards including an honor in partner's suit (or any three if partner is known to have at least a five-card suit).

"Excellent Trump Support"

Four-card support for partner's suit.

REMEMBER THIS! 

Eight trumps between you and your partner is the magic number.

LET'S TRY IT! 

1. Partner opens 1♠. Do the following holdings count as adequate trump support? (Remember partner has at least five spades.)

a) ♠ Q 5 2
b) ♠ A 2
c) ♠ 7 6 3
d) ♠ 5 4 3 2

Answers

1. a) This is perfect. You have found an eight-card fit and you have an honor for partner.
b) Two trumps are not enough.
c) This is fine. You have found an eight-card fit.
d) Excellent trump support! Your side has at least nine trumps.

Counting Your Points as Responder

Before you bid as responder, you need to count your points to give yourself a basis for deciding what to do. However, you are not under any obligation to do anything. In fact, with a very weak hand, you will just pass. First, add up those juicy high card points. Before counting distribution, there is one other thing to think about: can you support partner?

Remember the old joke? There are are three types of people in the world: those who can count and those who can't. Well, there are two types of bridge hands responder can have: those that have trump support and those that don't. If you have trump support for partner's major, then you are probably destined to be the dummy on this hand. So, instead of counting distribution points in the usual way, you count **dummy points**. Why? Partner has bid 1♠ and you have four spades and a diamond void. Imagine you are putting your hand on the table as dummy for partner in a spade contract. Your opponent leads the ♢A. Partner looks at your hand and smiles. He is smiling because he has no diamond losers. The opponents' ace is not a winner because your partner can trump it in your hand. It is wonderful to have short suits when you are dummy. As we will see in this chapter, partner can use your trumps to deal with any losers that he has in your short suits.

Here is how you do it:

REMEMBER THIS! 

If you are going to raise partner's suit, count dummy points, giving high value to your short suits. This replaces your usual method of counting distribution points.

Counting Dummy Points

Count your high card points and then add your dummy points to your total. To count dummy points, look at the short suits in your hand and for each short suit add:

5 points	for a void
3 points	for a singleton
1 point	for a doubleton

REMEMBER THIS! ☑

Shortness in opener's suit is not positive and is not worth any distribution points.

If you don't have support for partner's suit, count your points in the same way that you do when opening the bidding. Count both high card points and distribution points. However, no matter how you count points, you never count distribution points for shortness in opener's suit. It is not good thing to be short in partner's suit. If partner opens 1♡ and you have

♠ A 5 4 3 ♡ 2 ♢ K 10 9 8 ♣ Q 10 4 2

the singleton heart is not a positive feature of the hand. If partner had opened 1♠, then you would have been much happier — you would have counted that singleton heart for 3 dummy points! It is important to realize that hands get better or worse depending on partner's bids. We will talk more later about how your attitude towards your hand changes during the auction.

LET'S TRY IT!

1. Partner opens 1♠. Count up your dummy points on the following two hands:

a) ♠ K 9 3 2 ♡ 5 ◇ A 3 ♣ 8 6 5 4 3 2
b) ♠ A 5 4 2 ♡ K 4 3 2 ◇ — ♣ Q 7 5 3 2

2. How many total points do you have on this hand when your partner opens the bidding 1♡?

♠ A 5 4 3 ♡ K 5 4 3 ◇ Q J 3 2 ♣ 3

Answers

1. a) You have support for spades, so you have 4 dummy points: 3 points for the singleton heart and 1 point for the doubleton diamond.
b) You have 5 dummy points, all for the diamond void.

2. Since you like hearts, you have 13 total points: 10 high card points and 3 for the singleton club.

Biddable Suits

If you have adequate trump support for partner's major, most of the time you will **raise** partner — i.e. you will make a higher bid in his suit. We will talk about this in more detail shortly. However, suppose you do not have trump support for partner or he did not open a major — what can you bid instead? Basically, it is responder's job to help find the best place to play. You do this by suggesting alternative suits if you can't support partner's suit. So, while opener is not allowed to bid a four-card major on his very first bid, you as responder can. *Any* four-card suit is worth advertising by responder.

REMEMBER THIS!

After the opening bid, responder needs four cards in a new suit to bid it — any four!

Let's stop a moment and think about that. Suppose opener has bid 1◇ and you, responder, bid 1♡. What does opener know about your heart suit? Only one thing — that it contains at least four cards. The range of cards you could hold is still very wide. You could have ♡AKQJ987 or you could have ♡5432.

Could you have responded 1♡ with ♡AKQ? No! Remember, *length is more important than strength.* It may seem strange, but you cannot respond 1♡ with ♡AKQ, since you have only three cards in hearts. However, you can bid 1♡ with ♡5432, even though it is a weaker holding, because you have four hearts. You are trying to make sure that you have more trumps than your opponents, so length is the key, not strength.

And Now... Responder Bids!

One of our primary objectives during the bidding is to reach a game contract if we believe we can make it. We want that juicy game bonus. It usually takes 26 points between your hand and your partner's to make game in a major. That's easy to remember because it is twice the bridge magic number of 13. Game in a minor is harder because you have to take an extra trick (a total of eleven) and now you need about 29 points. When we play in notrump, we count only high card points and it takes about 25 HCP to make 3NT.

Here is a table that shows the approximate number of points you need to make various contracts. You don't need to memorize the whole table — just focus on the number of points needed for game. We have put those contracts in bold.

Points In Combined Hands Required	Contract
20 points	2♣ 2♢ 2♡ 2♠
23 points	3♣ 3♢ 3♡ 3♠
25 high card points	**3NT**
26 points	4♣ 4♢ **4♡ 4♠**
29 points	**5♣ 5♢** 5♡ 5♠
33 points	6♣ 6♢ 6♡ 6♠ 6NT
37 points	7♣ 7♢ 7♡ 7♠ 7NT

In order to make a final decision about what to bid as responder, you need to think about one more thing. Let's call it 'Who am I?' Are you too weak to bid anything and plan to pass? Are you going to bid once and leave the decision about going further to partner? Are you going to invite partner to bid a game? Are you going to make sure that your side gets to game? Or are you going to explore for slam? First, you need to decide how good your hand is and you do that by counting your points.

There are six point ranges for responder:

0-5	6-9	10-12	13-15	16-18	19+
very weak	one bid	invite game	game-going	invite slam	slam-going

Your first step should be to count up your high card and distribution (or dummy) points to determine what range your hand fits into. We are going to look at each category in detail, but for now let's concentrate on the first two ranges — 'very weak' and 'one bid' hands.

Responding With 0-5 Points

Partner has opened the bidding and your hand falls into the 0-5 range. What do you do? With a hand this weak, the answer is simple: always *pass*. Even if partner has a very good hand, you have so few points that game is very unlikely. It is safer just to keep quiet. Here are two tempting hands after partner opens 1♢:

♠ Q J 8 7 6 5 ♡ 3 2 ♢ 5 2 ♣ 10 3 2
♠ 10 7 6 5 4 ♡ J 8 7 3 2 ♢ 4 ♣ 5 9

It is true that spades might be a better trump suit than diamonds in the first example, or either major in the second example, but you don't know that for sure. Once you bid, partner is going to expect you to have at least 6 points and you might find yourself at the four-level before you know it. Just pass. It only hurts for a little while.

Responding With 6-9 Points

With 6-9 points, you are only going to bid once, unless partner pushes you to bid again. You have a minimum responding hand (with fewer points, you wouldn't bid at all), so partner must have a very good hand to come close to the 26 points or so between you that you need for game. For now, your plan is to make only one bid, so you want to make the most useful one available. There are several choices depending on whether partner opened one of a major or one of a minor, whether you have trump support, and so on. It may seem complicated at first as we go through the options, but there is a handy chart at the end of the section that summarizes them all.

With support for partner's major

If partner has opened one of a major and you have trump support (even three small), your priority is to raise partner's major and give him the good news.

over 1♠, bid 2♠
over 1♡, bid 2♡

This **single raise** is a very useful bid because it conveys a lot of information to partner. First, it shows that you have a hand in the 6-9 point range. Not only that, but it also shows that you have a fit for partner's suit, which will make him very happy. A bid that shows a specific point range is called a **limited** bid. Since partner knows you have at most 9 points, this bid is also **not forcing**, which means that partner can pass if he wants to. It's up to him. After all, partner can add your points (6-9) to his points and decide if game is possible. If you don't have enough for him, he will pass.

Bidding your own suit

If you do not have trump support for partner's major suit (or if partner did not open a major), then bid your own longest suit if you can do so at the one-level. Note that you are not allowed to bid a new suit at the two-level with fewer than 10 points. It is too dangerous to raise the level of the auction with a weak hand and no fit for partner. We reserve those bids for hands in higher point ranges. So if partner opens 1♡ and you have

♠ 5 4 3 2 ♡ 8 2 ◇ A Q 10 7 4 ♣ 5 2

REMEMBER THIS! ☑

You need at least 10 points to bid a new suit at the two-level.

sorry, but you can't bid 2◇. You must bid 1♠, since *any* four-card suit is biddable. It probably seems unnatural to bid a short weak suit rather than a long strong one, but bidding 2◇ would promise partner at least 10 points, and you don't have them.

If you have two or more four-card suits that you are able to bid at the one-level, bid the cheapest one on the bidding ladder. For example, partner has opened 1◇ and your hand is

	HCP	Distribution	Total Points
♠ Q 8 7 3 ♡ 9 8 7 6 ◇ 2 ♣ A Q 10 2	8	0	8

What do you bid?

You have 8 total points (no long suits and you don't count shortness in diamonds, partner's suit). You can bid either hearts or spades at the one-level. You should choose 1♡, the cheapest option. When you bid the cheapest suit, you leave partner with more bidding space, giving the partnership the best chance to find the right spot. If partner has spades, he can still bid them at the one-level. If partner has hearts, you have already found a fit.

One more point: when you as responder bid a new suit at the one-level, partner is never allowed to pass. Although you may have a weak hand, you will see in the next chapter that you would also respond this way on many very good hands. Bids by responder in a new suit are **forcing**. That means that opener *must* bid again if he wants to live through the day! Your response is forcing for now, but you'll let partner know with your next bid that you don't actually have very much.

Bid 1NT

If you cannot raise partner's major or bid your own suit at the one-level, you can bid 1NT. This bid is limited to 6-9 points and is not forcing. It is a catch-all bid. *This is one case where bidding notrump does not promise a balanced hand.* In fact, you may have a hand with quite a lot of distribution. For example, partner opens the bidding with 1♡ and your hand is:

♠ 3 ♡ 4 3 ◇ 5 4 3 2 ♣ A Q 5 4 3 2

You should respond 1NT. This tells partner that you have 6-9 points, no support for his suit and no suit of your own to bid at the one-level.

Raising partner's minor

Last and least, if you cannot raise partner's major or bid your own suit at the one-level, but you do have four-card or better trump support for partner's minor and shortness somewhere, raise partner's minor to the two-level. Just assume he has four cards, since it is rare that he will only have three. We suggest that in order to raise partner, you should have an unbalanced hand, e.g. you have a void, a singleton, two doubletons, etc. Why? With a balanced hand, it is probable that your side should be playing in notrump instead.Therefore, with excellent support for partner's minor *and* distribution

over 1♢, bid 2♢
over 1♣, bid 2♣

Responding with 6-9 points

Here are your options in order of preference:

Rank	Type of Hand	Bid	Shows
1.	Over one of a major with at least three-card support	Raise partner's major to the two-level	6-9 pts (3+ trumps)
2.	With one or more suits biddable at the one-level	*bid your longest suit *with two or more four-card suits, bid the cheapest	6+ pts, at least four cards in your suit
3.	No support for partner's major, no suit biddable at the one-level	Bid 1NT	6-9 pts
4.	Over one of a minor with at least four-card support and an unbalanced hand	Raise partner's minor to the two-level	6-9 pts

LET'S TRY IT!

1. Partner has opened 1♣. What do you respond with each of the following hands?

a) ♠ A 5 4 3 ♡ 7 6 ◊ 8 3 2 ♣ Q 5 4 3
b) ♠ A J 3 2 ♡ 9 8 7 6 5 ◊ Q 3 2 ♣ 7
c) ♠ Q 10 2 ♡ J 9 2 ◊ J 10 5 ♣ A 7 6 2
d) ♠ Q 10 2 ♡ J 9 2 ◊ 5 ♣ K 8 7 6 3 2

2. Partner has opened 1◊. What do you respond with each of the following hands?

a) ♠ A 5 4 3 ♡ 7 ◊ 8 3 ♣ Q 10 5 4 3 2
b) ♠ A J 3 2 ♡ Q 8 7 6 ◊ 10 3 2 ♣ 7 5
c) ♠ Q 10 3 2 ♡ J ◊ K J 10 5 ♣ 7 6 5 2
d) ♠ K 9 8 5 ♡ K 10 8 7 ◊ 8 7 3 2 ♣ 4

3. Partner has opened 1♡. What do you respond with each of the following hands?

a) ♠ A J 3 2 ♡ 8 7 6 ◊ 10 3 ♣ Q 7 5 2
b) ♠ Q 3 2 ♡ 7 ◊ 10 9 8 5 ♣ K Q J 7 6

4. Partner has opened 1♠. What do you respond with each of the following hands?

a) ♠ A 5 4 3 ♡ 7 2 ◊ 8 3 ♣ Q 9 5 4 3
b) ♠ K 10 ♡ K 8 7 6 2 ◊ 10 9 4 3 2 ♣ 7

Answers

1. a) Bid 1♠. We prefer bidding a major suit to raising partner's minor, as major suits score better than minor suits. Partner could still have a spade suit.

b) Bid 1♡. You bid the longest suit you can bid at the one-level and that is hearts.

c) Bid 1NT. You have four clubs to go with partner's, but with a balanced hand, it is better to bid 1NT rather than raise clubs.

d) Bid 2♣. You have terrific support for partner and you have some distribution as well.

2. a) Bid 1♠. Sure, your clubs are longer, but you do not have enough points to bid a new suit at the two-level.

b) Bid 1♡. With two four-card suits that you can bid at the one-level, bid the lower ranking.

c) Bid 1♠. It is more important to show the spade suit than to support partner's minor. We really don't like playing in minors if we can find another spot since they score fewer points. If partner doesn't like spades, we can support diamonds on the next round.

d) Bid 1♡. Although you do have support for partner, you would rather play in a major than in diamonds. With two four-card suits (spades and hearts), bid the lower ranking first.

3. a) Bid 2♡. Since partner is known to have five hearts, your three-card support is good enough to ensure at least an eight-card fit.

b) Bid 1NT. You are in the 6-9 point range. The singleton heart is not an advantage and does not add value to your hand. Although both diamonds and clubs are biddable suits, you do not have enough points to bid a new suit at the two-level.

4. a) Bid 2♠. Yes, your clubs are longer, but the most important and happiest thing you can do with a 6-9 point hand is raise partner's major.

b) Bid 1NT. You cannot raise partner's spades with only two trumps and you do not have enough points to bid a new suit at the two-level. So 1NT is your only choice, even though you don't really want to play in notrump with such a distributional hand. The response of 1NT is just an all-purpose bid promising 6-9 points and saying you do not like partner's major.

THE PLAY OF THE HAND

Planning the Play

One of the most important things you need to do when you play a bridge hand — and probably when you do other things in life too — is *make a plan.* Even bridge experts fail to do this at least some of the time and often regret it. The first step when playing a trump contract is to count your losers. Let's see how we do that. The easiest way is to look at only two hands to start with. Lay these hands out on the table:

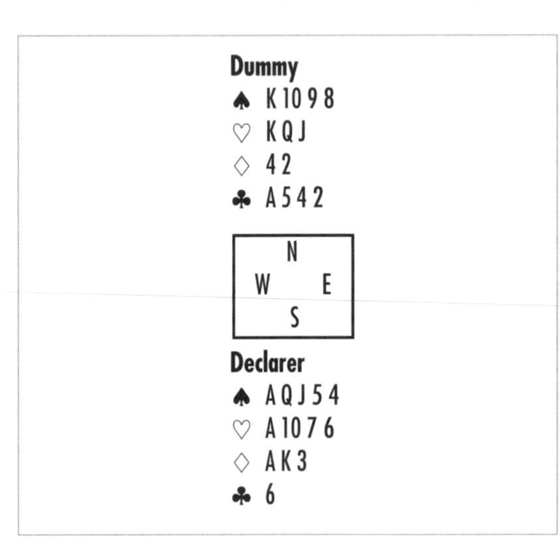

Declarer starts by counting losers *in his own hand.* He can 'borrow' high cards from dummy to fill in any gaps. For example, if you have three small spades in your hand, then you need the ace, king and queen of spades in dummy to compensate or you will have three losers. One simple way to think about losers is that any missing high cards are losers. If you are missing the ace of a suit, then you have one loser; if you are missing the ace and king of a suit, then you have two losers, and so on. If you are ever unsure about a card's ability to win a trick, count it as a loser.

Let's count up declarer's losers, suit by suit. First look just at the spade suit. Cover the other suits up for a moment.

♠ K 10 9 8

♠ A Q J 5 4

How many losers in spades? The answer is none. You have all of the top spades between the two hands. Declarer can borrow the king and even the ten from dummy. Can you see how it would go? When declarer plays the king from the North hand, he can play his four under it and win the trick. Next he plays the ten and can play the five from the South hand under it. Now all he has left is the ace, queen and jack, which are all winners.

Now uncover the heart suit. What about hearts?

♡ K Q J

♡ A 10 7 6

Can you see that declarer has no heart losers for the same reason? Now let's check diamonds.

♢ 4 2

♢ A K 3

There are no high cards in dummy to borrow. For now, we have to count the three of diamonds as a loser. Finally, the clubs:

♣ A 5 4 2

♣ 6

We have only one card in our hand and that will go under dummy's club ace. Thus we have no losers in clubs as we count losers in declarer's hand.

All together we have only one loser — a diamond.

Before we leave this deal, let's talk about making a plan. If you are playing the deal in notrump, you will take twelve tricks: five spades, four hearts, two diamonds and a club. At the end of the deal, the three of diamonds will actually still be a loser. However, suppose these are your hands in a contract of seven spades. Now you need all of the tricks, so you have to get rid of that diamond loser. If you play the ace and king of diamonds, dummy will have none left. You can then trump the last diamond in dummy with one of dummy's spades. (Of course, you will want to draw some of the opponents' trumps first. Just make sure to keep at least one trump in dummy to ruff the diamond loser.) So you see, one way to get rid of a loser is to trump it in the dummy — the short trump hand.

Let's try another deal. This time you are in 4♡.

How many losers do you have? Try counting before reading on.

Dummy
♠ 7 6 2
♡ K Q J 10
♢ 5 3 2
♣ K Q J

N
W E
S

Declarer
♠ J 9 3
♡ A 9 8 7 6 5
♢ A K 3
♣ A

You have four losers: three spades and one diamond. Let's say you are declarer in 4♡ (which means you can only afford to lose three tricks) and your opponents start by taking the first three spade tricks before switching to a diamond. You are on lead after winning the ♢A. Now let's make a plan. You cannot afford to lose any more tricks. How are you going to get rid of your diamond loser? You can't trump it because dummy is no shorter in diamonds than you are. However, you may recall from Chapter 2 that you can throw losers on dummy's winners and here dummy has club winners you can use.

Let's walk through the play. You need to draw trumps first. The opponents have only three hearts, so you will need to play at most three top trumps. Next, cash the

♣A to eliminate clubs from your hand and then lead a small heart to dummy. From there, play a second high club and discard your diamond loser on it. You could even throw the ♢K on the third club winner just for fun.

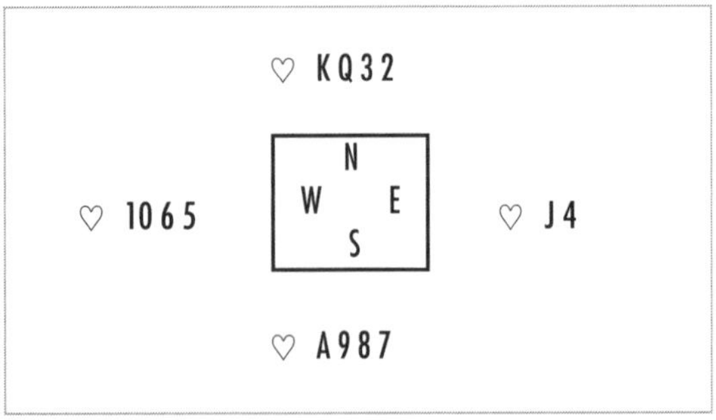

	♡ KQ32	
♡ 1065	N W E S	♡ J4
	♡ A987	

We have two more points to discuss before you attempt the practice deals. If you have more cards in a suit than your opponents do, not all of your small cards should be counted as losers. Any card left over after the rest of the suit has been played is capable of winning a trick.

In the suit to the left, it may seem that you have one heart loser — even after you borrow the ♡K and ♡Q from dummy, the ♡J is still missing, so the fourth heart has no 'big brother' to protect it from losing a trick. In actual fact, most of the time you won't lose that fourth heart. On this layout, once you have won three tricks with the ♡A, the ♡K and the ♡Q, your opponents will have played all of their hearts and your ♡9 will take a trick. This situation will arise often in the trump suit where you usually have lots of cards between the two hands.

REMEMBER THIS! ☑

An odd number of missing cards tend to divide evenly and an even number of missing cards tend to divide oddly.

The cards held by the opponents in a given suit tend to divide between them in predictable ways. When you are missing an odd number of cards in a suit, you can assume that they will split as evenly as possible between the opponents' hands (they won't all the time, but they will most of the time). So if you are missing five cards, you can assume they will break 3-2 — that is, one opponent will have three and the other will have two — which is as close to even as you can get. However, if an even number of cards is missing, most of the time the suit will not split evenly. If you are missing six cards, they will usually split 4-2; four missing cards will usually split 3-1.

Second, you will remember from the last chapter that you can create winners by knocking out the opponents' high cards. Once you've done that, you may be able to discard losers on them. Establish the winner and *then* discard a loser on it.

Now let's try some deals where you can put all this into practice. From now on, when we practice play, we are going to look at the auction as well. Of course, some of the bidding will go beyond the material we have covered so far, but we will still include it. Don't worry if you don't understand it just yet.

Deal 1 — Dealer South

West	North	East	South
			1♠
pass	2♠	pass	4♠
all pass			

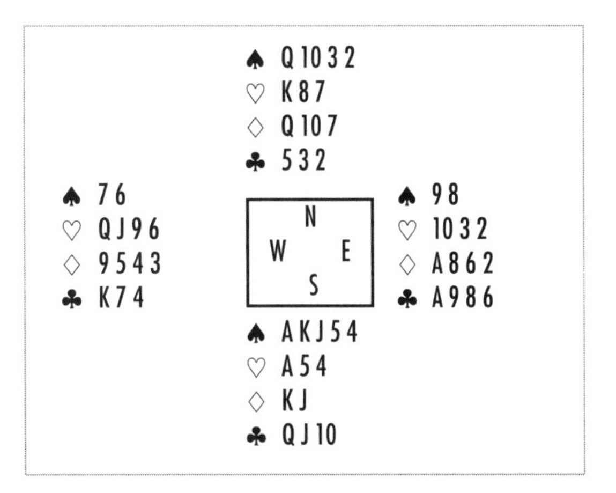

Did you think about opening 1NT on the South hand? With 19 HCP, you are just a little too strong for that bid. With five spades, South opens 1♠. With 7 points and excellent trump support, North can raise spades. Now South knows his partner has at least three-card support and 6-9 points. With a hand worth 20 points, South can bid game, knowing his partner has at least 6 points. West will likely lead the ♡Q, the top of a broken sequence.

South has four losers. He has no spade losers. He has one heart loser after borrowing dummy's king. He has one diamond loser. He also has two club losers, the ace and king. That comes to four, which is one too many — but declarer has a plan. After he forces out the diamond ace with his king, dummy's queen will be good (and dummy's ten as well). He can then discard one of his hearts on dummy's third diamond.

So South draws trumps and then plays a high diamond from his hand. East can win the diamond and play another heart. South wins this trick and plays diamonds, discarding the ♡5 from his hand on the third diamond. After that, South forces out the ♣A and ♣K to set up his tenth trick in clubs.

Deal 2 — Dealer West

West	North	East	South
			pass
1♣	pass	1♠	pass
2♠	all pass		

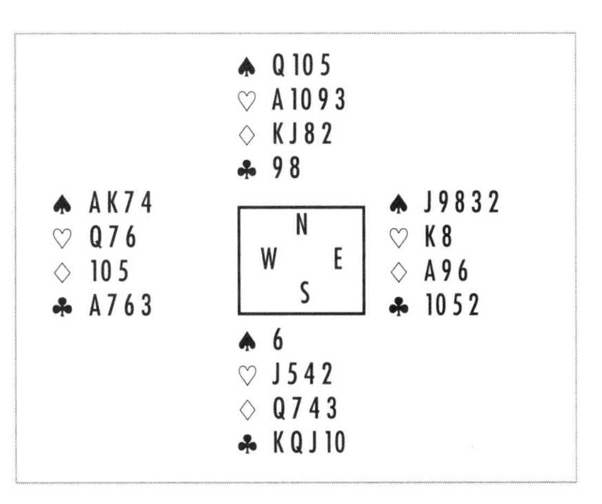

Although West has a balanced hand, with 13 HCP he is too weak to open 1NT. He opens 1♣, since he cannot open 1♠ with only four spades. His partner, East, is in the 6-9 point range and plans to make one bid; he bids 1♠, since that is his longest suit. This bid is unlimited and forcing (since West does not know how many points East has). Even though West has a minimum opener, he must bid again over responder's new suit bid. He raises to 2♠, which becomes the final contract. South leads the ♣K, the top of a sequence.

With four spades missing, an even number, we will assume that the suit does not split evenly. Declarer (East) counts one spade loser after borrowing the ♠A and the ♠K from dummy. There is one heart loser, the ♡A. Declarer also has two diamond losers and two club losers. That makes six losers, one too many. However, declarer can trump his third diamond in the West hand to make the contract.

Declarer draws two rounds of trumps, playing the ♠A and then the ♠K, and he does indeed have an unavoidable spade loser. He then plays the ♢A and then allows the opponents to win a diamond trick. When he regains the lead, he trumps a diamond in dummy.

Deal 3 — Dealer North

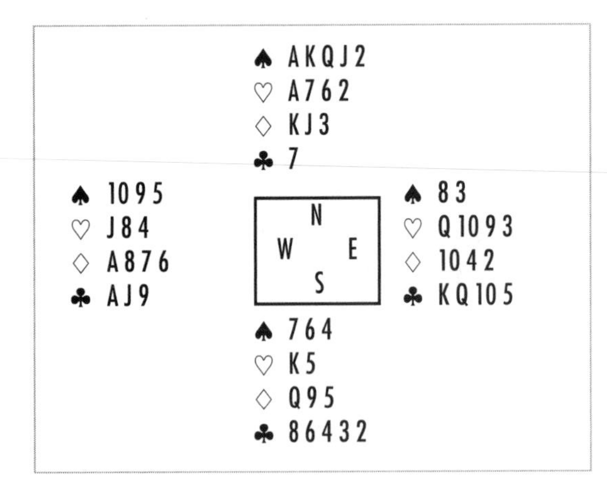

West	North	East	South
	1♠	pass	2♠
pass	4♠	all pass	

North has a great hand worth 19 or 20 total points. He opens 1♠. South has 6 points, so with three-card support for spades, he raises to 2♠. North can see that his side almost certainly has at least the 26 points needed for game, so he bids 4♠. East will lead the ♣K, top of a broken sequence.

North has four losers: two hearts, a diamond and a club. One too many. Remember, we assume that with an odd number of cards missing in a suit, they will split evenly, so we expect spades to split 3-2 this time. North needs to trump one of his hearts in dummy. This time he must play hearts before playing off three rounds of trumps to make sure dummy still has a trump to look after that heart loser. For example, North could win the ♡K, play only two rounds of trumps and then play a heart to the ace, followed by trumping a heart with dummy's last spade.

Deal 4 — Dealer East

West	North	East	South
		1♢	pass
1♡	pass	4♡	all pass

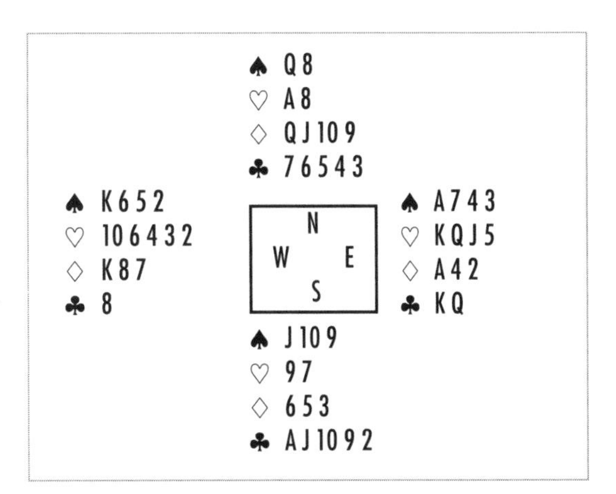

East has a balanced hand and 19 points — too many to open 1NT. He starts with 1♢ instead. West responds with 1♡, his longest suit, and East raises to 4♡. North should lead the ♢Q, the top of his perfect sequence. Even though he has a great 'poker straight' in clubs, it isn't a useful lead, since none of the clubs are honor cards.

West has four losers, one in each suit. One too many. We can count one spade loser, because we assume that the missing five spades will split 3-2. By the time our fourth spade is played, the opponents will have none left, and our small spade will actually be a winner. After the ♡A is gone, the hearts will be high, so there is one heart loser. The same is true in clubs. In diamonds, dummy can cover one loser with the ♢K, but there is still one diamond loser. Declarer can get rid of it, however, by establishing a club winner. This time he needs to do it before drawing any trumps. If he were to play a trump after winning the opening lead, North could win and continue diamonds. Declarer would win the second diamond, draw trumps and play a club, but South could win the ♣A and play a diamond winner. Therefore, declarer must play clubs right away to force out the ♣A and set up club winners before the ♢K is gone. The defenders will win the ♣A and lead back a diamond. Declarer must win the ♢A and now play dummy's high club, throwing away a small diamond from his hand. After this, he can draw trumps and eventually establish spades.

CHAPTER**SUMMARY**

A You get a big bonus for bidding and making a contract worth 100 points or more, a game contract.

B If responder doesn't have a fit for opener's suit, he counts his points exactly like opener and he does not value shortness in opener's suit.

C If responder has a fit for opener's suit, instead of counting distribution points in the usual way, he counts dummy points as follows:

- 5 for a void, 3 for a singleton and 1 for a doubleton.

D About 26 points are needed to make game in a major or notrump contract; 29 points are needed for a minor.

E Happiness is an eight-card trump fit. Adequate trump support for opener's suit is three cards in a major and four in a minor.

F Responder can bid any four-card suit, even four small, to help his side decide where to place the contract.

G Responder must determine the type of hand he has — from 'very weak' all the way to 'slam possible' — by looking at his point range:

- 0-5 points, responder always passes.
- 6-9 points, responder plans to make one bid:
    - With trump support, he raises partner's major.
    - With no support for partner's major, he bids a new suit at the one-level (but not the two-level).
    - If neither of the first two actions is possible, he can bid 1NT *OR* with an unbalanced hand and four-card or better trump support, he can raise partner's minor.

H When playing a hand in a trump contract, count losers — you may 'borrow' high cards from dummy to cover losers in your own hand.

I Always make a plan as declarer and you will be a star. If you have too many losers, see if there is a way to get rid of some of them. Consider trumping a loser in dummy or discarding a loser on a winner in another suit.

4 Responding to Opening Bids With Stronger Hands

DID YOU KNOW?

Millionaire American Harold S. Vanderbilt is credited with inventing the modern game of contract bridge in 1925, while on a cruise. His new scoring table changed the game of auction bridge by introducing the idea of 'vulnerability' and increasing the slam bonuses. His social influence contributed greatly to the popularity and spread of contract bridge, which rapidly took over as the only version of the game that was played.

WHAT YOU'RE GOING TO LEARN

In this chapter, we will complete our discussion of responding to an opening suit bid. We will start with a quick review of responder's role when responding with 0-5 and 6-9 points and then move on to the choices when responding with 10 points or more. We will also take another look at scoring. There is more than one kind of scoring system and in this book we use a method that is widely used in both social and competitive bridge today.

In the section on play, we will review counting losers and planning the play and then introduce a new way to get rid of some of your losers. After that, we will review opening leads and discuss the idea of leading from shortness rather than from strength.

More on Scoring

In the last chapter, we told you that a game contract is one that is worth at least 100 points. To get that game bonus, you have to bid at least 3NT, 4♡, 4♠, 5♣ or 5◊. When you do manage to score up a game, you receive a bonus of either 300 points or 500 points. How can you tell which? If you have been using duplicate boards (where the cards are placed in four slots, one for each player), you may have noticed that sometimes the slots are colored red. If you have a red slot, like a pool of blood in front of you, then you are said to be **vulnerable**. When you are vulnerable, everything counts more. You get 500 points for making game. When you are not vulnerable (no pool of blood), you get only 300 points.

> ***"Overtricks"***
> Tricks that the declaring side takes over and above the contract requirements.

When you fail to make your contract, you are said to have **gone down**. You are penalized for each trick you promised to take and didn't. For example, if you bid 2♠, promising to take eight tricks, and take only six tricks, you will be penalized for the two tricks you fell short. We call these **undertricks**. If you are not vulnerable at the time, your opponents get 50 points for each trick you go down. If you are vulnerable, they get 100 points per trick. You see? Everything counts more when you are vulnerable. Any tricks that you make over and above the number you contracted for are called **overtricks**. If you bid 2♡ (eight tricks) and make nine tricks, then you have made one overtrick. You will get the trick score for it (in this case, 30 points), but overtricks do not count towards making a game bonus.

> ***"Undertricks"***
> Tricks by which the declaring side falls short of making its contract.

If you bid and make a partscore (remember, that's a contract below game), you get a bonus of 50 points. You get the same bonus whether or not you are vulnerable. We have mentioned slams once or twice already. If you bid and make a contract of six in any suit or notrump, you have made a **small slam**. That is worth an additional bonus of 500 points not vulnerable and 750 points when vulnerable. Bidding and making a contract of seven, a **grand slam**, is worth 1000 points not vulnerable and 1500 points when vulnerable. The slam bonuses are in addition to both the trick score and the game bonus. So with a little arithmetic you can see that bidding and making 7♠ vulnerable is worth a whopping 2210 points. The trick score is seven times 30 or 210, plus 500 for game and another 1500 for slam. That's a lot more than bidding and making 2♠, which is worth only 110 points (60 for the contract and 50 for the partscore).

If you are not playing with duplicate boards, the simplest way to play is to rotate the vulnerability. On the first deal, play with no one vulnerable; on the second deal, North-South are vulnerable and East-West are not; on the third deal, East-West are vulnerable and North-South are not; and on the fourth deal both sides are vulnerable. At the same time, each player takes it in turn to be dealer, going clockwise. Then you can repeat the pattern. This form of the game is called **Chicago scoring**.

Scoring Summary

	Not Vulnerable	**Vulnerable**
Partscore	Trick Score +50	Trick Score +50
Game	Trick Score + 300 (Game Bonus)	Trick Score + 500 (Game Bonus)
Small Slam	Trick Score +300 (Game Bonus) + 500 (Slam Bonus)	Trick Score +500 (Game Bonus) + 750 (Slam Bonus)
Grand Slam	Trick Score +300 (Game Bonus)+ 1000 (Slam Bonus)	Trick Score +500 (Game Bonus) + 1500 (Slam Bonus)
Overtricks	Trick score for each	Trick score for each
Undertricks	50 each for the defending side	100 each for the defending side

There is another way to play called **rubber bridge**. It is based on the same principles, but your objective is to make two games (called 'winning the rubber') before the opponents do. Rubber bridge is still popular in home games, but it is not often played elsewhere anymore. We have included the rules and scoring for rubber bridge in an appendix in case you wish to play that form of the game with your friends.

Goals in the Bidding

You have two major goals in the bidding — deciding 'where' and 'how high' to play the deal. To answer the 'Where?' question, you need to find your partnership's best trump suit, giving strong preference to majors, because majors score better than minors. Without at least an eight-card major fit, you may decide to play in notrump. In fact, we suspect that as many as 90% of game contracts are played in notrump or a major. To answer the 'How high?' question, you need to decide whether to play the hand in partscore, game or slam. Since you have to bid game to get the game bonus, you really want to push to get there — but only when you have a good chance of making it. Of course, those slam bonuses are really nice too, and every bridge player is excited when they have a chance for one. However, slam deals are much less common than games.

Review of Responses With 0-5 and 6-9 Points

When partner opens the bidding, you will recall that as responder with fewer than 6 points, your bidding decision is easy: you pass. With 6-9 points, you plan to make only one bid, unless partner pushes you in some way. We will explore how partner can push you in the next chapter when we talk about opener's rebids. For now, suffice to say that partner can invite you to take another bid by asking you to pick between two suits or by asking you to bid game if your hand is at the top end of your range. Partner can even force you to bid again when he has a powerhouse hand and wants to go to game even though you have a weak hand. We saw in the last chapter that with 6-9 points, your first choice is to raise partner's major with adequate trump support (three cards) or better. Failing that, you can bid a new suit at the one-level (you need to have at least four cards in the suit you bid). If you can't do either of those things, you can bid 1NT, which in this one instance does not promise a balanced hand. Finally, as a last resort, with at least four-card trump support and some shortness, you can raise partner's minor.

Responding With 10-12 Points

Now you have a better hand. You are in the 10-12 point range and as a result you want to *invite* partner to bid game if he has a little extra. You can't be sure that you and partner have a combined 26 points, but if partner has just a little more than a minimum 13, you might be able to make game. You plan to take *two* bids to nudge partner towards game, unless you can show your values with one bid.

1) Raising partner's major

Partner is waiting to hear if you have support for his major. With excellent trump support (four cards) for partner's major, you are allowed to raise him to three of the major.

Partner	You
1♠	3♠

Partner	You
1♡	3♡

A raise to three rather than two tells partner that you have 10-12 points and four trumps — technically, this is known as a **limit raise**. It is a limited bid, meaning it tells partner exactly how many points you hold; it is also non-forcing. Opener can add your points to his to decide if game is possible. If he has more than a minimum opening bid, opener will bid game; with just a minimum, he will pass.

Notice that you have been able to tell partner that you have an invitational hand and excellent trump support with one bid. With only three-card support, wait until the next round to support your partner — you will show him some other feature of your hand first. It is still possible that there is a better place to play the deal and since you are planning to bid twice, you have time to provide partner with more information.

2) Bidding a new suit

If you don't have excellent trump support for partner's major, then your next choice is to bid a new suit of your own. Bid your longest suit (remember, length before beauty). With two suits of equal length, five cards or longer, bid the higher ranking first, planning to bid the lower ranking at your next turn. With two or more four-card suits, bid the cheapest first, as we saw in the previous chapter.

You will be happy to hear that with 10-12 points, you are not restricted to bidding new suits at the one-level. Your hand has grown up and now you can respond at the two-level if necessary. If you have

♠ 7 6 ♡ 3 2 ◇ A K Q 4 3 ♣ J 7 6 5

and partner opens 1♡, you can bid 2◇, your longest suit. Here are some examples of making a first response with 10-12 points:

♠ K Q 5 3 2 ♡ A J 8 3 ◇ 5 4 ♣ 7 6

Partner opens 1◇. You don't have support for partner's suit. You have 10-12 points. You respond 1♠, your longest suit.

♠ K Q 5 3 ♡ A J 8 3 2 ◇ 5 4 ♣ 7 6

Partner opens 1◇ and once again you have 10-12 points. This time you respond 1♡, since your hearts are longer than your spades. You would respond 1♡ even with a weaker heart holding as long as hearts were your longest suit. For example, with

♠ A K Q 5 ♡ J 8 7 3 2 ◇ 5 4 ♣ 7 6

you would still respond 1♡ over a 1◇ opening.

A bid of a new suit is **unlimited**, meaning that partner does not know how many points you have. You could have as few as 6 or as many as 18. Therefore, opener is forced to take another bid. With 10-12, you want to show him that you have something extra, not a just minimum 6-9. So, if you can't describe the strength of your hand in one bid by making a limit raise (1♠-3♠ or 1♡-3♡), you will have to bid *twice*.

REMEMBER THIS! ☑

With 10-12 points, you plan to invite partner to game. If you can't make an immediate limit raise, plan to bid twice.

3) Raising partner's minor

If partner has opened a minor, usually you will not raise even if you have excellent trump support. Your first choice should be to suggest another suit if you have one that is at least four cards long. Make a limit raise of partner's minor only if you do not have any other bid and you have at least four-card trump support for the minor.

Partner	You
1♢	3♢

Partner	You
1♣	3♣

Again, this kind of bid is limited and not forcing.

In the following examples, partner has opened 1♣:

♠ K Q 5 3 ♡ 8 3 ♢ 5 4 ♣ A 7 6 3 2

Bid 1♠ rather than raising clubs, since you have another four-card suit to bid.

♠ K 8 5 ♡ 3 2 ♢ Q 5 4 3 ♣ A J 6 3

Bid 1♢. Tell partner about your diamonds — you may be able to get to a game in notrump rather than trying for eleven tricks in clubs.

♠ A 8 ♡ 7 4 3 ♢ 9 8 7 ♣ A Q 6 3 2

Bid 3♣. You have excellent support for partner's clubs and no other sensible bid.

Summary: Responding With 10-12 (First Bid)

Choice	Type of Hand	Bid
1.	Excellent trump support (4+) for partner's major	Raise partner to the three-level.
2.	Fewer than four of partner's major and one or more five-card suits	Bid your longest suit (or the higher ranking of the two).
3.	Fewer than four of partner's major and one or more four-card suits	Bid your cheapest four-card suit.
4.	Excellent support for partner's minor (4+) and no other bid	Raise partner to the three-level.

Bids 1 and 4 are not forcing, since they show exactly 10-12 points. Partner can pass if he doesn't think the partnership has enough for game.

LET'S TRY IT!

1. Partner opens 1♢. What do you respond with each of these hands? Remember to refer back to the chart on the previous page (you couldn't have memorized it yet!). On hand (b), remember that shortness in diamonds does not improve things.

a) ♠ A J 7 4 ♡ K 9 ♢ Q 9 8 3 2 ♣ 3 2
b) ♠ K 9 8 7 ♡ 10 9 8 3 2 ♢ A 2 ♣ K 2
c) ♠ 10 4 ♡ K 3 2 ♢ A 10 9 8 5 ♣ Q 10 9
d) ♠ K 8 5 4 ♡ A 8 6 2 ♢ Q J 3 ♣ 5 4

2. Partner opens 1♡. What do you respond with each of these hands? On hands (a) and (c), remember that shortness in hearts is not a plus.

a) ♠ A 10 9 3 2 ♡ 7 6 ♢ K 9 8 7 ♣ K 3
b) ♠ A 10 9 3 2 ♡ Q 10 5 4 ♢ 3 2 ♣ A 2
c) ♠ K 3 2 ♡ 10 2 ♢ K 3 ♣ A 10 9 5 3 2
d) ♠ 3 ♡ A J 2 ♢ Q 10 9 8 7 ♣ K 10 3 2
e) ♠ A 10 9 3 ♡ Q 5 4 ♢ 3 2 ♣ A J 6 2

Answers

1. a) Bid 1♠. You have wonderful diamond support, but you should check first to see whether you have a spade fit. A major-suit game at the four-level is easier than a minor-suit game at the five-level. You can support diamonds later.

b) Bid 1♡. Length before strength. Even though the spade suit is prettier, you always bid the longer suit first.

c) Bid 3♢. You have no other suit to bid and excellent trump support. Time to raise partner.

d) Bid 1♡. With more than one four-card suit, bid the lowest suit first.

2. a) Bid 1♠. With only two hearts, you can't raise partner. Bid your longest suit.

b) Bid 3♡. You have excellent trump support — partner will be delighted.

c) Bid 2♣. You don't have support for partner. Bid your longest suit.

d) Bid 2♢. With only three-card support, you are going to raise hearts at your next turn. Bid your longest suit now.

e) Bid 1♠. With two four-card suits, clubs and spades, bid the cheaper one on the bidding ladder. Again, you plan to support hearts with your next bid.

Responding With 13-15 Points

What happens if you pick up a hand worth an opening bid and hear partner open the bidding before you have a chance to do the same? Actually, that's great news! Partner has at least 13 points and you have 13 points. With 26 points in the combined hands, that is usually enough for game! Now you know that your side has enough for game and it is your responsibility to make sure that you get there. While you still have to answer the question of what game contract you should play in, there is now the possibility that you can make a slam.

REMEMBER THIS! ☑

The sequences 1♠-4♠ and 1♡-4♡ are reserved for responding hands in the 6-9 point range with at least five trumps. Some players call this a 'weak freak'.

When you have a hand in this point range, your first choice is to bid a new suit. You will do this even if you have support for partner's major. Since a raise to the two-level shows 6-9 points and a limit raise to the three-level shows 10-12, it probably seems logical that a jump to the four-level (1♡-4♡) should show the next higher range, 13-15. However, while that bid does get you to game quickly, it does not allow your partnership much room to explore for slam, since it uses up all the bidding space. The direct jump to game is more useful for another purpose — we use it to try to take away the opponents' bidding space on a weak hand with a lot of trumps. (This kind of bid is called a **preempt**, and we'll talk about it a lot more in Chapter 11.)

Instead of jumping to game, you should simply make a descriptive bid: bid your longest suit first (at the two-level if necessary). Remember that when responder bids a new suit, it is completely forcing — opener must bid again. Your plan, when you have support, is to jump to game in opener's suit next round. The auction will go something like this:

Partner	You
1♡	2♣
2♢	4♡

or

Partner	You
1♡	1♠
2♣	4♡

Both of these auctions show a responding hand with 13-15 points and at least three-card trump support. They also tell partner something about your side suit. In the first example, partner knows you have some clubs along with good support for hearts. In the second example, he knows that you have some spades.

With two five-card suits, bid the higher ranking first, planning to bid the other one next. For example, suppose you have:

♠ K J 6 5 4 ♡ A J 7 6 2 ♢ K 3 ♣ 7

Partner opens 1♢ and your hand is in the 13-15 range (did you remember that the diamond doubleton is not an asset?) You respond 1♠, which is forcing. Now partner bids 2♢ and you can bid 2♡. This bid is also forcing — a new suit bid by responder is always forcing.

With two or three four-card suits, bid the cheapest first.

♠ Q J 6 3 ♡ K 10 7 2 ♢ A K 3 ♣ 4 2

Partner opens 1♢ and your hand is in the 13-15 range. You bid 1♡; perhaps partner can raise hearts or rebid 1♠, showing four of that suit.

Your final choice is to make an immediate bid of 2NT. Since this response takes up so much bidding space, we need it to provide a lot of information. In order to respond 2NT, you need 13-15 HCP, no four-card or longer major, no support for partner's major, stoppers in the unbid suits and a balanced hand. 'What is a stopper?' you may ask. A **stopper** is a high card that will prevent the opponents from taking all of the tricks in their long suit. An ace is clearly a stopper, since it will take the first trick when the opponents play that suit. A king-queen combination is also a stopper. The opponents may take the ace on the first round, but after that you will win the next trick in the suit. For bidding purposes, we consider any of the following holdings to be stoppers:

A Kx Qxx Jxxx

(The little x's mean any small card in that suit: Kx could be K3 or K8, and so on.)

As you can see, the response of 2NT shows a very specific hand.

"Stopper"
A likely winner in a suit that will prevent the opponents from taking lots of tricks in the suit right away.

LET'S TRY IT!

1. You hold:

♠ K 10 7 6 ♡ A Q 3 ♢ K 9 ♣ J 5 3 2

Partner opens:

a) 1♣
b) 1♢
c) 1♡
d) 1♠

What do you respond in each case?

2. Partner opens 1♢. What do you respond with each of the following hands?

a) ♠ K 10 7 ♡ A Q 3 ♢ K J 4 ♣ 6 5 3 2
b) ♠ K 10 7 ♡ A Q 3 ♢ K 9 6 ♣ J 5 3 2

Answers

1. In each of the first three cases, you bid 1♠, your longest suit. Example (d) is a peculiar case: the only time you don't bid spades is when partner bids them! Although you have four-card support, you are too strong to bid 3♠, so your first move should be 2♣. You will raise to game in spades next round.

2. a) You have no four-card major, but no club stopper either. Even though this is a balanced hand, you have to start with 2♣, not 2NT.

b) This hand is perfect for a 2NT response.

Responding With 16-18

Holding 16-18 points, your responses are similar to those you make with hands in the 13-15 point range. You are certainly going to keep bidding until your side reaches game, but you should also keep yourself open to the idea that you might have a slam. Your first response is exactly the same as if you have 13-15, with one exception: with a balanced hand, you may be able to respond 3NT. Your hand needs to meet the same specific requirements as those for a 2NT response (no four-card or longer major, no support for partner's major and stoppers in all the unbid suits), but this time you are in the 16-18 HCP range.

You need at least 33 points between you and partner for a small slam. This means that even with your 16-18 points, you are going to need more than a minimum opening hand from partner. If you have the opportunity to do so at your second or later bid, you will show partner your extra values. Generally, you will not bid past game unless partner shows extra too. More about this in later chapters.

Responding with 13-15 and 16-18 points	
With support for partner's major	Bid a new suit and then jump to game in partner's major. If opener's rebid promises anything extra, you may be interested in going further.
With two or more suits of equal length	Five-card suits: bid your higher-ranking. Four-card suits: bid your cheapest. You may make your first bid at the two-level if necessary; keep bidding until you get to game. Usually you will try to find a major-suit fit, and failing that end up in 3NT.
With one longest suit	Bid your longest suit, at the two-level if necessary; keep bidding until you get to game.
With no four-card major, no support for partner's major, a balanced hand and stoppers in all unbid suits	With 13-15 HCP, bid 2NT. With 16-18 HCP, bid 3NT.

Responding With 19 or More

Suppose you pick up your cards and you find you have been dealt:

♠ A K 2 ♡ A J 5 ◇ A Q 10 6 5 2 ♣ 8

You are thinking, 'This is my best hand of the whole night' — and then your partner opens the bidding 1♠! You can hardly believe there are enough high cards left for him to do that. You have 21 points in support of spades. Partner has at least 13. Slam seems possible; in fact, slam seems almost certain. On those rare occasions when you have a hand as good as this one as responder, it is your responsibility to drive the partnership towards slam. If (as in the example) your hand contains a five-card or longer suit, you can employ a special bid to let partner know just how good your hand is.

You start off with a bid called a **jump shift**. A jump shift means that you bid a new suit — that's the *shift* — one level higher than you have to — that's the *jump*. As always, bid your longest suit first. Notice that even if you have good trump support, you do not raise partner immediately; you jump shift first. A jump shift forces partner to keep bidding at least until game has been reached.

"Jump Shift"

A jump bid in a new suit. When responder makes a jump shift at his first bid, it shows 19+ points and is game-forcing.

Let's look at an example:

Partner	You
♠ Q J 10 6 5	♠ A K 2
♡ Q 7	♡ A J 6
◇ K 8	◇ A Q 10 6 5 2
♣ A 9 7 2	♣ 8
1♠	3◇

You will support spades next round.

If you do not have a five-card suit or better, simply bid a new suit as you would with 16-18 points. Your plan is to keep bidding until your side reaches slam or it becomes clear that slam is not possible.

Responding With 19 Points or More	
With a good five-card suit or better	Jump shift in your longest suit.
Any other hand	Bid a new suit and keep bidding until you reach at least a small slam, unless it becomes clear that slam is not possible.

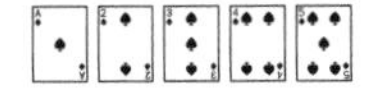

LET'S TRY IT!

On each of the following hands, partner has opened the bidding with 1♡. What is your response in each case?

1) ♠ 6 ♡ A 10 9 8 ◇ K Q 5 4 3 ♣ A J 2
2) ♠ 6 ♡ A Q 9 8 ◇ K Q J 4 3 ♣ A J 2
3) ♠ A 3 ♡ 4 2 ◇ A K Q 2 ♣ K 5 4 3 2
4) ♠ K Q 3 ♡ 5 ◇ A K Q J 6 3 ♣ A J 2
5) ♠ A Q 5 4 2 ♡ A K 10 ◇ 5 ♣ Q 6 5 4
6) ♠ A J 2 ♡ 5 4 ◇ K Q 3 2 ♡ K Q J 2

Answers

1) Bid 2◇. You have too many points (17) to raise hearts immediately. Start with your longest suit and support hearts next.

2) Bid 3◇. Jump shift to show your five-card suit and 19+ points. You will show your heart support on the next round of bidding.

3) Bid 2♣. Bid your longest suit first. You have too much distribution to consider bidding 3NT (two doubletons).

4) Bid 3◇. Jump shift into your terrific diamond suit.

5) Bid 1♠ and raise hearts at your next turn. A new suit bid by responder is 100% forcing.

6) Bid 3NT. You have support for all the unbid suits, no support for hearts, 16 HCP and no four-card major. This bid describes your hand perfectly.

THE PLAY OF THE HAND

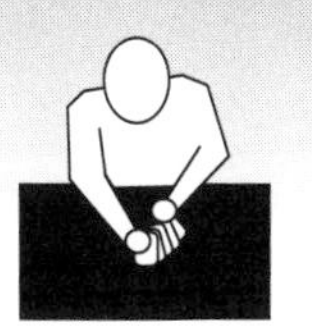

Counting Losers and Making a Plan — One More Time

In the last chapter we talked about counting losers and making a plan. This is one of the most important concepts in dummy play, so let's do a complete review of it. When you count losers, you look at your high cards and 'borrow' dummy's high cards to determine how many losers you have in a suit. If you are missing only one top card, then you have only one loser. All the rest can be counted as good cards. For example, if you have KQJ in a suit, you have exactly one loser. What if you have AQJ in a suit? Again, you have one loser.

If you have AK76 and dummy has Q543, you can borrow the queen from dummy to cover one of your small cards, the six. What about the seven — is it a loser? If you have length in a suit, your spot cards can probably be set up as winners. Of course, this involves an assumption about the distribution of the cards in the opponents' hands. If you are missing an odd number of cards, assume that the suit will split as evenly as possible. In this example, you are missing five cards and they will probably split 3-2. However, if you are missing an even number of cards, one opponent usually has more than the other. Therefore, if you are missing six cards, you should expect them to divide 4-2, not 3-3, while four missing cards are more likely to divide 3-1 than 2-2. Remember, this is just an assumption; when you find out the actual situation as you play the deal, you may have to adjust your approach.

In the last chapter, we looked at two ways to get rid of losers: we can trump them in dummy when dummy is short in the suit, or we can set up winners on which to discard our losers. Generally, we like to draw trumps as soon as possible, but sometimes our plan may require us to delay drawing trumps until we have set up a winner or a ruff.

Here is another way to get rid of losers. Sometimes you can set up winners in your hand and throw a card from dummy. After that dummy can ruff your own loser in the suit you discarded from dummy. Let's look at a quick example. The contract is 4♠.

The opponents cash their ace and king of clubs and then switch to the queen of hearts. Count the losers. You have four: one in hearts, one in diamonds and two in clubs. One too many. However, after you draw trumps, you can force out the diamond ace and throw one of dummy's hearts on a diamond winner. Then you can trump your losing heart in dummy. Do you see how it works?

Dummy
♠ K 8 7 6 4
♡ K 3 2
◇ 3
♣ 9 8 7 6

(N / W E / S)

You
♠ A Q 5 3 2
♡ A 4 5
◇ K Q J
♣ Q 2

We are using both of the tactics we looked at before — we are establishing winners *and* trumping losers in dummy.

Playing High Cards from the Short Hand First

When you are cashing high cards in a suit, it is good technique to win your tricks in the short hand first. For example:

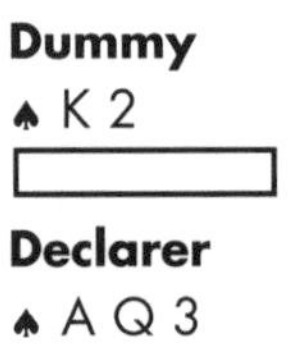

It is a good idea to win the first trick with the king and then cash the ace and queen later. Why is this? Let's look at what happens if you win the first trick with the queen. You will have this left:

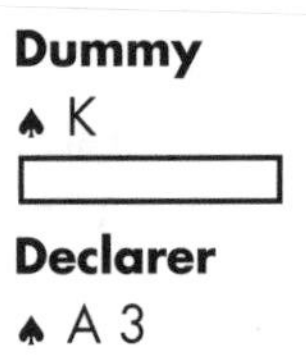

It is true that you can still take two tricks in the suit. You can very carefully take the king and then play the ace later when you are back in your hand. (You definitely don't want to play the king under the ace — that will waste a trick.) *The problem is that after cashing the king, you have to be able to get back to your hand in a different suit.* Sometimes that will be impossible. Remember this jingle. Learn it as if it were your favorite television commercial:

Use up your high cards from the short side first

Say it out loud a few times. (It's best to avoid doing this when you are in a group of non-bridge-playing friends.)

Another Opening Lead Idea

We have talked about leading the top card from a sequence of honors or the ace from ace-king. We have also mentioned BOSTON for spot-card leads: **B**ottom **O**f **S**omething, **T**op **O**f **N**othing. Here is one more great idea for a lead against a suit contract: you can lead from a short suit (not trump). The idea is that if your partner gets the lead before trumps are gone, he can give you a ruff in the suit you led. Let's say you have a singleton diamond and you lead that against a 4♡ contract. You also have three little hearts. On a happy day, partner might be able to win the ♡A when declarer leads trumps and then return a diamond for you to trump. Even a doubleton can sometimes be a good lead. When you lead from a doubleton, lead your higher card ('top of nothing'). This lead needs a little more help from the bridge gods to work. A very helpful partner might even have the ace-king in your doubleton suit.

So be on the lookout for chances to lead short suits. Sometimes you might have both a sequence and a singleton. On hands like those, you have to decide which lead will be more effective. There is no easy rule. Generally, with the ace-king in a suit, we prefer that lead. Then, if we want to lead the singleton after we see the dummy, we still have time to do it.

Deal 1 — Dealer South

West	North	East	South
			1♠
pass	2♠	pass	4♠
all pass			

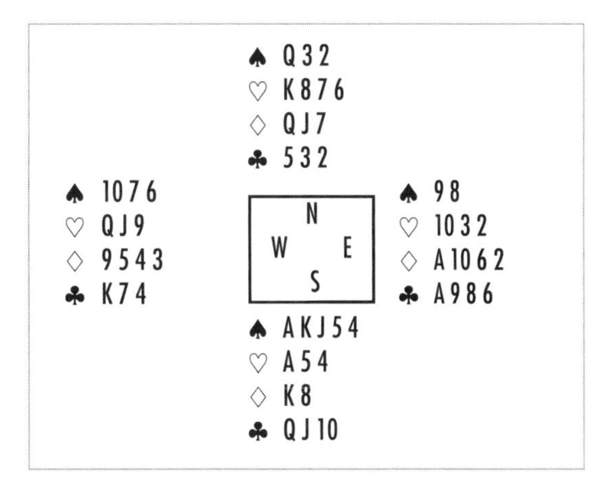

With five spades, South opens 1♠ (with 18 HCP, he is just a little too strong to open 1NT). With 8 points and three-card trump support, North can raise to 2♠. South knows his partner has at least three spades and 6-9 points, so he can bid game, knowing his side has about 26 points. West will probably lead the ♡Q, the top of a broken sequence.

Declarer has four losers: none in spades, one heart loser after borrowing dummy's king, one diamond loser (the ace) and two club losers, the ace and king. This is one too many, but declarer has a plan. He can discard one of his hearts on dummy's third diamond. He wins the ♡A (he may need the ♡K to get to dummy later), draws trumps and then leads the ◇K, playing his high card from the short hand first. East can win the diamond and return a heart. Declarer wins and plays the queen and jack of diamonds, discarding the ♡5 from his hand. After that, he can force out the ♣A and ♣K to set up his tenth trick.

Deal 2 — Dealer West

North:
♠ 7 4
♡ K 3 2
◇ A 8 6
♣ Q 9 5 3 2

West:
♠ K Q J 10
♡ J 10 8 7 6
◇ J 3
♣ 6 4

East:
♠ A 8 3 2
♡ Q 9 4 2
◇ K Q 4 2
♣ A

South:
♠ 9 6 5
♡ A
◇ 10 9 7 5
♣ K J 10 8 7

West	North	East	South
pass	pass	1◇	pass
1♡	pass	3♡	pass
4♡	all pass		

Neither West nor North has enough points to open the bidding and so they both pass. With no four-card major, East opens 1◇. West bids his longest suit first, hearts, even though his spades are much prettier than his hearts. With excellent trump support and 18 points, East raises to 3♡. West has enough extra to bid 4♡.

North leads the ♠7 from his doubleton, hoping to be able to trump a spade later. Declarer wins the spade and counts his losers. He has two heart losers and a diamond loser. Things are looking very good, but he still needs to make a plan. The only risk in this contract is that the opponents will be able to trump one of declarer's high cards, probably a spade. Declarer leads a trump. If declarer leads a heart from his hand, North must not play the king. Otherwise, he will find that it disappears under his partner's ♡A. South wins and leads a spade back. Declarer wins the spade and plays a second trump, which North wins. Unfortunately, North cannot get his partner in to give him his spade ruff. If only he could pass the diamond ace under the table to his partner! Declarer wins whatever North continues and draws the last trump. At some point, he will give up the ◇A to North and make his contract.

Deal 3 — Dealer North

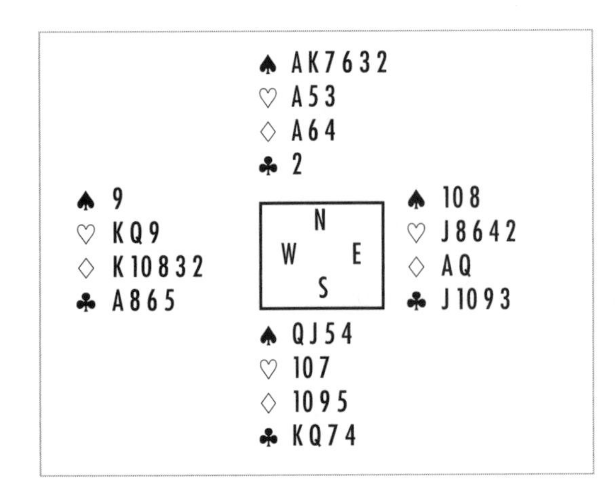

West	North	East	South
	1♠	pass	2♠
pass	4♠	all pass	

North opens with his longest suit, 1♠. With 9 points in support of spades and excellent trump support, South raises to 2♠. North has enough extra to bid game. (After reading the next chapter, you will understand this better.)

East leads the ♣J from his perfect sequence. Declarer covers with an honor from dummy and West wins the ♣A. Declarer has a lot of losers: a club, two diamonds and two hearts. Too many by two. One of the diamonds can be discarded on South's club winner and declarer can trump one heart loser in dummy. Notice that it will do no good to throw a heart on the club winner. Declarer cannot trump diamonds in dummy and he will still have three red-suit losers.

North plays two rounds of trumps ending in dummy and leads his club winner, throwing a diamond. He can then play the ♡A and another heart, allowing the opponents to take their heart winner; later he ruffs a heart in dummy. Eventually, the opponents will take their diamond winner as well. Declarer has lost only three tricks: one diamond, one heart and one club.

Deal 4 — Dealer East

West	North	East	South
		1♢	pass
1♡	pass	1♠	pass
2♢	all pass		

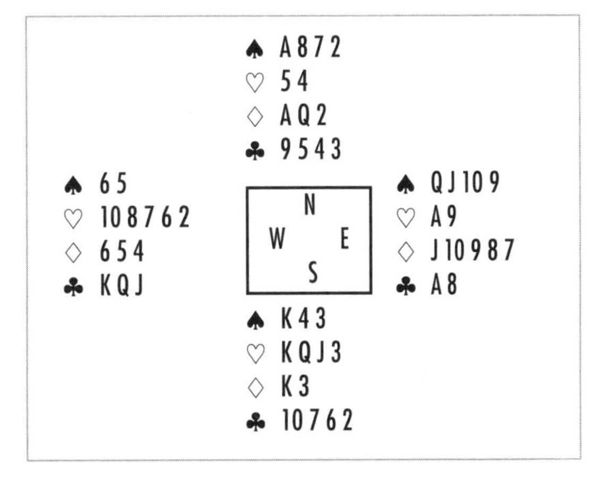

East opens 1♢, his longest suit. Although West doesn't have much, he has enough to bid 1♡. East rebids 1♠ and West bids 2♢, since he likes diamonds better than spades.

South leads the ♡K, the top of his sequence. Declarer wins the heart with his ♡A. He has six losers: two spades, three diamonds and a heart. One too many, but there is hope, as he can throw his heart loser on dummy's clubs. However, if he tries to play trumps first, the defenders will win, cash their heart winner and defeat the contract. Declarer must play three rounds of clubs right away to discard his heart loser. He must be careful: if he plays a club to dummy's king first, he will have only one club left in his hand, the ♣A. He will not be able to get to dummy to cash dummy's other club winner. The right order to play the clubs is first the ace, then a small club to dummy's king and queen. Remember to use up high cards from the short side first.

CHAPTER**SUMMARY**

A A popular way to play bridge is to use Chicago scoring: vulnerability rotates around the table, and bonuses are awarded for making partscore, game or slam.

B With 10-12 points, when partner opens the bidding, choose among the following actions:

- With excellent trump support, jump raise partner's major (a limit raise).
- Bid your longest new suit, at the two-level if necessary; with two five-card suits bid the higher-ranking. Otherwise bid your cheapest four-card suit.
- With four-card trump support in an unbalanced hand, jump raise partner's minor.

C With 13-15 points, when partner opens the bidding, choose among the following actions:

- With trump support, make a descriptive bid in a new suit, then raise partner's major to game.
- Bid your longest new suit, at the two-level if necessary; with two five-card suits bid the higher-ranking. Otherwise bid your cheapest four-card suit. Keep bidding until you get to game.
- Bid 2NT – this shows a balanced hand, 13-15 HCP, no four-card or longer major, no support for partner's major, and stoppers in the unbid suits. This bid is game forcing.

D With 16-18 points, when partner opens the bidding, your first response is exactly the same as if you have 13-15, with one exception: with a balanced hand, you may be able to respond 3NT. Your hand needs to meet the same specific requirements as those for a 2NT response but the 3NT response shows 16-18 HCP. Keep in mind that if partner has anything extra, you may be in the slam range (33+ points).

E With 19+ points, start with a jump shift – a bid in a new suit one level higher than necessary. This is game forcing. You will keep bidding until a slam is reached, or until it becomes clear slam is not possible.

F When cashing your tricks in a suit as declarer, it is usually right to use up your winners from the short side first, to avoid blocking the suit.

G Against a suit contract, it is often a good idea to lead a short suit (a singleton or doubleton) in the hope of getting a ruff.

5 Opener's Rebid

DID YOU KNOW?

Ely Culbertson was the first great promoter of bridge. His books, starting with the Contract Bridge Blue Book in 1930, sold millions of copies world-wide, while his bidding and teaching methods dominated the game. Culbertson's radio show was a huge hit. He won numerous national and international titles, many in partnership with his wife, Josephine. *The Bridge World*, the magazine Culbertson founded in 1929, still appears monthly.

WHAT YOU'RE GOING TO LEARN

In this chapter, you're going to see how the bidding continues after the first round. We'll assume that you have opened the bidding with one of a suit (auctions after an opening 1NT bid are covered in the next chapter). Partner has responded and it is now your turn to bid again.

We will look at a variety of situations: those where partner has raised your suit and those where he has bid notrump or a new suit of his own. When partner has raised your suit, your hand has improved, and we will see how you can revalue your hand to reflect this. To decide how high to bid, you will need to consider all of the information that partner has provided and also your own point range.

In the play section, you will learn about one of the primary tools of declarer play, the finesse. This is a method for making more tricks by leading towards your high cards. It doesn't always work, but when it does, it is almost magical how extra tricks appear.

The Auction Continues — Opener's Rebid

Let's assume you have made an opening bid of one of a suit. You will recall that partner's response may be either forcing or non-forcing. If responder has made a forcing bid, opener must bid again; he doesn't have a choice. Forcing bids are usually **unlimited** bids — that is, they have a floor but no ceiling. Here are two examples of unlimited bids.

Opener	Responder
1♡	1♠

Opener	Responder
1♡	2♣

In the first case, responder's 1♠ bid is unlimited. The floor for this bid is 6 points because with less responder would pass, but there is essentially no ceiling — you know the bottom, but you don't know the top. Responder may have a weak hand or a very strong one or something in between; opener just doesn't know yet. In the second case, responder's floor for 2♣ is higher. He has at least 10 points, but once again there is no ceiling. New-suit bids by responder are always forcing.

You know that there are also bids by responder that are limited and non-forcing. Opener may choose to pass them. Here are two examples:

Opener	Responder
1♡	1NT

Opener	Responder
1◇	3◇

These bids have both a floor and a ceiling. In the first case, responder has at least 6 points (the floor) and no more than 9 points (the ceiling). In the second case, responder has at least 10 points and no more than 12 points.

Opener's Rebid After a Limited Response

When your partner has made a limited bid showing an exact point range, you can often place the contract simply by adding your own points to partner's. So when partner makes a limited bid, you are 'He Who Knows'. As a result, you get a promotion: you are now the **captain** of the auction. You are in charge.

When partner has raised your major suit, the question 'Where should we play?' has been answered. You are going to play in your major. The next decision is 'How high?' Before you make it, there is a little more work to do. Once partner has raised your suit, you have to revalue your hand.

Blooming and Wilting — Revaluing Your Hand

During any bridge auction, the value of your hand goes up and down as the bidding progresses. For example, if you have a singleton club and four hearts, then your hand gets better if partner bids hearts: your hand blooms. But if partner bids clubs, your hand gets worse: it wilts. One of the happier moments at the bridge table occurs when partner raises your suit, especially if it is a major. Now your hand has really bloomed; it is worth a lot more. We are not going to lay down any exact rules for adding and subtracting points. Let's just say that you should be more aggressive with a blooming hand — if it is borderline, you can upgrade it to the next range. Likewise, you should be more careful with wilting hands and downgrade them if they are borderline.

Once you know the trump suit, extra unexpected length in trumps is worth a lot and this is definitely worth an upgrade whether you are declarer or dummy.

♠ A K 10 8 6 4 ♡ A 3 ◇ 6 3 ♣ Q 10 3

When you first picked up this hand and decided to open the bidding, it was worth 15 points: 13 HCP and 2 for distribution. If partner bids 2♠, your hand is worth even more and you should move it from the 13-15 point range into the 16-18 point range.

Counting Dummy Points as Opener

Suppose partner has responded in a suit that you are going to support. Even though you opened the bidding, it seems that you are destined to be the dummy. Partner is going to trump his losers in your hand if you have short suits. Once again, short suits are wonderful for partner. So just like responder, instead of counting distribution points the usual way, you should count dummy points. We apologize to the mathematically challenged, but you do have to recount. Take your high-card point total and add dummy points: 5 for a void, 3 for a singleton and 1 for a doubleton. This is the new point value for your hand.

Opener's Rebid After a Raise by Partner

You	Partner
1♡	2♡[1]

1. 6-9 points

You	Partner
1♡	3♡[1]

1. 10-12 points

Both of these bids by partner are limited and non-forcing. In the first example, you need a very strong hand to make game, since partner is contributing only 6-9 points. In the second example, you need just a bit more than opening values to bid game. You are the captain. Simply add your points to partner's (after revaluing your hand) and see if the total comes to 26 points or so. Then make your decision as to whether to bid again.

In the first auction, you would pass with a minimum hand (13-15). You simply can't have enough to reach 26 points. In the second, if you had 15 points, you would bid game, since on average partner will have 11 points. With a maximum hand (19+), you would bid game in both cases, since you have at least 26 points (or close enough — it isn't that scientific). With a moderate hand of 16-18 points, you can definitely go to game over the limit raise, since you know you have at least 26 points between you. However, in the first auction, if you have 17 or 18 points, you cannot be sure whether or not your side has enough for game. It depends on whether partner has a maximum (8 or 9) or a minimum (6 or 7). What to do? Ask partner. You are not allowed to shout across the table, but you can make a bid that asks the question: 3♡. Partner is expected to pass with a minimum hand (6-7) and bid game with a maximum (8-9).

Opener's Rebid After 1NT by Partner

When partner bids notrump, he has also limited his hand. You are therefore still the captain. For example:

You	Partner
1♡	1NT[1]

1. 6-9 points

First, just as before, think about how high you want to bid by adding your points to partner's. Do you want to play at a minimum level, invite to game or just bid game? This time, you must also think about the best spot to play in.

Suppose you have a minimum hand. There is no chance for game, so you should pass, right? Not necessarily. While it is true that you probably can't make game, a notrump contract might not be the best place to play. Remember, partner may have bid 1NT without a balanced hand. Therefore, if you have a balanced hand, you can pass, but with an unbalanced hand, you should choose one of these actions: (1) rebid your own suit or (2) bid a new suit if it is lower-ranking than your first suit.

When you bid a new suit, you are asking partner to pick which of your suits he likes better. If he likes the second suit better, he will pass; if he likes the first suit better, he will go back to it. Remember, you don't want to rebid a higher-ranking suit and force partner to bid at the three-level if he likes your first suit better. Here are some examples:

You	Partner
1♡	1NT
2♡	?

You	Partner
1♡	1NT
2♣	?

In the first auction, you expect partner to pass 2♡. In the second, he will give you **preference**: he will either pass 2♣ or take you back to 2♡. He's not showing anything more than his 6-9 minimum by doing this.

If you have enough points for game when you add everything together, and if you know where you want to play, just bid the game.

You	Partner
1♡	1NT
4♡	

You	Partner
1♡	1NT
3NT	

In the first example, you will have a good six- or seven-card heart suit. In the second, you have a strong balanced hand.

If you have a strong unbalanced hand with more than one suit, you want to ask partner for his opinion about where to play. Suppose you have both majors — the most common case. You will have opened 1♠, the higher ranking of your two suits. Over partner's 1NT, you jump to game in hearts, your second and lower-ranking suit. Now if partner likes your first suit better, he can go back to it without raising the level. To be clear, here is that auction:

You	Partner
1♠	1NT
4♡	

Partner will pass with better hearts and bid 4♠ with better spades.

If you are unsure about whether you should be in game after a 1NT response from partner, you can issue an invitation. If you have a balanced hand, you can bid 2NT. Recall that with a balanced hand of 15-17, you would have opened 1NT and with 13 or 14, you would have passed 1NT. Therefore, you must have exactly 18 or 19 points to make this 2NT bid. Partner should pass with a minimum (6-7) or bid 3NT with a maximum (8-9). With a good six-card major, you can rebid three of your major over 1NT.

You	Partner
1♡	1NT
3♡	?

You are asking partner to bid 4♡ with a maximum or pass with a minimum.

With a very strong hand (19+), you can also bid a new suit — just make sure that you bid one level higher than you would if you had a minimum or partner won't understand how good your hand is (this is called a **jump shift** — we encountered it last chapter for responder, and we'll discuss it a little more later on in this chapter).

You	Partner
1♡	1NT
3♣[1]	

1. Jump shift: 19+, game-forcing.

LET'S TRY IT!

1. Your hand is:

♠ A K J 7 6 5 4 ♡ K 10 4 ◇ A 3 ♣ 6

You open 1♠ and partner bids 2♠.

a) Has your hand bloomed or wilted?
b) What is your rebid?

2. You have:

♠ 7 6 ♡ A J 9 5 3 2 ◇ K J 7 ♣ A 3

You open 1♡ and partner raises hearts.

a) Has your hand improved?
b) What is your rebid if partner has bid 2♡?
c) What should you do if partner has bid 3♡?

3. You open 1♡ and partner bids 1NT. What is your rebid on each of these hands?

a) ♠ K 10 3 2 ♡ A K J 6 4 3 ◇ 6 ♣ 10 3
b) ♠ A 2 ♡ A K Q 10 5 4 ◇ K 3 2 ♣ 4 2
c) ♠ A 10 ♡ A K Q 10 9 8 ◇ A J 2 ♣ 4 2

Answers

1. a) Your hand has improved. You started out with 18 points: 15 HCP and 3 for distribution. Your hand should be upgraded to the 19+ range.
b) Rebid 4♠, since you have enough for game.

2. a) Your hand has improved and should be moved up from the 13-15 point range to the 16-18 point range.
b) Bid 3♡. Ask partner if he has a maximum. If partner has a maximum 8 or 9 points, he will bid 4♡. If partner has only 6 or 7, you are a touch short. He will pass 3♡.
c) Bid 4♡. You have enough for game opposite partner's 10-12.

3. a) Bid 2♡. You do not have enough for game and your hand is too distributional to want to play in notrump. Partner will pass your 2♡ bid, since you are the captain. Don't bid 2♠, since spades are higher ranking than hearts. In any case, partner can't have four spades or he would have bid 1♠ instead of 1NT.

b) Bid 3♡. You want to play in hearts, but you cannot be sure that your side has 26 points. If partner has a maximum, he will bid 4♡; otherwise, he will pass.

c) Bid 4♡. You have enough to play in game even if partner has a minimum and very little heart support.

Opener's Rebid After a New Suit by Responder

If partner's first bid is a new suit, you do not know how many points he has. True, you know that partner has enough to respond, since he didn't pass, and if he has bid a new suit at the two-level, then he has at least 10 points. However, partner could have a great deal more. It is your job as opener to bid again.

We know this 'open-endedness' of the first response is a tough nut to swallow. To make it a little clearer, look at these four hands for responder and imagine that in each case the opening bid has been 1♢:

♠ A K 7 5 3	♠ A K 7 5 3	♠ A K 7 5 3	♠ A K 7 5 3
♡ 5 4	♡ 5 4	♡ 5 4	♡ 5 4
♢ 8 6 2	♢ 8 6 2	♢ 8 6 2	♢ 8 6 2
♣ 4 3 2	♣ A 3 2	♣ A K 2	♣ A K Q

REMEMBER THIS! 

When responder bids a new suit, opener may not pass. He must make a bid, since a new suit by responder is a forcing bid.

On all four of these hands, the first bid by responder will be the same — 1♠! However, as you can see, they fall into very different point ranges: 6-9, 10-12, 13-15, and 16-18 respectively. Opener has no idea how many points responder actually has when he bids a new suit. Opener's responsibilities are to keep the bidding alive and to continue to describe his own hand with his rebid. Responder will then be able to add his points to opener's and decide how high to go.

Your side is still trying to answer the question 'Which suit should be trumps?' You also have to keep in mind exactly what type of hand you have: 13-15, 16-18, 19+. We will see how you should bid with each of these types of hand.

Opener's Hand Type

13-15 points	Minimum Hand
16-18 points	Intermediate Hand
19 or more	Maximum Hand

Once you, as opening bidder, describe your hand accurately, partner will be able to decide whether the hand belongs in partscore, game or even slam.

Rebids by Opener with a Minimum Hand (13-15 points)

Most of the time, when you are the opening bidder, you will find yourself holding a minimum hand. That's life. However, it is important that you bid very carefully with hands in this range. You don't want to mislead partner by showing more than a minimum. You have two simple options you should consider first. If partner has bid a major suit and you have support for it, then raise partner at the cheapest level. With a balanced hand and stoppers in the unbid suits, bid the cheapest number of notrump. If your hand doesn't fit either of these options, you have a chance to get creative. Basically, you choose the rebid that best describes your hand from the following list (they are not in any particular order — go for the one that fits your hand best):

a) Rebid your first suit at the cheapest level (you need at least five);
b) With trump support, raise partner's suit at the cheapest level. You would like to have four trumps to do this, but if no other choice appeals, then it's okay to raise with three if you have an honor in that suit;
c) Bid the cheapest number of notrump if you have stoppers in the two unbid suits;
d) Bid a new suit at the one-level;
e) Bid a new suit at the two-level. You may bid a new suit at the two-level only if it is *lower ranking* than the suit you opened (otherwise, if partner likes your first suit better, he will have to return to it at the three-level and you are too weak to ask partner to bid that high).

Here are some auctions where opener shows a minimum hand:

You	Partner
1♡	1♠
2♠	

You	Partner
1♡	1♠
1NT	

You	Partner
1♡	1♠
2♡	

You	Partner
1♡	1♠
2♣	

You	Partner
1◇	1♡
2◇	

You	Partner
1◇	1♡
1♠	

You	Partner
1♣	1◇
1♠	

You	Partner
1♣	1◇
2◇	

Notice that most of your rebid choices show that you have a minimum hand, but when you bid a new suit of your own, you could have as much as 18. (New suit bids are unlimited.)

Opener's Rebid With an Intermediate Hand (16-18 points)

Once again, your first choice is to raise partner's major with excellent trump support, but with 16-18 points, you *jump*:

You	Partner
1♢	1♡
3♡	

You	Partner
1♢	1♠
3♠	

You have answered the question, 'In what suit shall we play the deal?' Partner will now be able to decide how high to bid by adding your points to his.

With a balanced hand and no support for partner's major, you will rebid notrump. If you had a balanced hand in the 15-17 range, you would have opened 1NT in the first place. With 18 or 19 points, a balanced hand and stoppers in the unbid suits, you jump in notrump.

You	Partner
1♢	1♠
2NT	

Otherwise, pick one of these options:

a) With a six-card suit, jump to three of your own suit.
b) Bid a new suit at the cheapest level. You don't have to jump. Bidding a new suit doesn't show a minimum and if partner doesn't pass (with a very weak hand), you can make another move towards game. With 17 or more, you can even bid a higher-ranking suit than your first suit at the two-level, since you are strong enough to play at the three-level if partner likes your first suit better.

Both of these auctions are possible if you are in the 16-18 range:

You	Partner
1♡	1♠
2♢	2♡
3♡	?

You	Partner
1♢	1♠
2♡	?

c) If partner has raised your major, you can make an invitational bid:

♠ A 2
♡ A Q 8 7 4 3
♢ K J 3
♣ 7 4

You	Partner
1♡	2♡
3♡	

With 6 or 7 points, he will pass. With 8 or more, he will go on to game.

Rebidding with a Maximum Hand (19+)

If, after hearing partner's response, you know you have enough for game and you know where to play, just bid the game. For example, if you have excellent support for partner's major, you can just bid game in the major.

You	Partner
1♢	1♡
4♡	

You	Partner
1♢	1♠
4♠	

Also, as we saw earlier, if partner made a minimum raise of your suit, you can bid game.

You	Partner
1♡	2♡
4♡	

You	Partner
1♠	2♠
4♠	

We have already discussed some of the other possibilities with a maximum hand. With a balanced 18-19 HCP, you can jump in notrump. However, on most strong hands, your rebid will be a jump shift, as we mentioned earlier. This promises at least 19 points and it is forcing to game, because even if partner has a mere 7 points, you have the 26 points needed for game.

REMEMBER THIS! ☑

A jump shift by opener shows 19+ points and is a game force.

Summary of Rebids After Partner Makes an Unlimited Bid

Here is a summary of the bids you can make when partner has bid a new suit over your opening bid of one of a suit. The top two bids are your first choices. After that, pick the bid that best describes your hand.

Summary of Opener's Rebid After Responder Has Bid A New Suit			
Opener has	**Minimum (13-15)**	**Moderate (16-18)**	**Maximum (19+)**
Excellent trump support for partner's major	Single Raise	Jump Raise	Raise to Game
Balanced Hand	Rebid notrump at the minimum level	With 18 HCP, jump in notrump	With 19 HCP, jump in notrump
Five-card or longer suit of your own	Minimum bid in your suit	Jump in your suit (six-card suit or better)	Bid game in your suit (if it is solid) or jump shift
New suit at the one-level	Bid at cheapest level	Bid at cheapest level	Jump shift
New suit at the two-level	Bid at cheapest level, but don't bid a suit higher ranking than your first	Bid at cheapest level, but you may bid a higher-ranking suit if necessary (17+ points)	Jump shift
Excellent support for partner's minor	Single Raise	Jump Raise	

LET'S TRY IT!

1. You have:

♠ A 2 ♡ K 7 6 5 ◊ A J 3 2 ♣ Q 10 3

You open 1◊. What is your rebid in each of the following auctions?

a)

You	Partner
1◊	1♡
?	

b)

You	Partner
1◊	1♠
?	

c)

You	Partner
1◊	2♣
?	

2. You have:

♠ A K ♡ K Q J 6 3 2 ◊ 7 2 ♣ K 4 3

You open 1♡ and partner bids 1♠. Has your hand improved? What is your rebid?

3. You have:

♠ A K 10 8 ♡ K Q 7 ◇ A Q 10 3 2 ♣ 2

a) You open 1◇ and partner bids 1♡. What is your rebid?
b) What is your rebid if partner's response is 1♠ instead?

Answers

1. **a)** Bid 2♡. You have a minimum hand with excellent trump support for partner.
b) Bid 1NT. You have a balanced minimum hand.
c) Bid 2NT. You have a balanced minimum hand. This is not forcing.

2. No, you have not yet found a fit, so your hand has not improved. Bid 3♡: you have a moderate hand with a good six-card suit.

3. **a)** You have a maximum hand. You should rebid 2♠, a jump shift.
b) Bid 4♠. Even if partner has a minimum, you have enough for game.

Practice Bidding

You have now begun to see the way bidding works. It is beautiful and fun, but it does need practice. We suggest that you deal out two hands and practice bidding them (if you take some of the low spot cards out of the deck, you'll find you get more opening bids). Bid a few hands whenever you have time. A friend of ours, a well-known bridge expert, always carries a deck of cards and deals them out once he has ordered in a restaurant! If you can practice with your favorite partner, that is the best method of all. Bridge is a partnership game and you want to be on the same wavelength as your partner. It is also fun and helpful to discuss the outcome after you bid. Did you get to the right spot? Was partner expecting your hand to be similar to the one you held?

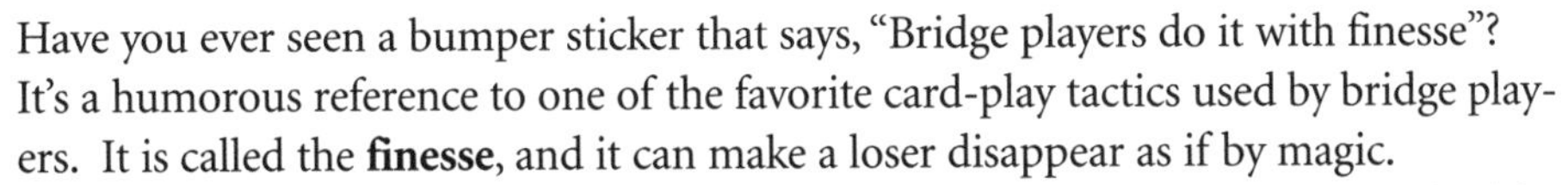

THE PLAY OF THE HAND

Finessing

Have you ever seen a bumper sticker that says, "Bridge players do it with finesse"? It's a humorous reference to one of the favorite card-play tactics used by bridge players. It is called the **finesse**, and it can make a loser disappear as if by magic.

Let's lay out some cards. Take the spade suit and give South two little spades (the ♠4 and the ♠5 in the example we are using). Give North across the table the A-Q of spades. Lay these cards face up on the table. This is what you should see:

♠ A Q

♠ 5 4

How many spade tricks are you going to take? There is one sure trick, the ace, but what about the queen? You could play the ace and hope the king falls, but that doesn't seem very likely. Is there any other way for you to take a trick with the spade queen? Actually, there is, but it depends on exactly where the spade king is. Take the king of spades and put it in the hand on your left (the West hand) with another spade. Put two other spades in the hand on your right (the East hand). Now you have a layout something like the one to the right.

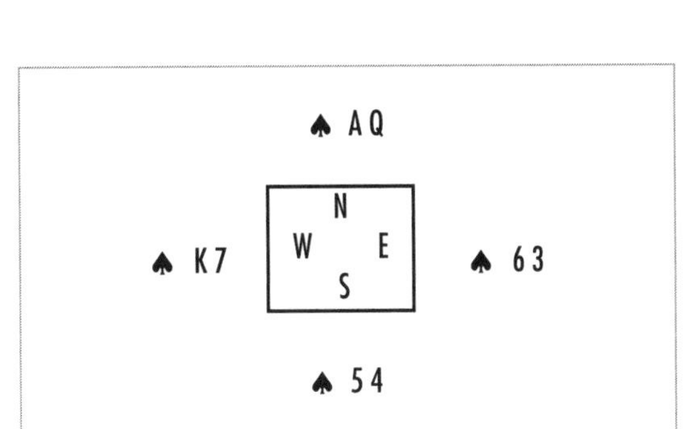

Lead the ♠4 from the South hand. The plan is to play the ace only if your left-hand opponent plays the king. If he plays a low card, you will play the queen... and it will win the trick! Go ahead, try it.

Congratulations — you have just taken your first finesse. For this play to work, you have to lead from the weaker side of the suit *towards* the stronger. If you lead a spade from the North hand, it doesn't matter whether you lead the ace or the queen — you will take only one spade trick.

Now trade the East and West hands. You will see something like this (lower right).

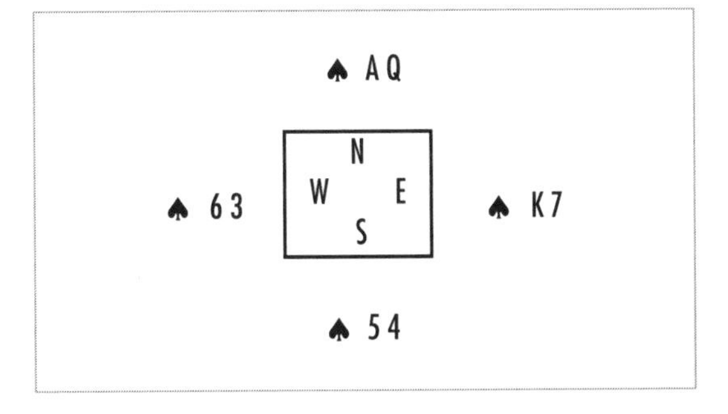

How many spade tricks can you take now? This time you will only be able to take one, the ace. This time when you lead a spade towards dummy's A-Q, your right-hand opponent will win his king if you play the queen and play a low card if you play the ace. *Finesses depend on the position of the*

missing honor and so they work only half of the time. But that is definitely better than nothing!

There are many positions where you may be able to win extra tricks by finessing. Let's look at some more examples. It is a good idea to lay out the cards as they appear in each diagram and then try the play for yourself.

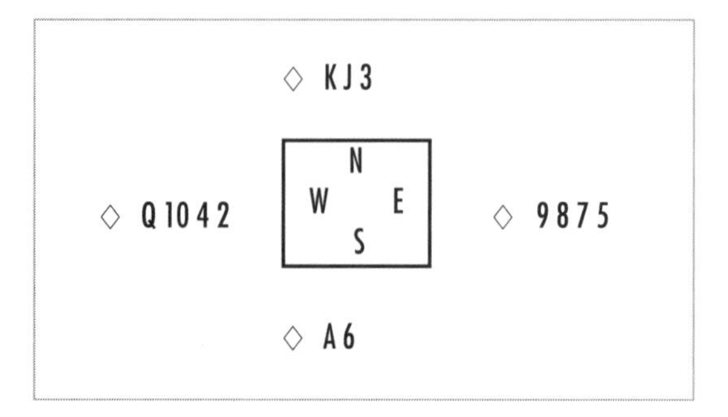

If you want to try to take three tricks, you can cash the ace first and then lead the six — *towards* the jack, the honor that you want to finesse. If West plays a small diamond, you play the jack... and hope! In this layout, no matter what your left-hand opponent does, he cannot prevent you from taking three tricks in this suit: the ace, the king and the jack.

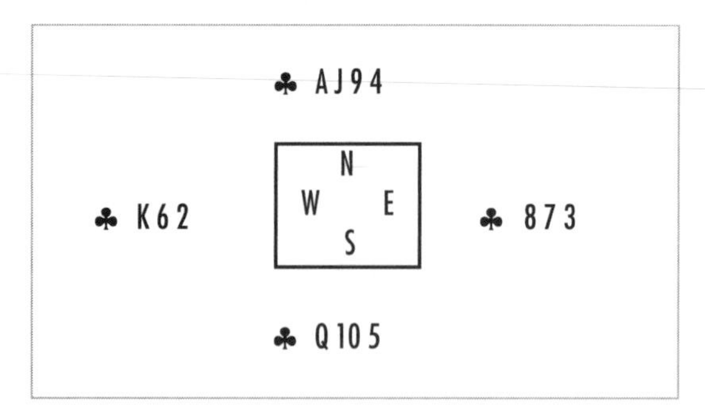

We're sure you know by now that you have to lead towards the ace. This time you should lead the queen and play low from dummy if West does not produce the king. If the queen wins the trick, you will still be in the proper hand to take another finesse. You should always lead an honor to a finesse when you own all the neighboring cards in the combined hands. However, without those to help, it won't work.

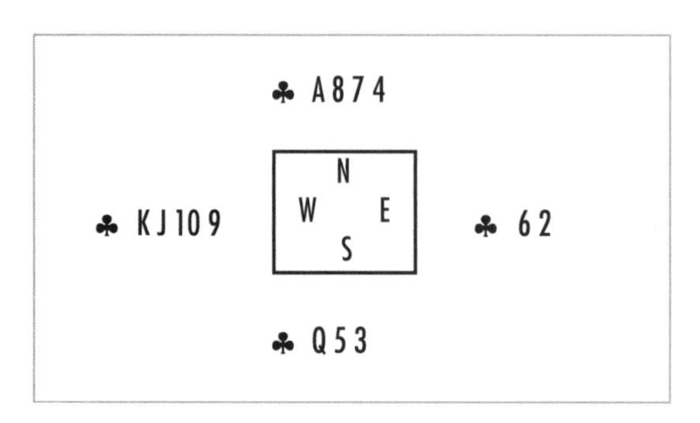

In this position, if you lead the queen, West plays his king. Now when you take your ace, the jack, ten and nine have become winners. Thus, you must not lead the queen. After all, you have no neighbors. If you have this holding, you should lead the three to the ace and then the four towards the queen, hoping that East has the king. As the cards lie in the diagram, you will only be able to get one club trick— the ace.

Look for chances to take finesses in the practice deals. Don't forget to count your losers and make a plan.

Deal 1 — Dealer South

West	North	East	South
			1♠
pass	2♠	pass	3♠
pass	4♠	all pass	

North
♠ J932
♡ AQ5
◇ J98
♣ J53

West
♠ 76
♡ K932
◇ 7643
♣ KQ10

East
♠ 108
♡ J1087
◇ A5
♣ A9876

South
♠ AKQ54
♡ 64
◇ KQ102
♣ 42

South opens the bidding with 1♠, and North, with excellent trump support, raises to 2♠. With an intermediate hand, South can make game if North has a maximum, so South asks North by bidding 3♠. Today South is lucky and his partner goes on to 4♠.

West leads the ♣K, the top of a broken sequence. East and West will probably try to take three rounds of clubs, but declarer will trump the third round. He needs to take ten tricks. He has already lost two clubs. There are no spade losers and exactly one diamond loser. He can borrow the ♡A from North, but still has another heart loser. That makes four losers, one too many. However, if West has the ♡K, then declarer can finesse the ♡Q and make his heart loser disappear. First, he should draw the opponents' trumps. Then he can give up the ◇A and establish his diamond winners. Later, he will lead a heart from his hand towards the ♡A-Q. If West plays low (as expected), declarer will put in the queen (with his fingers crossed). On this deal, the queen will win the trick and South will make 4♠.

Deal 2 — Dealer West

West	North	East	South
1♡	pass	2◇	pass
2♡	pass	4♡	all pass

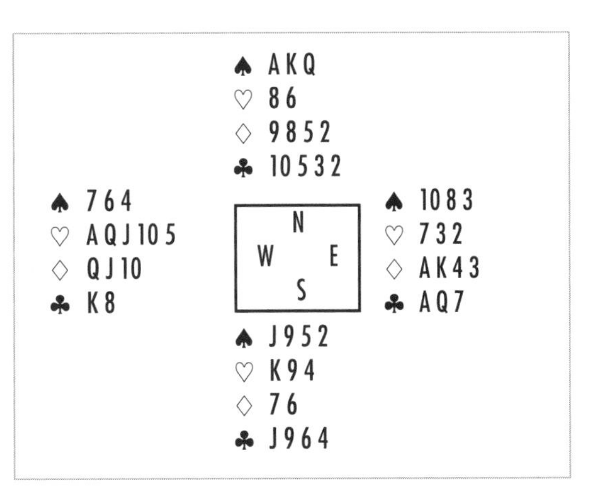

With a five-card heart suit, West opens 1♡. Although he is balanced, he is too weak to open 1NT. East has a game-going hand with 13 points and shows his partner his diamond suit. West rebids 2♡, lacking the spade stopper for a 2NT bid. East now knows exactly what to do and bids the game in hearts.

North finds the wonderful lead of the ♠A. He will probably be very happy to take the first three spade tricks. Declarer counts his losers and finds that, after losing the first three spades, he is solid in every other suit except hearts. The opponents hold the king of hearts. His best hope is that the heart finesse will work. Notice that this time he has to take the heart finesse twice to avoid losing a heart trick. Let's say that North plays a diamond after cashing the three spades. Declarer wins in dummy and immediately takes the heart finesse. When that works, he returns to dummy with one of his winners in clubs or diamonds to take the heart finesse again. Finally, he can draw the last trump and claim his contract.

Deal 3 — Dealer North

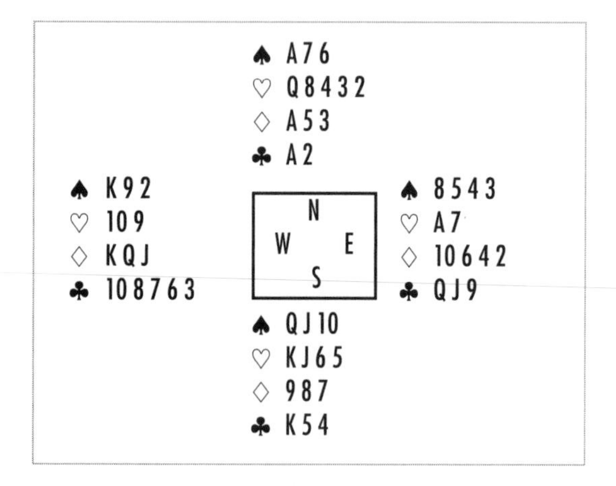

West	North	East	South
	1♡	pass	3♡
pass	4♡	all pass	

North opens 1♡. With 10 points and four trumps, South bids 3♡. North's hand is worth upgrading after South supports him, and so he bids game.

East will probably lead the ♣Q from his broken sequence. Declarer wins the first trick and counts his losers. He has one spade loser, one heart loser and two diamond losers: one too many. Fortunately, he has a plan. He can take the spade finesse and avoid a spade loser. First, he needs to get the kiddies off the street — he doesn't want any of his side winners ruffed. He leads a heart; East wins and plays another club. Declarer wins this, draws the last trumps ending in dummy and takes the spade finesse. This position is a little different — this time he leads the ♠Q from dummy. It works! If West plays the ♠K on the ♠Q, then declarer plays the ♠A. After that, dummy's ♠J and ♠10 will be high. If West doesn't play the ♠K, then declarer plays low from his own hand as well and the ♠Q will win the trick. Remember, this type of finesse works because declarer owns all of the neighbors of that spade queen in the combined hands.

Deal 4 — Dealer East

West	North	East	South
		1♢	pass
1♡	pass	1♠	pass
3♢	all pass		

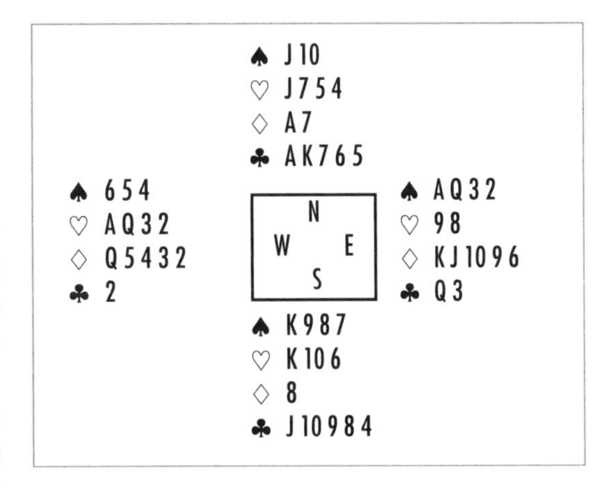

East opens 1♢ and West bids his four-card major instead of raising diamonds right away. When East rebids 1♠, West shows his diamond support and 10-12 points by jumping to 3♢. East has a minimum hand and passes.

South leads the ♣J, the top of his sequence. Declarer has a lot of losers: three potential spade losers, a heart loser, a diamond loser and two club losers. All of this adds up to seven: three too many. However, declarer has a plan. He will draw trumps. Even if trumps are 3-0, there will still be two left in dummy, so eventually declarer can trump his second club and his fourth spade in dummy. At this point, he will still have one loser too many. His plan is to take finesses in both hearts and spades. If either finesse works, declarer will make his contract; if both work, he will make an overtrick.

The play goes this way: North wins the club and switches to the ♠J. Declarer finesses the ♠Q and it loses to the ♠K. South continues a spade, won by declarer with the ace. Declarer forces out the ♢A. After he gets the lead back, he draws the last trump and then takes the heart finesse. Happiness! The heart finesse works. Later, declarer will trump his club loser and one spade loser in dummy.

CHAPTER**SUMMARY**

A When responder raises your suit, especially if it is a major, your hand has bloomed in value. If you are debating whether to bid on, go for it!

B When responder raises your major suit, add your points to partner's and place the contract. You are the captain.

- If you cannot have at least 26 points, pass.
- If you have 26 or more points for certain, bid game in your major.
- If you *might* have 26 points, invite partner to bid game with a maximum. He will pass with a minimum.

C When responder bids 1NT, he has 6-9 points. You are the captain.

a) With a minimum hand (13-15), pick from this list:

- With a six-card suit or longer, rebid your suit.
- Bid a new suit (if it is lower ranking).
  - If you bid a new suit, partner will give you preference.
- Pass.

b) With 16-18, invite to game by picking from this list:

- With a balanced hand, bid 2NT.
- With a good six-card or longer suit, bid three of that suit.
- Bid a new suit.

c) With 19 or more, you have enough for game:

- With a good six-card or longer major suit, bid game in the major.
- **jump shift** in a new suit. This is forcing to game.
- With a balanced hand, bid 3NT.

D When responder bids a new suit, it is forcing. Opener must bid again.

E After a new suit by responder:

a) With a minimum hand (13-15), pick from this list:

- With adequate trump support, raise partner's suit at the cheapest level.
- Rebid your first suit at the cheapest level (you need at least five).
- With stoppers in the two unbid suits, bid the cheapest number of notrump.
- Bid a new suit at the one-level.
- Bid two of a new suit if it is lower ranking than your first suit.

b) With extra values (16-18), pick from this list:

- Jump raise partner's suit with excellent trump support (4+ cards).
- With a good six-card suit or better, jump in your first suit.
- Bid a new suit at the cheapest level (it doesn't show a minimum); it is allowed to be higher ranking than your first-bid suit.

c) With a game-going hand (19+), pick a rebid from this list:
- With excellent trump support (4+ cards), raise partner's major suit to game.
- With a balanced hand and stoppers in the unbid suits, jump in notrump with 18-19 HCP.
- Bid game in your suit if it you know you have at least 26 points between your hands.
- Jump shift.

F You can sometimes make a loser disappear by taking a finesse: play a card from the weaker hand towards the stronger hand. A finesse is dependent on the position of the missing honor and works only 50% of the time.

6 Notrump Bidding

DID YOU KNOW?

Charles Goren, a Philadelphia lawyer, took over from Ely Culbertson as 'Mr. Bridge' in the 1950s. His 'point-count' bidding eclipsed the use of the old-style Culbertson Honor Tricks and established a standard method of bidding that has endured through the last half-century. A world champion in 1950, he was also a prolific book author who hosted a TV show on bridge and penned a regular *Sports Illustrated* column on bridge. In 1958, he was featured on the cover of *Time* magazine.

WHAT YOU'RE GOING TO LEARN

In the last few chapters, we have concentrated on trump contracts, but you can also play contracts in notrump. In fact, in notrump, you only have to commit to nine tricks to make game, whereas major-suit games demand ten and minor-suit games eleven. As a result, 3NT is the favorite game contract of most bridge players.

In this chapter, we will look at auctions that start with an opening bid of 1NT. A 1NT opening is a very specific bid that defines opener's hand within narrow limits. Since responder knows so much about the hand opposite, he can often select the best contract right away. Even if that isn't possible, he often needs only a little more information from partner to decide where to play. We will look at responder's role in notrump auctions, how he can use a special bid to get information he needs, and how his point range affects the bid that he selects.

After that, we will look at how to play notrump contracts. In notrump contracts, we count the number of winners rather than the number of losers. We will look at exactly how to count sure winners and then how to make a plan to get the number of tricks we need. Notrump is a race between declarer and the defense to see who can take their winners first. We will look at the hold-up play, where you refuse to win a trick, and how that can help you to win the race. Finally, we will look at how to select the opening lead against a notrump contract.

Notrump Auctions

Two quick reminders: (1) when bidding notrump, you only count high card points and (2) an opening bid of 1NT shows exactly 15-17 HCP and a balanced hand. A balanced hand has at most one doubleton and no singletons or voids at all. The most balanced hand has a distribution of 4-3-3-3 — four cards in one suit and three in each of the others. Hands that have 4-4-3-2 or 5-3-3-2 shape are also balanced. However, 4-4-4-1 and 5-4-2-2, for example, are not balanced hand patterns: the first contains a singleton and the second contains two doubletons.

Also remember:

25 HCP makes 3NT (game)
26 points makes 4♡, 4♠ (game in a major)
33 HCP makes 6NT (small slam)
37 HCP makes 7NT (grand slam)

Responder will use those point ranges as a guide to decide how high to bid.

Responses to Partner's 1NT Opening Bid

Most bridge players enjoy opening 1NT. For one thing, it announces quite a good hand. For another, a 1NT opening provides your partner with a lot of information about your hand. Partner knows that you have 15, 16 or 17 HCP and a balanced hand. This is very powerful information. Compare that to what partner knows when you open one of a suit. You can have anything from 13 points to more than 20. You can be balanced or unbalanced, and if you open one of a minor, partner can't even be sure that your minor is four cards long!

It is fun to be responder when partner opens 1NT. As responder, you are going to take charge, since you know so much about partner's hand. You are the captain of the auction. You are in a great position to answer the two fundamental questions of bidding, 'Where?' and 'How high?' Sometimes you can just place the contract. On other occasions, you might want to ask partner a few questions. Let's see how that works.

We will look at responding to notrump by range. When responding to notrump, you don't count any points for distribution. However, with a good five-card suit (one headed by an ace or king), go ahead and add an extra point. With a good six-card suit, add 2 points. You know that partner has at least a small fit for you, because he has two cards or more in every suit. A good five-card suit will be useful either in notrump or in a suit contract. With an unbalanced hand, you can count all of your distribution, but only after you decide that you are going to play in a suit contract.

REMEMBER THIS! ☑

The responder to a 1NT opening bid should add an extra point for a good five-card suit (headed by the ace or king) even if he plans to play in notrump. With a good six-card suit, add 2 points.

Responding to 1NT With 0-7 Points

Let's start with weak hands. If you have 0-7 points, you know that game is unlikely. When you add your points to those of your partner, you can see that you cannot have 25 points, even if partner has his maximum 17 points. Therefore, your goal is to keep the contract low, but 1NT might not be the right place. If you have a five-card major suit, you will usually be better off with your suit as trumps. That way, your weak hand will be able to take a few tricks. Say you have this hand

♠ 10 9 8 4 3 ♡ K 5 ◇ Q 4 3 2 ♣ 3 2

or worse still

♠ 10 9 8 4 3 ♡ 6 5 ◇ 5 4 3 2 ♣ 3 2

If partner opens 1NT, it will very difficult for him to make that contract. However, if you can arrange for spades to be trumps, knowing that partner has at least two of them (since he opened 1NT), that will be much better. Now you will be able to take some tricks with your small spades, whereas they would be useless to partner in 1NT. There is a special way to get to a major-suit contract after a 1NT opening bid.

Jacoby Transfers

This is an exciting moment in your bridge career. You are about to learn your first **convention**. A convention is a bid that does not mean what it says — it is an **artificial bid**. The convention we are going to describe is called the **Jacoby Transfer**.[1]

If partner opens 1NT and you bid 2♡, you expect it to promise hearts and to suggest that your side play in a heart contract. As we will see, that's not always true. If you and your partner have agreed to play Jacoby Transfers, the 2♡ bid does not say anything about hearts.[2] In fact, it shows something quite different.

A transfer is a convention that *requires* partner to make a bid in a different suit, specifically the next suit up from the actual transfer bid. Using Jacoby Transfers, you bid 2◇ to tell partner to bid 2♡, and use 2♡ to tell partner to bid 2♠. If you bid 2◇, you are promising at least five cards in the heart suit; if you bid 2♡, you are promising at least five spades.

> ***"Convention"***
> **A bid with a specific agreed-upon artificial meaning. It may not say anything about the suit bid.**

1. Many bridge conventions are named after the person who first invented or popularized them. This one is named after Oswald Jacoby, one of the premier American bridge players of the twentieth century.
2. You will encounter some people who do not play Jacoby Transfers. In that case, when they bid 2◇ over 1NT, they have diamonds, and when they bid 2♡, they have hearts. You must agree with your partner about whether or not you are playing transfers before starting to play. Transfers are very common in modern bidding.

Partner	You
1NT	2♢[1]
2♡[2]	

1. Transfer to hearts.
2. Partner must bid this.

Partner	You
1NT	2♡[1]
2♠[2]	

1. Transfer to spades.
2. Partner must bid this.

"Jacoby Transfer"

A response to an opening 1NT bid. A bid of 2♢ asks partner to bid 2♡; a bid of 2♡ asks partner to bid 2♠. This promises at least five cards in the transfer suit.

Thus, 2♢ over 1NT says absolutely nothing about diamonds and 2♡ over 1NT says absolutely nothing about hearts. The 2♢ bid is simply a way to get partner to bid 2♡ and the 2♡ bid is a way to get partner to bid 2♠. Instead of bidding 2♡ or 2♠ yourself, you have 'transferred' the bid to partner. He makes it instead of you. We call the suit partner must bid the **transfer suit**. Remember, using a Jacoby Transfer promises at least five cards in the transfer suit.

Bridge is a game of full disclosure. That means that your opponents are entitled to know what your bids mean if you have an agreement with your partner. When you and your partner are using a convention, you have a responsibility to tell your opponents when you use it. Make sure that your opponents know that you are playing Jacoby Transfers so that they will be able to follow the auction.

Partner has opened 1NT. If you have a weak hand with hearts, you bid 2♢, Jacoby Transfer. Now, when partner bids 2♡, as you requested, you pass. You are in the contract that you, the captain, have selected, but partner is declarer.

Why do we go to so much trouble to get partner to play the contract? Certainly not because he is a better declarer! It turns out that when one hand is very weak and another is strong and balanced, the contract plays better when the strong hand is declarer. When the opponent on partner's left makes the opening lead, partner plays last. He can save his high cards until he sees which card he needs to play — that alone can often be worth an extra trick in the play. In this case, getting partner to be declarer is the first job of the person responding. As we explore Jacoby Transfers further, you will also see that using this convention allows you to describe a lot of different hands, not just the weak ones.

REMEMBER THIS! ☑

After an opening bid of 1NT, responder with 0-7 points and a five-card or longer major should transfer to the major and then pass. With 0-7 and no five-card major, pass and hope for the best.

If you have a weak hand with a long minor, you are out of luck. By adopting transfers, you have lost your ability to bid 2♢ to show a diamond suit, and, as we shall see later, 2♣ is reserved for something else. If you have one of those hands, you just have to pass 1NT and hope for the best. This is the downside of using conventions: you lose the natural meaning of your artificial bid. So you have to be sure that you are gaining more than you are losing.

LET'S TRY IT!

1. Partner opens 1NT. What do you respond on each of the following hands?

a) ♠ Q J 9 8 7 ♡ 5 4 ◇ 8 7 3 2 ♣ 3 2
b) ♠ K 4 3 ♡ 5 4 ◇ Q 10 8 7 ♣ Q 6 5 4
c) ♠ 4 ♡ 9 8 7 6 5 4 ◇ Q 3 ♣ 10 9 8 7
d) ♠ J 10 5 4 ♡ 10 3 2 ◇ 9 8 7 6 4 ♣ 5

2. Partner opens 1NT. How many points do you have on each of these two hands?

a) ♠ 5 4 3 ♡ Q 4 3 ◇ A 5 4 3 ♣ 9 3 2
b) ♠ 5 4 ♡ Q 4 3 ◇ A 5 4 3 2 ♣ 9 3 2

Answers

1. a) Bid 2♡. This hand will almost surely play better in spades than in notrump. When you have a five-card major, use a Jacoby Transfer. Partner will bid 2♠ and you will pass.

b) Pass. You have 7 HCP, a decent hand for partner, but not enough for game. He will be happy to be playing in 1NT.

c) Bid 2◇, Jacoby Transfer. You want to play in hearts, but you have way too little for game. You will pass partner's 2♡ rebid.

d) Pass and hope for the best. With only four spades, you must not transfer to spades (partner may only have two of them) and there is no way to play in 2◇, since that bid is a transfer to hearts.

2. Hand (a) is worth 6 points and hand (b) is worth 7 points (even for notrump, you add 1 for the five-card suit headed by the ace). Both hands fit within the 0-7 point range.

Responding to 1NT With 8 or 9 Points

With 8 or 9 points, you can see that if you add your points to partner's, you may have enough for game if partner has a maximum. However, if partner has only 15, you do not have the 25 points that you need for game. We consider hands in this 8-9 range to be invitational. So, as captain, you want to invite partner to bid game. If you don't have a long major suit, your invitational bid is 2NT. Partner will pass with a minimum and bid 3NT with a maximum. However, if you have a five-card major, then you want to offer partner the option of using that as a trump suit as an alternative to playing in notrump.

Therefore, if you have a five-card major, you again start with a Jacoby Transfer. However, this time you don't pass when partner completes the transfer. Let's look at what happens next. Let's say you have:

♠ Q 10 8 7 5 ♡ A 3 ◇ Q J 4 ♣ 10 7 6

This hand is worth 9 points in notrump — not quite enough to be sure of game — so you start by bidding 2♡, Jacoby Transfer. Of course, partner does his part by bidding 2♠.

REMEMBER THIS!

When you are responding to 1NT and your major is only five cards long, you can show it to partner by transferring. After that, you may not bid the suit again. Your next bid must be the correct number of notrump.

Partner	You
1NT	2♡
2♠	?

Now you bid again to invite partner. However, since partner may have only two-card support for spades, this deal may play better in notrump. Bid 2NT now. This tells partner that you have exactly five spades and 8 or 9 points. Partner can decide what to do. With a maximum, partner accepts your invitation. If he also has three or more spades, partner bids 4♠, but with only two spades, he bids 3NT. With a minimum, partner refuses the invitation. With only two spades, he passes 2NT, but with three or more spades, he bids 3♠, since these hands will play better in spades than notrump with that magic eight-card fit. Don't give in to temptation and bid again over 3♠. You gave your partner a choice and he made it: he doesn't want to play in game.

Here are the possible spade auctions:

Partner	You
1NT	2♡
2♠	2NT
pass[1]	

1. Minimum, two spades.

Partner	You
1NT	2♡
2♠	2NT
3♠[1]	

1. Minimum, three or more spades.

Partner	You
1NT	2♡
2♠	2NT
3NT[1]	

1. Maximum, two spades.

Partner	You
1NT	2♡
2♠	2NT
4♠[1]	

1. Maximum, three or more spades.

Here's a summary chart of opener's options after 1NT-2♡; 2♠-2NT:

	Two spades	Three or more spades
Maximum opener	Bid 3NT	Bid 4♠
Minimum opener	Pass	Bid 3♠, which responder will pass

Of course, there are four similar auctions available to you that begin with a transfer to hearts.

With a six-card or longer major suit, things do not need to be quite this complicated. If you have six or more cards in your major suit and 6-7 HCP, you know you want to play there; so after partner accepts your transfer, raise him.

Partner	You
1NT	2♡
2♠	3♠

REMEMBER THIS!

After partner opens 1NT, if you have 8 or 9 points, invite partner to game.

This auction offers partner a choice of passing 3♠ or going on to 4♠. This time, 3NT is not an option. The captain has spoken and said that this deal will be played in spades.

Responding to 1NT with an invitational hand (8-9 points)	
With a balanced hand	Bid 2NT
With a five-card major	Transfer to the major and then bid 2NT
With a six-card major	Transfer to the major and then raise the major to the three-level

This table is not yet complete. There are some more options and we will add them in the next chapter.

LET'S TRY IT!

1. Partner has opened 1NT. What do you respond with each of the following hands? How do you plan to continue the auction?

a) ♠ K 10 5 4 3 ♡ Q 3 2 ◊ K 10 2 ♣ 4 2
b) ♠ K 4 ♡ J 10 9 8 7 6 ◊ Q J 2 ♣ 10 4
c) ♠ 7 6 3 ♡ K J 2 ◊ Q 10 3 2 ♣ K 9 7

2. The auction has gone:

You	Partner
1NT	2◊
2♡	2NT
?	

a) What is partner asking?

b) What would you do now if you held this hand:

♠ A Q 3 ♡ 4 2 ◇ K Q J 4 ♣ A J 3 2

Answers

1. a) Bid 2♡ (transfer). You have 9 points: 8 HCP and 1 for the fifth spade. When partner bids 2♠, bid 2NT to invite to game in either notrump or spades.

b) Bid 2◇ (transfer). You have 7 HCP and 2 for distribution since you are going to play in hearts. You have enough to invite. When partner bids 2♡, bid 3♡ to invite to game in hearts.

c) Bid 2NT to invite partner to bid 3NT. You have a very balanced hand. Notrump is the spot.

2. a) Partner is asking you to choose between playing hearts or notrump and also whether you have a maximum or a minimum.

b) You have only two hearts, but you do have a maximum. Bid 3NT.

Responding With 10-15 Points

When you are in this range, you know that you have enough for game, but not enough for slam (that usually takes at least 33 combined points). As we look at your choices, you will see that they are quite similar to bidding with an invitational hand.

If you have a balanced hand with no five-card major, you will usually simply bid 3NT. Well done, captain. If you do have a five-card major, once again you do responder's first job — you use a Jacoby Transfer. However, this time you won't stop short of game. For example, if you have a balanced hand with only five hearts, then after partner completes the transfer, you bid 3NT (rather than 2NT as you did with only 8-9 points). Partner can now pick which game he prefers: with three or more hearts, he will bid game in hearts; with only two hearts, partner will pass and play 3NT.

Partner	You
1NT	2◇
2♡	3NT
pass	

Partner	You
1NT	2◇
2♡	3NT
4♡	

If you have lots of your major (six or more), transfer to the major and then bid game. Again, the captain has spoken.

Partner	You
1NT	2♡
2♠	4♠

Partner	You
1NT	2◇
2♡	4♡

Responding to 1NT with game values	
With a balanced hand	Bid 3NT
With a five-card major	Transfer to the major and then bid 3NT
With a six-card major	Transfer to the major and then raise the major to the four-level

Again, as you'll see in the next chapter, this table is not yet complete.

LET'S TRY IT! 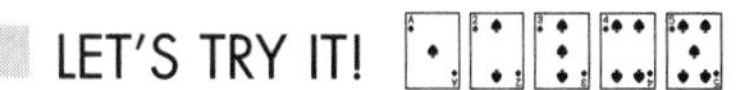

1. Partner opened with 1NT. What do you respond with each of the following holdings? How do you expect the auction to continue?

a) ♠ Q J 10 5 4 3 ♡ A 4 2 ◇ Q 3 ♣ 7 3
b) ♠ K 3 ♡ A K Q 5 4 ◇ 7 6 3 ♣ 5 3 2

2. Your hand is:

♠ A 10 3 ♡ K 5 3 ◇ Q 10 2 ♣ A Q 10 2

The auction has been:

You	Partner
1NT	2♡
2♠	3NT
?	

What is partner asking and what do you do now?

Answers

1. a) Start with a transfer to spades and then bid 4♠. With a six-card suit, you want to play the deal in your major.
b) Transfer to hearts and then bid 3NT. Give partner a choice of games. If partner doesn't have at least three hearts, chances are this deal will play better in notrump.

2. Partner has five spades and is asking you to bid 4♠ with three or more spades or to pass with two. Even though you have a perfectly balanced hand, your partner does not. You do have three spades, so bid 4♠.

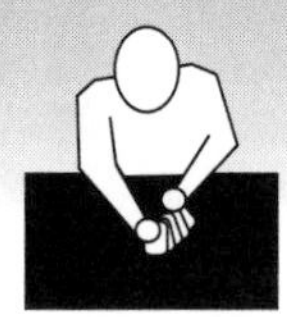

THE PLAY AT NOTRUMP

Counting Sure Tricks

Playing in notrump requires different thinking than playing suit contracts. It has some special challenges because you don't have a trump suit to keep control of the action. As you will see, when you play notrump, losers are not as important as winners. Therefore, the very first action you take when you are declarer in a notrump contract is to count sure winners. A sure winner is a trick you can take without giving up the lead — that means without losing any tricks in that suit. If you have an ace, you have one sure trick. If you have the ace and king in a suit, you have two. To count winners, look at both your own hand and dummy. You can borrow both high cards and length from dummy's cards.

If your holding in a suit is

AK3

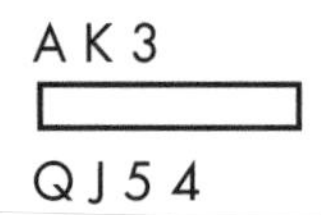

QJ54

you have four sure tricks.

A sure winner means that there is no risk in that suit at all. If you have a suit that needs a favorable split, it is not a sure trick. Suppose you hold:

AK32

QG54

"Winner"
A trick that you can take without giving up the lead.

How many winners do you have? We count this as only three winners. Of course, most of the time you will get four tricks, since with an odd number missing, you expect the suit to split evenly (in this case 3-2) and your fourth card will become high. If you had the jack as well, then you would have four winners — you would not need a favorable split.

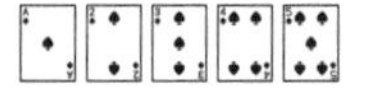

LET'S TRY IT!

In each of the following suits, how many sure winners do you have?

a)	b)	c)
Dummy	**Dummy**	**Dummy**
♠ A Q 5	♠ A Q 5	♠ K Q J
You	**You**	**You**
♠ K 3 2	♠ 6 4 3	♠ 10 9 8 7

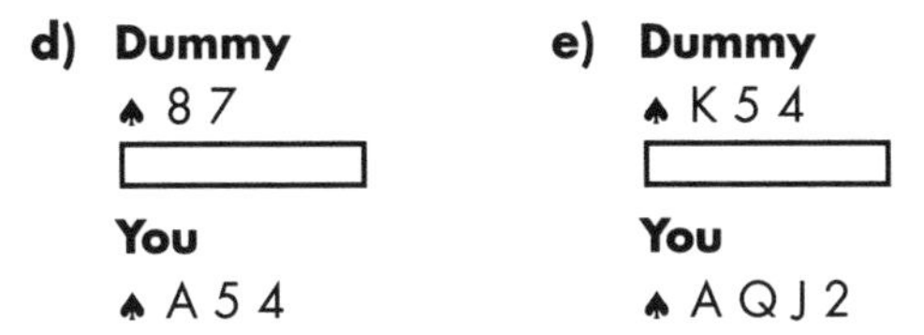

2. Count the number of sure winners you have in the following hands.

You
♠ A 4 3
♡ A K 5
◇ K Q 9 8
♣ Q J 5

Answers

1. a) You have three sure winners.

b) You have one sure winner. You may make another trick if the finesse works, but that is not a sure winner.

c) You have no ace and therefore no sure winners. You can, however, establish three tricks in this suit by knocking out the ace.

d) You have one sure winner, the ♠A.

e) You have four sure tricks.

2. You have two sure tricks in spades, three in hearts, three in diamonds and none in clubs. That makes a total of eight sure tricks. Remember — no ace, no winner!

Developing More Tricks

After you count your sure winners, you will find that most of the time you will not have enough tricks to make your contract. You will need to develop additional tricks. So the next step is to look for the best suit to produce extra tricks. You are going to make this suit your 'project suit'. How can you locate a good project suit? Start by eliminating suits that *can't* produce any more tricks. Look at this holding:

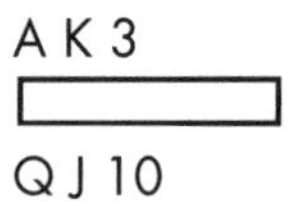

You have all of the high cards and three winners. However, once you've played three rounds of this suit, you'll have no more winners. You can't get blood from a stone — this suit simply will not produce more than three tricks even if you play it very slowly! This is not a suit to make your project suit. You need to look elsewhere to find more tricks. What about this?

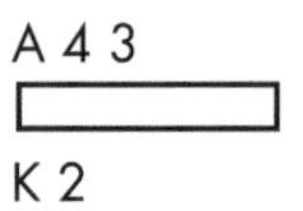

You have two sure winners in this suit, but you are unlikely to make three. You only have five cards in this suit, so the bad guys have eight; all of their cards will be higher than yours after you play the ace and king. This is another suit that you can eliminate as a project suit.

Now let's look at a suit with some potential. Suppose you have:

K Q J 10

6 5 4 3

You have counted nothing for this suit yet, since without the ace you have no sure winners. However, if you give up the ace to the opponents, you can develop three winners. A suit like this makes an excellent project suit.

Now that you have found the project suit, the next step is to attack it before touching any other suits. When should you do this? The minute you get the lead! When playing a deal without enough sure winners, establishing the extra winners is your first priority. Yes, it's comforting that you have sure winners in other suits, but get into the good habit of establishing extra winners first, instead of playing off your sure winners in other suits.

Finally, remember that when you are cashing winners, you should use up the high cards from the short hand first, just like in a trump contract.

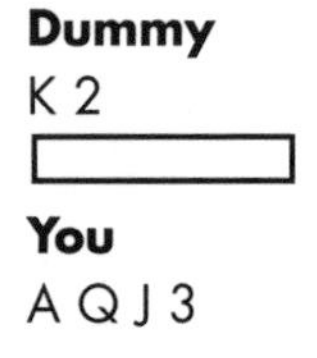

The first high card you play in this suit should be the king. The second high card should be the ace. Playing the suit this way will ensure that you can play all of your winners in the suit without any problems. Note that you could also play the three from your hand towards the king in dummy. You do not have to *lead* the high card from the short side first, but you do need to 'use it up'.

Stopping Your Opponents' Suits

If the opponents have a good suit, then you are going to need some high cards in that suit to prevent them from taking tricks in it. You may recall that we called high cards like these 'stoppers', since they stop the opponents from running their suit. Typical stoppers might be the ace, the king and another, the queen with two bodyguards or a four-card suit headed by the jack. Why do you need this length? The idea is that when the opponents play their high cards, you follow with your small cards; eventually your high card becomes a winner and you can take a trick.

Let's see how it works with Q-5-2 as a stopper. The opponents start off with the ace and you play the two. They play the king and you play the five. Now they play their jack, but it isn't good enough — you win with the queen. If you had started with Q-5 (without that third card), then the queen would have fallen ignobly under their king. So Q-5 is not good enough to be a stopper.

One stopper is handy, but having just one might not always be enough. Let's look at an example. Lay out this deal.

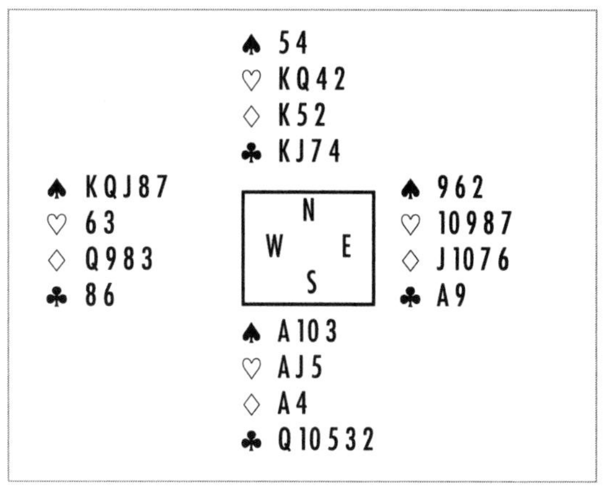

South opens 1NT and North bids 3NT. West makes the unfriendly lead of the ♠K, top of his sequence. Let's look at what might happen. You do have a stopper, the ♠A, so you can win the first trick with it. Let's count the sure winners. You have seven sure winners: four in hearts and two in diamonds to go along with the ♠A. However, your side needs nine tricks. Clubs looks like an excellent project suit and you will have four club winners once the opponents take their ♣A. There is a fly in the ointment, though. When you give up the lead, the opponents will be able to cash four spade winners. When you add that to their club winner, they will have taken five tricks, leaving only eight for you: not enough. Try playing it out to test this scenario, if you like.

Notrump contracts are like a race, and the defenders have the advantage — they get the opening lead, so they have a head start. In this case, they got their spade tricks set up and were able to take them before you could get your project suit established. But wait: perhaps this contract is not doomed after all...

The Hold-Up Play

Oh, the fascination of playing bridge! It is full of thrust and counter-thrust as the opponents and declarer battle it out. Let's try that last deal again, because there is a way that declarer can make this contract. Suppose that you had taken a peek at East's hand. You didn't see anything except that East has the ♣A. You can guarantee making 3NT as long as West has led his longest suit. The key is this: when West leads the ♠K, *you don't have to win your spade trick right away*. There is no harm in playing a small card on the ♠K. When West plays the ♠Q, you withhold your ♠A again. If West plays another spade, you have no choice, you have to take the ♠A, but notice what has happened. Since East started out with only three spades, when he gets the lead with the ♣A, he has no spade to play. You can win whatever suit East returns and now you can take the rest of the tricks. If East had in fact started with a fourth spade, that would simply mean that the eight spades between the opponents were split 4-4. The opponents would have been able to cash one last spade, but that would have been it. They would have taken three spade tricks and one club trick. Play the deal out and try it for yourself.

> ***"Hold-up"***
> A strategy of refusing to win a trick with a high honor, saving the winner for a later trick.

There is a name for this strategy: it is called a **hold-up** play. You are holding up your stopper and taking it later, so that you can exhaust one of the defenders of the suit they are attacking.

The Opening Lead Against Notrump

As you have seen, notrump contracts are a race and the winner will be whichever side can set up their long suit first and take their winners. It doesn't matter so much if declarer can set up nine tricks to make 3NT if you can take five tricks first on defense. Since your goal in a notrump contract is to establish your side's long suit, normally you will lead your own longest suit. With two suits of equal length, pick the strongest. If you have a sequence in your long suit, then lead the top of the sequence; otherwise, lead BOSTON. However, we would like to make one suggestion. When you have an honor in your long suit, don't lead the very bottom card — lead your fourth-highest card instead. So if your longest suit is four cards long, lead the lowest; if it is five cards long, lead the second lowest, and so on. Like this:

REMEMBER THIS! ☑

Lead your longest and strongest suit against notrump.

K 7 5 **2**   K 7 5 **3** 2   K 9 7 **5** 3 2

When you lead your fourth highest partner can get an idea of how long your suit is and can decide whether to continue playing that suit or change direction.

Deal 1 — Dealer South

West	North	East	South
			pass
pass	1NT	pass	3NT
all pass			

	North	
	♠ A Q 8 ♡ K 7 6 ◇ K J 9 3 ♣ A 3 2	
West ♠ 10 9 5 3 ♡ Q J 3 2 ◇ 6 5 4 ♣ 5 4	N / W E / S	**East** ♠ J 7 6 ♡ 10 5 4 ◇ A 2 ♣ Q J 10 9 8
	South ♠ K 4 2 ♡ A 9 8 ◇ Q 10 8 7 ♣ K 7 6	

South doesn't have quite enough to open the bidding, so he passes. North opens 1NT. South is captain. He knows that his side has at least 27 points, since partner must have a minimum of 15 to open 1NT. With a balanced hand, South can place the contract in 3NT.

East leads clubs, his longest suit. Since he has a perfect sequence, he leads the top of the sequence, the ♣Q. Declarer stops to count his sure winners. He has three spade winners, two heart winners and two club winners. That makes seven. Once the ◇A is gone, he will have three diamond winners. Diamonds is the project suit. Declarer wins the opening club lead and goes right after diamonds. It is imperative to play your project suit before touching any other suits. At some point, East will win the ◇A. Declarer can win the return and take his tricks. He will make ten tricks: three diamonds in addition to his seven sure winners.

Deal 2 — Dealer West

North:
♠ 10 4 2
♡ K Q 8 7 6
◇ A 3 2
♣ 9 8

West:
♠ A K Q
♡ A 2
◇ 10 9 8
♣ K J 10 6 5

East:
♠ 7 6 3
♡ 5 4 3
◇ K Q J 7
♣ A Q 3

South:
♠ J 9 8 5
♡ J 10 9
◇ 6 5 4
♣ 7 4 2

West	North	East	South
1NT	pass	3NT	all pass

West opens 1NT. With a balanced hand and 12 points, East, the captain, can place the contract in 3NT.

North leads the ♡7, the fourth highest from his longest suit. Declarer counts his sure winners: he has five clubs, three spades and a heart. Nine winners! Enough for his contract. He can hold up on the heart for one round, but after that, he should take all nine of his winners. Yes, diamonds is a great project suit, but with nine tricks already, you don't need it. If you play diamonds before taking your nine tricks, the opponents can take five tricks, four hearts and a diamond to defeat the contract. It would be a shame to go down in a game contract when you have all the tricks you need!

Deal 3 — Dealer North

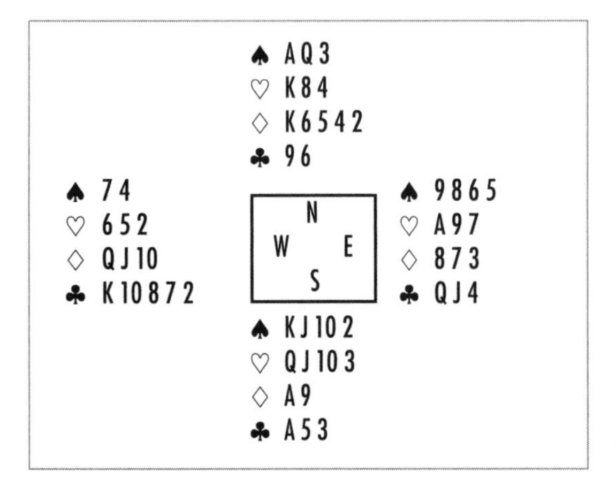

West	North	East	South
	pass	pass	1NT
pass	3NT	all pass	

South has a perfect 1NT opening bid with 15 HCP and a balanced hand. With 11 HCP, North knows that his side has at least 26 points, enough for game. Looking at a balanced hand and no five-card major, North just bids 3NT.

West should lead the ♣7, his fourth-highest club. It is a better lead than the ◇Q, since clubs are much more likely to be the longest suit for the defense. West's goal is to set up his long club suit. Declarer counts his sure tricks. He has seven of them: four spades, two diamonds and a club. He can establish the extra three tricks by setting up his heart suit. If he plays hearts, the opponents will have to take the ♡A eventually and his remaining hearts will be winners. So hearts makes an excellent project suit. The danger is that the defenders will take five tricks: a heart and four clubs. By holding up the ♣A twice, declarer can reduce the risk. He wins the third round of clubs and immediately starts on his project suit. As it happens, East wins the ♡A and has no clubs to return. Declarer can win the next trick in whatever suit East plays now and make ten tricks.

Deal 4 — Dealer East

West	North	East	South
		1NT	pass
3NT	all pass		

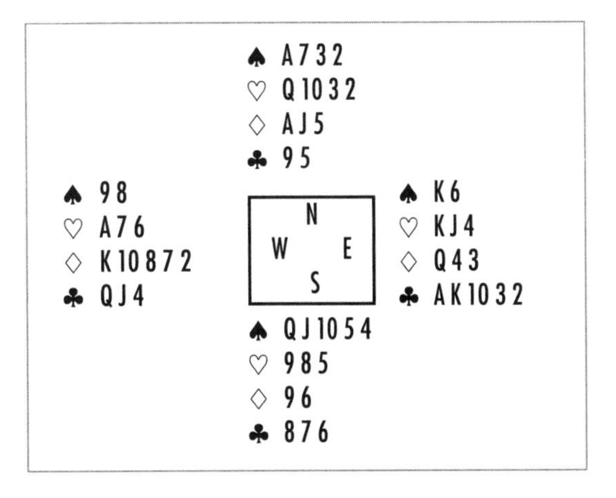

East opens 1NT. West has 10 points and an extra point for the fifth diamond, for a total of 11. We need only 25 HCP to make 3NT, so West bids game.

South leads the ♠Q. Spades are his best suit and he leads the top of his perfect sequence. North wins the ♠A and continues spades, declarer's ♠K winning. Declarer has eight sure tricks: five clubs, two hearts and a spade. Diamonds look attractive as a project suit, but do you see the problem? If you let the opponents gain the lead with the ◇A, they will cash three more spade winners, making a total of five tricks for the defense. Too many. You need to make your ninth trick without giving up the lead. The best chance to do that is to lead a heart to the ♡A and then finesse the ♡J. If the ♡Q is held by North, then declarer will make his ♡J, which will be his ninth trick. The bridge gods are kind on this deal and declarer can score up his game.

CHAPTER SUMMARY

A Responder is the captain of the bidding, since opener has already described his hand by opening 1NT.

B Responder adds 1 point for a five-card suit headed by the ace or king, and adds 2 points for a six-card suit headed by the ace or king.

C With a five-card or longer major, responder uses a Jacoby Transfer to "transfer" the major-suit bid to opener.

D Responder adds his points to opener's to decide at what level to play the deal.

E With 0-7, responder plans to play in a partscore. If he has a five-card or longer major, he transfers to the major and then passes. Otherwise, he just passes.

F With 8 or 9 points, responder invites to game.

- With a five-card major, use a Jacoby Transfer and then bid 2NT.
  - With a minimum: opener passes with two cards in the major and bids three of the major with three or more cards.
  - With a maximum: opener will bid 3NT with two cards in the major and four of the major with three or more.
- With a six-card major, Jacoby Transfer and then bid three of the major. Opener raises to four with a maximum and passes otherwise.
- With no five-card major, bid 2NT. Opener bids 3NT with a maximum and passes otherwise.

G With 10-15 points, responder bids game:

- With a five-card major, use a Jacoby Transfer and then bid 3NT. Opener passes with two cards in the major and bids four of the major with three or more cards.
- With a six-card major, use a Jacoby Transfer and then bid four of the major.
- With no five-card major, bid 3NT.

H When playing a notrump contract:

- Count winners, not losers. Start by counting sure winners — those you can take without giving up the lead.
- Pick a project suit that can produce the extra winners you need and play it immediately.

- Hold up a winner to try to prevent the opposition from taking tricks in that suit.

(I) Against notrump contracts, lead your longest suit or the strongest of equal suits. Lead top of a sequence. From a holding without a sequence, lead BOSTON, but instead of leading the bottom card from a suit headed by an honor, lead the fourth highest.

7 Improving Notrump Auctions

DID YOU KNOW?

By 1933, bridge had become so popular that Hollywood made a movie about it. *Grand Slam*, starring Loretta Young and Paul Lukas, can still be seen occasionally on late night television. The film was based on a novel by B. Russell Herts, *Grand Slam: the rise and fall of a bridge wizard* and was loosely based on some of the events in the Culbertson era.

WHAT YOU'RE GOING TO LEARN

In this chapter, we will continue our discussion of bidding in notrump auctions. You will see how to use another convention, the Stayman convention, to find out about any four-card major in opener's hand. You will learn the appropriate use of this convention and how the auction continues afterwards. We will then complete our discussion of responding to 1NT opening bids with a look at how you respond with a very good hand.

In the play section, we will spend more time on the play in notrump contracts. We will look in more detail at selecting the correct project suit and at more advanced hold-up plays.

One More Response to 1NT

We have seen that Jacoby Transfers work well after an opening bid of 1NT when responder has a five-card or longer major. However, what if responder has one or two four-card majors? If opener has four of responder's major, then the partnership has at least an eight-card fit. The partnership is likely to take more tricks playing in their major-suit fit than in notrump.

Why is that? Consider this suit:

If you are playing in notrump, you will take exactly four tricks in this suit. However, if you play in a trump contract, you can often take one or two extra tricks by trumping losers in one of the hands. If you can trump two losers in responder's hand, then in this example you will be able to take six tricks with this suit rather than the four you would take in notrump. Another advantage of playing in a trump contract is that trumps give you the ability to prevent opponents from taking tricks in their long suits. It is therefore safer to play in a trump-suit contract than in notrump; hence our eternal quest to find an eight-card major-suit fit.

In general, you can expect to take one extra trick if you play in a 4-4 major-suit fit. Therefore, it is often important to find out if the opening 1NT bidder has a four-card major, and which one it is.

Where a need in bridge exists, there is a usually a convention, and this case is no exception. In fact, the one that suits this particular purpose is one of the two most commonly used bridge conventions in the world: Stayman. (In a later chapter you will be introduced to the other top convention, Blackwood.) This particular convention was popularized in the 1940s by American expert Sam Stayman — hence the name. Sam Stayman was a world bridge champion, but he is best known today for writing about this convention.

The beauty of the Stayman convention is its simplicity. When partner opens 1NT and you want to find out whether he has a four-card major, you simply bid 2♣. This bid says absolutely nothing about clubs. Instead, it asks partner the question 'Do you have a four-card major?' Opener does not have any discretion as to his reply: his job is simply to answer the question. If he has no four-card major, he rebids 2♢ (this bid says nothing about diamonds). If he has four hearts, he rebids 2♡, and if he has four spades, he rebids 2♠. If he happens to have four cards in both majors, his bid is 2♡. That's it. Simple and elegant. Remember, though, that you can no longer bid 2♣ to play in clubs when partner opens 1NT. If you bid 2♣, partner will treat it as Stayman and show you his major suits. Unfortunately, you cannot have it both ways.

REMEMBER THIS! ☑

After a 1NT opening, responder can bid 2♣ to initiate a Stayman auction.

OPENER REBIDS	
2♢	No four-card major
2♡	Four hearts (and maybe four spades)
2♠	Four spades, but not four hearts

Opener does not have a choice. He has to make the rebid that describes his hand for responder. He can't make any other rebid.

When Should You Use the Stayman Convention?

On most hands that include a four-card major, you want to know if partner has a fit for your major, so you use Stayman. There are, however, a few hands that are not suitable. If you have a hand worth fewer than 8 points, it is too risky to bid at all. Suppose your partner opens 1NT and you hold:

♠ 9 8 7 5 ♡ J 10 4 2 ♢ J 3 2 ♣ 4 2

While it's true that if partner has a four-card major suit you may be better off playing in two of that major than in 1NT, it is just too risky to bid. With fewer than 8 points, you always pass 1NT, unless you have a five-card or longer major (on those hands, you transfer to the major).

If you do have a five-card or longer major, then you don't need to use Stayman. Just transfer to the major, after which you either insist on your major or offer partner the choice of playing in notrump.

LET'S TRY IT!

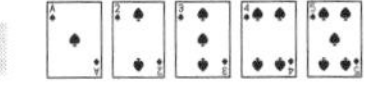

1. On each of the following hands, you have opened 1NT and partner bids 2♣ (Stayman). What do you bid now?

a) ♠ A J 2 ♡ K J 2 ♢ 4 3 ♣ A Q J 5 4
b) ♠ J 10 5 4 ♡ A K 2 ♢ K Q J 4 ♣ K 10
c) ♠ A Q 3 2 ♡ 10 9 8 2 ♢ A 4 ♣ K Q 2

2. Partner opened 1NT. What should you bid on each of these hands?

a) ♠ K Q 3 2 ♡ Q 5 4 2 ♢ 4 3 ♣ 5 4 3
b) ♠ A J 5 4 ♡ 3 2 ♢ A K 2 ♣ Q 5 4 3
c) ♠ 7 6 ♡ Q 10 8 7 2 ♢ A Q 5 ♣ K J 2

3. Your hand is:

♠ A 2 ♡ K Q 6 2 ◇ 3 2 ♣ 10 9 4 3 2

What would you bid now in each of these auctions?

a)

Partner	You
1NT	2♣
2♡	?

b)

Partner	You
1NT	2♣
2◇	?

Answers

1. a) Bid 2◇. It doesn't matter that you have only ◇43 — this bid simply says that you do not have a four-card major. You aren't saying anything about diamonds.

b) Bid 2♠. Tell your partner about your four-card spade suit. It might be just what he's looking for.

c) Bid 2♡. Yes, your spades are better, but with both majors, you bid 2♡.

2. a) Pass. With only 7 high card points, you are too weak to use Stayman.

b) Bid 2♣ (Stayman). If partner has four spades, you are probably better off playing in that suit; if not, you can play in notrump. In either case, you plan to bid game.

c) Bid 2◇ (Jacoby Transfer). You intend to give partner a choice between 3NT and 4♡. With a five-card suit, there is no need to use Stayman: partner has a fit with you even if he has only three trumps.

3. a) Great! Partner has hearts too. You can now add dummy points to your high card points, since you are going to play in a suit. You have a hand worth 11 points in hearts, enough for game opposite partner's 15-17. Bid 4♡.

b) Sadly, partner does not have four hearts, so you plan to play in notrump. Since your hand has only 9 HCP, invite to game by bidding 2NT.

Putting It All Together

Let's look at the whole structure of how you respond to a 1NT opening with different types of hand.

First, with 0-7 points, you either (a) pass or (b) transfer to your long major suit and then pass.

If you have an invitational hand with 8-9 points, you have plenty of choices. Start by looking at your major suits. If you have a six-card or longer major suit, you transfer to that major and then raise to invite partner to bid game. With a five-card major suit, you transfer and then bid 2NT, giving partner a number of choices: he can opt for game or partscore in either notrump or your major. If you have one or two four-card majors, start with Stayman. If partner holds four cards in your major, what do you think you do next?

♠ 7 6 ♡ A 7 5 2 ◇ K J 9 3 ♣ 9 8 7

Partner	You
1NT	2♣
2♡	?

Using Stayman, you were able to find the best place to play, but don't pass now! Passing would end the auction and you want to invite partner to game. Bid 3♡ instead. Partner will bid 4♡ with a maximum opener.

What if partner doesn't bid your major? For example, suppose on this hand partner bids 2♠ instead of 2♡. Now you bid 2NT: you still want to invite partner to game, but it will be a notrump game this time.

With a game-going hand (10+ points), you follow the same approach. With a six-card major, you start with a transfer and bid game in the major. With a five-card major, you start with a transfer and then bid 3NT, offering partner a choice of games. With one or more four-card majors, you start with Stayman. If partner picks your major, you (the captain) can jump to game in the major. If partner doesn't bid your major, then you bid 3NT. Can you see why everyone loves the Stayman convention?

Finally, let's make one subtle point. You hold:

♠ J 6 4 2 ♡ A Q 6 4 ◇ A J 5 ♣ K 8

You	Partner
1NT	2♣
2♡	2NT
?	

What does partner have? He used Stayman, so he must have 8 or more points and at least one four-card major. Since he didn't like hearts, he must have four spades. That means there's an eight-card fit in spades. Therefore, even though you have a minimum, don't just pass 2NT — bid 3♠ and partner will pass. If you had a maximum and four spades, you would bid 4♠ in this auction.

LET'S TRY IT!

1. Partner has opened 1NT. What do you respond with each of the following hands?

a) ♠ K J 10 7 4 ♡ 4 3 2 ◇ 5 4 ♣ K J 2
b) ♠ 9 8 7 ♡ 3 2 ◇ K Q J 5 4 ♣ A J 2
c) ♠ 7 6 5 4 ♡ A 2 ◇ K Q 5 4 2 ♣ 10 5

2. Your hand is:

♠ Q 5 4 2 ♡ K 5 4 3 ◇ K 3 ♣ 5 3 2

The auction has been:

Partner	You
1NT	2♣
2♠	?

What do you bid now?

Answers

1. a) Bid 2♡, transfer to spades. You don't need to use Stayman, since you have five spades. Your plan is to bid 2NT next and invite partner to pick between spades and notrump and between game and partscore.

b) Bid 3NT. You have enough points for game and your diamonds will be useful as tricks in notrump. We like to avoid playing in a minor suit if we can, because game in a minor requires eleven tricks while game in notrump requires only nine tricks.

c) Bid 2♣, Stayman. If partner has four spades, then spades is likely to be the best contract. If partner responds 2♠, you will bid 4♠ next. Otherwise, you will bid 3NT. (Don't worry about the quality of your spade suit — quantity not quality is what matters!)

2. Bid 3♠. You can count a point for your doubleton now that you have found a spade fit, but even so, you still have only 9 points. Invite partner to bid 4♠ with a maximum.

Responding to 1NT With Very Strong Hands

Before we finish our discussion of responding to partner's opening 1NT bid, let's take a brief look at what you should do if partner opens 1NT and you have a balanced hand with more than 15 HCP.

It takes about 33 HCP to make a small slam in notrump (twelve tricks) and about 37 to make a grand slam and take all thirteen tricks. If you have 16 or 17 HCP, you may have enough for slam if partner has a maximum. With a balanced hand, you bid 4NT. You are asking partner to pick between passing and playing there or bidding the slam. Partner will bid 6NT with a maximum and pass with a minimum.

If you are lucky enough to have 18 or 19 HCP, then when you add them to partner's 15-17, your side has 33-36 HCP. You have enough points to make 6NT, but not enough for 7NT. So just bid 6NT. We know twelve sounds like an awful lot of tricks, but your side has plenty of high cards and you will get the nice slam bonus.

With 20 to 21 HCP, you bid 5NT. This asks partner to bid 6NT with a minimum and 7NT with a maximum. Partner cannot pass your 5NT bid: he must bid either 6NT or 7NT. Finally, if you have 22 or more points, you know your side has at least 37 points and you can bid 7NT.

In summary, if you know you want to play in notrump (i.e. you have no four-card or longer major), you make one of the following bids over partner's 1NT opening:

HCP	**Bid**
0-7	pass
8-9	2NT (partner will bid 3NT or pass)
10-15	3NT
16-17	4NT (partner will bid 6NT or pass)
18-19	6NT
20-21	5NT (partner will bid 6NT or 7NT)
22+	7NT

All of these auctions can also start with either Stayman (with a four-card major) or a Jacoby Transfer (if you have a five-card major). For example:

You	**Partner**
1NT	2♡
2♠	4NT
?	

Partner has five spades and 16-17 points — a slam-invitational hand. If you have only two spades, you will pass with a minimum or bid 6NT with a maximum; with three or more spades, you should bid either 5♠ or 6♠, depending on whether you have a minimum or a maximum.

LET'S TRY IT!

1. Partner has opened 1NT. What do you respond on this hand?

♠ A Q 3 ♡ K Q 2 ◇ A 10 4 3 ♣ K 7 6

2. Partner has opened 1NT. What do you respond? What do you expect partner to do?

♠ K Q 3 ♡ K 5 ◇ A J 10 4 3 ♣ K 7 6

Answers

1. Bid 6NT. You have a balanced hand worth 18 points. Even if partner has only 15 HCP, it will be enough for slam.

2. You have a hand worth 17 points: 16 HCP and 1 point for the fifth diamond. Bid 4NT. You expect partner to bid 6NT with a maximum and pass with a minimum.

THE PLAY OF THE HAND

More About the Play at Notrump

We have already seen how to count your winners at notrump right at the beginning of the play. Winners are sure tricks won by your top honors. Do you remember that if you don't have an ace in a suit, you have no sure tricks in that suit? What if you have a suit like this?

When we talked about counting winners, we said that if you are missing an odd number of cards in a suit (here five), then most of the time they will split as evenly as possible. That means that most of the time you will have four winners in this suit. The opposing cards will break 3-2 and your last spot card will become a winner. So you count this suit as three winners, but keep in mind that it may in fact turn out to be four.

When you have this holding, you can definitely count only three winners. If you are missing an even number of cards in a suit (in this example, six), the suit will not split perfectly evenly most of the time. You should expect that one of the opponents will have at least four cards in this suit and that your ♠5 will not take a trick. Sometimes the suit will split evenly and you will get a happy surprise, but it's best not to base your plans on it.

After you count your winners, work out how many tricks you need to develop and then look for the most likely suit in which to get them — we called this your project suit. Usually, the best place to find your project suit is the longest suit containing the most high cards, but this is not always true. Which of these suits is the better project suit?

The answer actually depends on how many tricks you need. If you need only one trick, and there is some risk that the opponents will establish some fast winners of their own, then the first suit is better. It will provide your one trick faster. However, it will never produce more than one extra trick, while the second one will eventually produce three. When you look for a project suit, you are looking for a suit that will provide the number of additional tricks you need to make your contract. Therefore, after you count winners, subtract them from the total number of tricks you need and work on the suit or suits that will provide those missing tricks.

In the last chapter we looked at different ways to develop the extra winners you needed to make your contract. We looked at forcing out honors to set up your suit, and in one of the example deals we took a finesse to develop a trick. Let's look at one more way to develop tricks. It is similar to forcing out the opponents' high cards to establish winners in a suit, but in this case we are deliberately going to lose a trick to a lower card. Suppose this is your project suit:

You have only two winners in the suit initially, but if you give up a spade, then you can probably establish more tricks after the opponents have taken their spade winner. Let's say this is how the spades are distributed around the table.

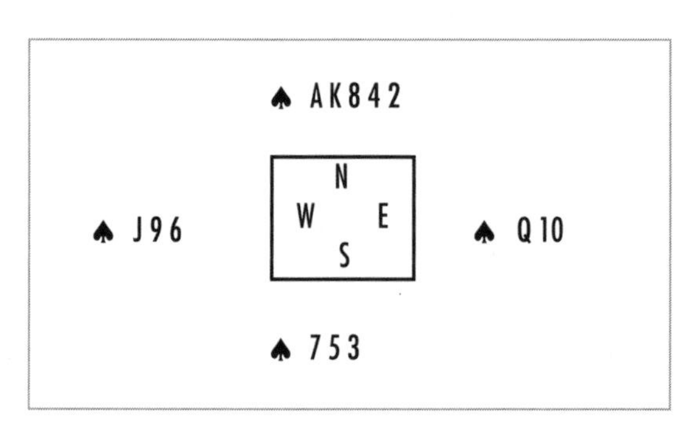

After you play the ♠A and the ♠K, there will be only one spade left in the opponents' hands. You let West have his spade trick, setting up two more spade winners for you. Alternatively, you can get the same effect by letting the opponents have the first spade trick and then playing your ♠A and ♠K later. This is often a good way to play a suit such as this one, because you will still have spades in the South hand to reach North's spade winners. Try it both ways and see how it works.

More About the Hold-Up Play

Remember that notrump contracts are a race. You are trying to score the tricks you need before the defense can take enough tricks to defeat your contract. The defense has a project suit too and they are trying to set it up for the winners they need – from your point of view, this is the danger suit. In the last chapter, we saw that sometimes when the opponents lead a suit you should not take your winner in that suit right away. Instead, you should hold it up: you refrain from taking your winner as long as you can. Your hope is that whichever defender gets the lead later in the deal will not be able to play the danger suit because he won't have any left.

REMEMBER THIS! ☑

If in doubt, assume the opponents have led from a five-card suit and plan any hold-up play based on that.

However, every deal you play is different and each one needs its own plan. You can't just go on auto-pilot. Even when you have only a single stopper in a suit, you may not want to hold up. Why not? Perhaps there is a risk that the opponents will attack another suit where you don't have a stopper at all! If another suit is more dangerous (or just as dangerous), you can't afford to hold up a winner. Here is an example:

Partner
♠ A 6 2
♡ J 4 2
♢ K J 5 4 3
♣ J 4

N
W E
S

You
♠ 10 8 7 4
♡ A K Q 5
♢ Q 10 6
♣ A 2

You	Partner
1NT	3NT
pass	

You opened 1NT and partner raised to 3NT. Your opponent led the ♠3. Let's count winners. You have six top winners: the ♠A, the ♣A and four tricks in hearts. If you force out the diamond ace, you will have four more tricks. The only danger is that the opponents might take five tricks before you take nine tricks. Are you tempted to hold up the ♠A? Look at what happens if you hold up the first spade and the opponents switch to clubs. It is almost certain that they will take enough club tricks to defeat the contract.

Meanwhile, it is very unlikely that the opponents can set up four winners in spades. Just win the ♠A, mentally thanking the opponents for not being nasty enough to lead a club, and get to work on diamonds.

Deal 1 — Dealer South

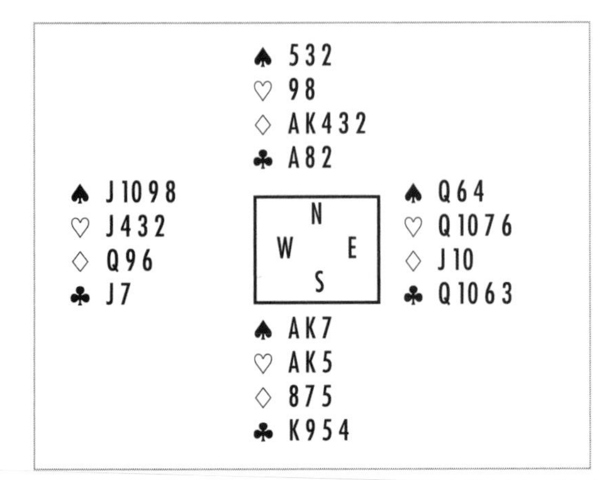

West	North	East	South
			1NT
pass	3NT	all pass	

South opens 1NT with his balanced 17 HCP. North has 11 points, enough for game. With no major suit, North raises 1NT to 3NT. West decides to lead a spade, his longest suit: he leads the ♠J, top of the sequence.

Declarer stops to count his winners. He has eight top winners: two spades, two hearts, two diamonds and two clubs. Diamonds look most promising as the project suit. If diamonds break evenly (3-2), three rounds of diamonds will use up all of the defense's cards in the suit and the extra diamonds in dummy will be winners.

At Trick 2, declarer plays a low diamond from each hand, allowing the defense to win their diamond trick. (This is the correct technique, so it's good to get into the habit; however, on this deal, it will work just as well if declarer plays his top two diamonds first.) When declarer regains the lead, he will then play the ◇A and ◇K. On this deal, the diamonds break 3-2, so dummy's fourth and fifth diamonds are winners and declarer will take ten tricks.

Deal 2 — Dealer West

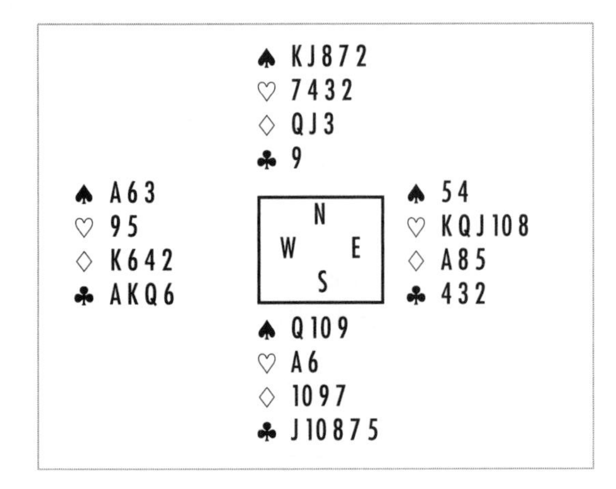

West	North	East	South
1NT	pass	2◇	pass
2♡	pass	3NT	all pass

West opens 1NT. With five hearts, East bids 2◇ (Jacoby Transfer) and West dutifully bids 2♡. With enough for game, East bids 3NT to give West a choice between 3NT and 4♡. With only two hearts, West passes 3NT. North leads the ♠7 (fourth highest).

Declarer holds up the ♠A until the third round. He has six winners: one in spades, two in diamonds and three in clubs. He does not count the fourth club, since most of the time the clubs will not split evenly with six missing. Hearts looks like an excellent project suit. If declarer can force out the ♡A, he will have four extra tricks. He hopes that the defense will not be able to take five tricks first. If North started with five spades, declarer will have to hope he does not have the ♡A as well. Declarer starts on hearts immediately. South has the ♡A, so all is well and declarer makes ten tricks.

Deal 3 — Dealer North

West	North	East	South
	1NT	pass	3NT
all pass			

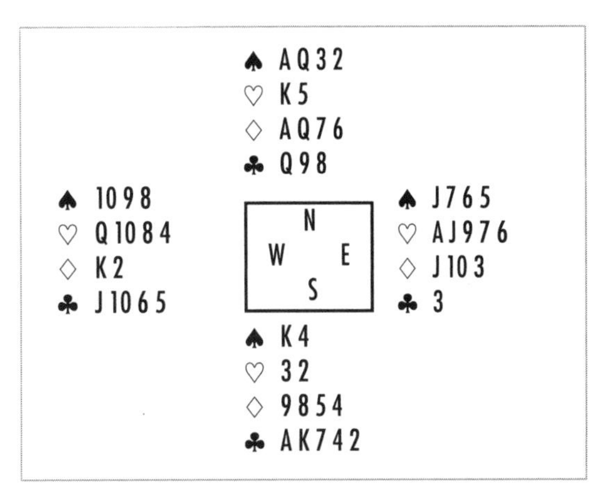

North opens 1NT. With 10 HCP, South has enough to raise directly to 3NT. East leads the ♡7, his fourth-highest heart.

Declarer has to win the ♡K and then stops to count his winners. He has three spades, one heart, one diamond and at least three clubs. An odd number of clubs is missing. Most of the time they will divide more or less evenly (3-2) and declarer will have five club winners. He tests this theory immediately by playing three rounds of clubs, ending in the dummy. On this deal, declarer is unlucky and the clubs are not 3-2. However, he still has one string left to his bow. He takes the diamond finesse. This will work only half of the time, but it's better than nothing. On this layout, the diamond finesse works and declarer makes his contract.

Often we try to look for more than one chance to make our contract. If one line doesn't work, another might. This deal is a good example. Notice that in order to make the most of your chances, you have to try clubs first. If you take the diamond finesse first and it loses, you will go down right away without ever getting to see if the clubs would have behaved.

Deal 4 — Dealer East

	North	
	♠ J 8 4 ♡ A J 7 ◇ A 9 7 2 ♣ 10 5 3	
West ♠ 10 7 6 2 ♡ 4 2 ◇ Q 6 ♣ A Q 9 7 6	N / W E / S	**East** ♠ A Q 5 ♡ K 10 3 ◇ K 8 5 ♣ K 8 4 2
	♠ K 9 3 ♡ Q 9 8 6 5 ◇ J 10 4 3 ♣ J	

West	North	East	South
		1NT	pass
2♣	pass	2◇	pass
2NT	all pass		

With a balanced 15 HCP, East opens the bidding with 1NT. West uses Stayman to see if his partner has four spades and East responds 2◇, showing no four-card major. With a hand worth 9 points, West has enough to invite to game and bids 2NT. East passes with a minimum. South will probably lead the ♡6, fourth highest from his longest suit.

North wins the ♡A and continues with a heart. Declarer should hold up the ♡K (although it won't hurt on this particular deal to win the second heart) and win the third round of hearts. (When you make your plan, you should always assume that the lead is coming from a five-card suit.) Declarer counts seven winners: one spade, one heart and (probably) five clubs. He needs one more winner. He could take the spade finesse or he could force out the ◇A, setting up a diamond winner. Which is safest? Giving up the diamond is completely safe, as the defense can take at most four hearts and the diamond ace. Taking the finesse works only 50% of the time. On this deal, the finesse would lose and South would win the ♠K. The defense would prevail by taking four hearts, a spade and a diamond.

CHAPTER**SUMMARY**

A Over 1NT, if responder has one or two four-card majors and at least 8 points, he can use the Stayman Convention.

B 2♣ over 1NT is the Stayman Convention. Opener rebids:

2♢	no major
2♡	four-card heart suit (may have four spades too)
2♠	four-card spade suit (and not four hearts)

C If responder finds a fit using Stayman:
- with 8-9 points, raise the major to invite partner.
- with 10-15 points, bid game.

D If responder does not find a fit:
- with 8-9 points, he rebids 2NT (invitational).
- with 10-15 points, he rebids 3NT.

E Responder should not use Stayman with fewer than 8 points.

F With a big hand and no four-card or longer major, responder bids as follows:

16-18	4NT (partner will bid 6NT or pass)
18-19	6NT
20-21	5NT (partner will bid 6NT or 7NT)
22+	7NT

G With a five-card or longer major and a big hand, responder can start with Jacoby and then go to the appropriate level in either notrump or a suit, as he deems appropriate.

H With a four-card major and a big hand, responder can start with Stayman and then go to the appropriate level in either notrump or a suit, as he deems appropriate.

I Don't play the hand on auto-pilot.
- When you pick your project suit at the beginning of the deal, make your choice based on the number of extra winners you need. Pick the safest suit that can deliver the number of tricks you need.
- Don't hold up a winner unless the suit is truly dangerous to you, especially if there is another suit the opponents could attack.

8 Competing in the Bidding

DID YOU KNOW?

Bridge has often featured in fiction. In *Cards on the Table*, by Agatha Christie, detective Hercule Poirot is able to solve a murder by examining the scoresheet of the bridge game that his suspects were playing when the crime occurred. Somerset Maugham, a keen bridge player, wrote several stories that involved bridge scenes. C.C. Nicolet's *Death of a Bridge Expert* was published in 1932, and many of its characters were thinly disguised portraits of the leading players of the day. *Trick Thirteen*, by Terence Reese and Jeremy Flint, and *Takeout Double*, by Jim Priebe, are both murder mysteries where the motive for the crime is related to cheating at bridge tournaments!

WHAT YOU'RE GOING TO LEARN

In this chapter, we will start to explore the world of competitive bidding and the variety of actions you can take to get into the auction when the other side has opened. When one opponent has opened, the requirements for you to make a bid are not the same as those for opening the bidding. That is because your goals are often different. For example, you may simply be trying to make sure that partner knows what suit to lead. At other times, you may have exactly the same goal as the opening bidder — to win the auction and get to play in your trump suit.

In the play section, we will look at finesses again and introduce you to some new types of finesses. Also, since both sides are now involved in the auction, we will look at a new idea for opening leads — leading the suit your partner bid.

In every deal you have seen so far, the opponents have done nothing except pass. It's like going to an auction where no one bids against you. In real life, however, this doesn't always happen. Your opponents will usually be quite happy to bid if they have good cards even if you have opened the bidding. By the same token, you should be eager to get into the auction yourself even when the other side has started the ball rolling.

The cornerstone of competitive bidding is the **overcall**. What is an overcall? It is a bid made in a new suit or notrump *after* one of your opponents has opened the bidding. Where did it get that name? Well, a 'call' is actually another name for a 'bid', so an *over*call means a bid you make *over* your opponent's 'call'. Here are some examples of an overcall:

West	North	East	South
1♢	**1**♡		

West	North	East	South
1♢	**1NT**		

West	North	East	South
1♠	pass	1NT	**2**♡

When you overcall, your objectives are different than when you open the bidding. Your goal might simply be to suggest to partner that he lead your suit; alternatively, you may have quite a good hand and want to compete with the opponents to win the contract. You may want to take away some of the opponents' bidding space or you may want to push them to bid to a higher level where it is possible to defeat them. Sometimes you have all of these objectives.

"Overcall"
A bid of a new suit or notrump after an opponent has opened the bidding.

REMEMBER THIS! ☑

An overcall has one or more of these objectives:
1. Suggest a lead.
2. Compete and win the contract.
3. Push the opponents to bid higher.
4. Take away your opponents' bidding space.

Overcalling in a New Suit

It is not necessary to have a very good hand to make an overcall in a suit at the one-level. You need at least 8 points to overcall (including distribution) and at least a five-card suit. If you have only 8-12 points, you should have a very good suit that you wish partner to lead. The primary purpose of bidding with this kind of hand is to suggest the lead of the suit you have bid. We suggest that you have a suit packed with honors — two of the top three honors (ace, king and queen) or three of the top five honors (ace, king, queen, jack and ten).

If you have 13 points or more, you can overcall a five-card or longer suit of poorer quality. With this kind of hand, you want to compete for the contract and your high cards will make up for the lack of suit quality.

Here are some example hands on which you would overcall 1♠ after an opponent's opening bid of 1♢:

♠ A K J 9 3 ♡ 9 8 ♢ 7 6 ♣ 5 4 3 2
♠ K J 7 4 3 ♡ A 3 ♢ 6 2 ♣ A J 4 2

The first hand does not have a lot of high card points, but it does have an excellent spade suit, one that you certainly want partner to lead. The second hand has a weaker spade suit, but contains more points.

Here are some hands that really do not qualify as a good overcall of 1♠ over an opening 1♢ bid:

♠ K 8 7 6 2 ♡ A 8 ♢ 7 6 ♣ 5 4 3 2
♠ A J 10 9 4 ♡ 9 8 ♢ 7 6 ♣ 5 4 3 2

The first hand has enough points, but the suit is too weak for an overcall in this range. The second hand has a good suit, but you have too few points to overcall.

Look at this hand, though:

♠ K 8 7 6 2 ♡ A 8 ♢ A 6 ♣ K J 3 2

With 15 HCP, you can't afford not to be in the bidding. You should overcall 1♠ even with a suit as poor as this; your high-card strength will compensate for the bad spades. An overcall can be made on a very good hand indeed, but with 18 or more points, you should take some other action, as you will see in the next chapter.

Sometimes you can't make your overcall at the one-level. Suppose your opponent opens 1♠: whatever suit you bid is going to take you to the two-level. To overcall at the two-level, you need to have a hand that is a bit stronger. You should have an opening bid (13 total points or more), with at least a good five-card suit (and preferably six or more). So with

♠ 10 9 8 7 ♡ A K J 10 9 ♢ K 8 ♣ 7 6

bid 2♡ over 1♠, but with

♠ 10 9 8 7 ♡ A K 10 9 3 ♢ 9 8 ♣ 7 6

you just aren't good enough to overcall at the two-level. If your opponent opens the bidding with 1♠, you have to pass. You would really like to bid to get that heart lead, but it is just too dangerous. On a bad day, you might make as few as three tricks in 2♡ with this hand, and that can be very expensive.

With a *really* good suit, you can cheat a little:

♠ 9 8 7 ♡ 4 3 2 ◇ 8 6 ♣ A K Q J 2

If your opponent opens 1♡, you really want to tell partner to lead a club. Here, your suit is so good that you should bid 2♣ anyway.

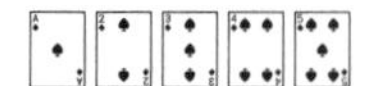

LET'S TRY IT!

1. Your hand is

♠ A K J 3 2 ♡ 7 6 4 ◇ 5 3 2 ♣ 3 2

Your opponent has opened 1♣ and it is your turn. What do you bid and what is your purpose in doing so?

2. The auction has been:

Opponent	You	Opponent	Partner
1♡	?		

What do you bid on each of the following hands?

a) ♠ 10 9 ♡ 7 6 ◇ A K Q J 5 ♣ Q 8 5 3
b) ♠ 7 6 ♡ 10 3 ◇ A Q J 10 5 2 ♣ 9 4 2
c) ♠ K 10 9 8 3 ♡ A 3 2 ◇ K 4 ♣ K 5 3
d) ♠ A J 9 8 7 ♡ 5 ◇ 9 8 7 ♣ 9 8 7 6

Answers

1. You should bid 1♠. Your main purpose is to recommend a spade lead if partner is the opening leader. A spade is very likely to be the best lead for your side.

2. a) Bid 2◇. You have a great five-card diamond suit and enough points to bid at the two-level.
b) Pass. You have only 9 total points, not enough to bid at the two-level.
c) Bid 1♠. You don't have a very good suit, but you have a good hand, so you should overcall.
d) Pass. You have a decent suit, but you don't have enough points to overcall, even at the one-level.

Responding to a Suit Overcall

When partner overcalls, you can be sure that he has at least a five-card suit and almost always a very good suit. Therefore, you only need three-card trump support to have the magic eight-card fit. However, remember that partner didn't open the bidding, so he could have as little as 8 points for a one-level overcall; when you respond, you need to take that into consideration. With at least three-card trump support and 8-11 points, raise one level (for example, raise 1♠ to 2♠, or 2♣ to 3♣). With 12-14 points and three trumps or more, raise two levels (e.g. 1♠ to 3♠). With 15 points or more, raise partner's suit three levels or to game, whichever is lower.

What if you don't have support for partner? If you have 10 or more points, you can bid a five-card suit of your own. This bid is unlimited and therefore forcing, since partner does not know how good a hand you have. You can make this bid with 10 points, but you might have 18 points or even more. The only exception occurs if you have already had a chance to open the bidding but passed, since that limits your hand to fewer than 13 points. If you are a passed hand, the bid of a new suit is not forcing.

So here your 1♠ bid is forcing:

West	North	East	South
	Partner		*You*
1♢	1♡	pass	1♠
pass	?		

but here:

West	North	East	South
	Partner		*You*
			pass
1♢	1♡	pass	1♠
pass	?		

it is not forcing because you passed at the very beginning of the auction.

If partner is forced to bid again over your new suit and rebids his suit, he is not promising six of them. He simply had to bid something.

If you don't have support for partner, you can also bid notrump over your partner's overcall. You should have a balanced hand and stoppers in the opponents' suit. With 8-11 HCP and one stopper, bid notrump as cheaply as you can. With 12-14 HCP and 1½ stoppers (e.g. AQ), jump in notrump, and with 15+ HCP, just bid 3NT.

Summary of Suit Overcalls

Overcall

8-12 and at least a very good five-card suit	Overcall at the one-level only.
13-17 points and a good five-card suit	Overcall at the one-level or at the two-level if you have to.

Responses to an Overcall

8-11 points and three-card or better trump support	Raise one level.
12-14 points and three-card or better trump support	Raise two levels.
15+ points and three-card or better trump support	Raise three levels.

Bid a New Suit

10+ points	Bid a new suit at the cheapest level with a good five-card or longer suit (forcing except by a passed hand).

Bid Notrump

8-11 HCP and one stopper in opponents' suit	Make cheapest notrump bid.
12-14 HCP and 1½ stoppers	Jump in notrump.
15+ HCP and 1½ stoppers	Bid 3NT.

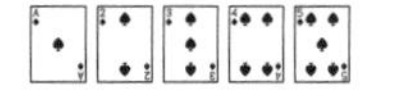

LET'S TRY IT!

1. This is the auction so far:

West	North	East	South
	Partner		*You*
1♡	1♠	pass	?

What do you bid with each of the following hands?

a) ♠ 9 8 7 ♡ 7 ◇ A 7 6 5 ♣ K Q 9 8 2
b) ♠ 6 5 ♡ A K 2 ◇ K Q 3 2 ♣ J 10 9 8
c) ♠ K Q 5 4 ♡ 9 2 ◇ A K 5 3 2 ♣ 6 2
d) ♠ Q 9 ♡ K 5 3 ◇ A K Q 6 5 ♣ 7 6 5

2. The auction so far is:

West	North	East	South
	Partner		*You*
1♡	2◇	pass	?

Your hand is:

♠ K Q J 10 9 ♡ A 2 ◇ 5 4 ♣ 10 8 7 6

a) What is the minimum number of points partner can have?
b) What bid should you make now?
c) If you bid 2♠, can partner pass?
d) If partner then rebids 3◇, how many diamonds does he promise?

Answers

1. a) Bid 2♠. You have support for partner and 8-11 points.
b) Bid 2NT. You don't have support for partner, but you do have 13 HCP and a double stopper in hearts.
c) Bid 3♠. You have great support for partner and 12-14 points.
d) Bid 2◇. You have 10+ points (but remember to downgrade for shortness in partner's suit). You do not have a good enough heart stopper to jump in notrump, so bid your good five-card suit.

2. a) Partner probably has at least 13 points.
b) Bid 2♠. You do not have enough diamonds to support partner, but you do have an excellent five-card spade suit of your own. You have enough points to bid it.
c) No. This is a forcing bid. Your hand is unlimited, so partner cannot pass.
d) He promises the same five diamonds he has already shown with the overcall. You forced him to bid and he may not have another good bid.

Overcalling 1NT

Now let's look at another type of overcall. On occasion you will pick up your hand and think, 'Great, I have a balanced hand in the 15-17 range — I can open 1NT', only to hear your right-hand opponent bid one of a suit before you can open. Undeterred, you can still *overcall* 1NT. This overcall shows the same hand as an opening 1NT bid (15-17 HCP and a balanced hand). In addition, it promises at least one and a half stoppers in the opponents' suit. A half stopper simply means that it is a stopper depending on the location of the opponents' high cards. For example, AQ is really 1½ stoppers. Let's see why in an example.

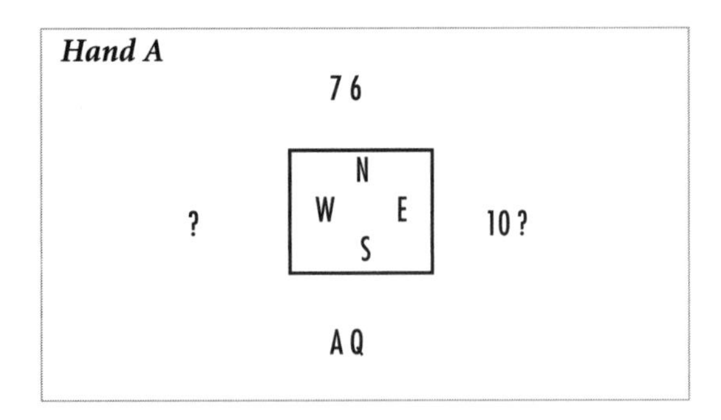

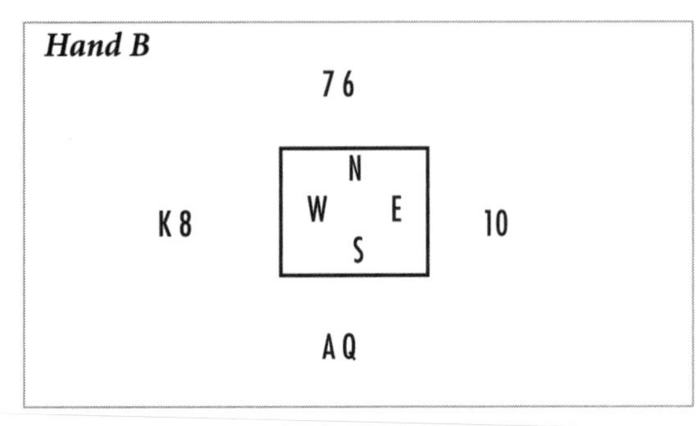

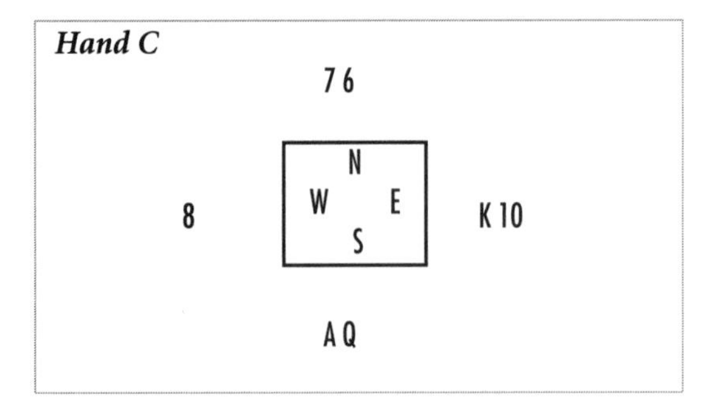

In this diagram (Hand A), suppose East leads the ten. Now South needs a successful finesse for the queen to hold up as a second stopper.

If West has the king (Hand B), South will only be able to stop the suit one time.

Whereas if East has the king (Hand C), then the queen works as a second stopper.

However, if instead West leads the suit, the AQ is always two stoppers. It doesn't matter who has the king because South plays last. Compare this to the AK, which is always two stoppers. All of these holdings in the opponents' suit are good enough to overcall 1NT:

AQ   AK   KQ6   KQJ   AJ10   KQ10

Here is an example of a hand where you might overcall 1NT over an opening bid of 1♡:

♠ 10 8 3 ♡ A K 10 ◇ K Q 10 3 ♣ K J 3

How should the bidding continue after your partner has overcalled 1NT? We suggest you respond exactly as you would if your partner had opened 1NT. You can use both notrump conventions (Jacoby Transfers and Stayman) in just the same way as before. Suppose you hold

♠ 10 9 8 3 ♡ A Q 5 2 ◇ K 5 ♣ Q 3 2

and this is the auction:

West	North	East	South
	Partner		*You*
1◇	1NT	pass	?

What do you bid? You should bid 2♣, Stayman, to see whether partner has a four-card major fit with you. If partner bids a major, you can raise him to game in that major. If partner bids 2◇, showing no major, then you can bid 3NT. You see, it is just the same as if partner had *opened* 1NT. Even if your opponent had opened 1♠, you would still use Stayman.

LET'S TRY IT!

1. Your opponent opens 1♢. Should you overcall 1NT on the following hands?

a) ♠ A Q 7 3 ♡ K 10 3 ♢ Q 5 4 ♣ A J 6
b) ♠ A 9 7 ♡ K 10 3 2 ♢ K Q 5 ♣ A 10 6
c) ♠ Q 9 7 ♡ J 3 2 ♢ A K Q 5 ♣ J 10 6

2. The auction has been:

West	North	East	South
	Partner		*You*
1♢	1NT	pass	?

You have

♠ A K J 10 9 5 ♡ 9 7 ♢ Q 4 3 2 ♣ 7

What do you bid now and what is your plan for the rest of the bidding?

Answers

1. a) No. Although you have 16 HCP, your diamond stopper just isn't good enough.
b) Yes. This is the perfect hand for an overcall of 1NT.
c) No. You have diamonds very well stopped, but only 13 HCP.

2. Use a Jacoby Transfer (2♡). Partner will bid 2♠ and your plan is to bid 4♠ next, since you have enough for game. Partner has at least two spades, so you know that you have at least an eight-card spade fit.

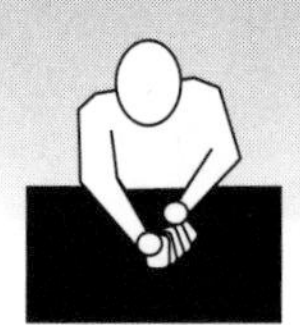

The Play of the Hand

Finesses

Previously, we showed you how to take a finesse when you are missing the king in a position like the one below.

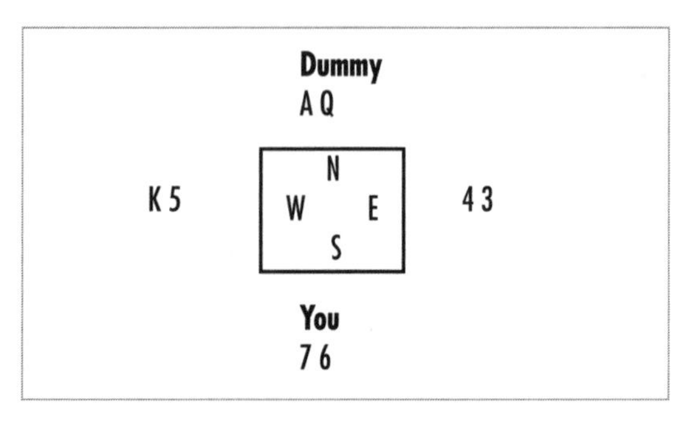

You lead a small card towards the dummy, hoping that West has the king. If he plays low, you play the queen, while if he plays the king, you play the ace. The whole scheme works because West has to play before dummy. You decide on dummy's card based on what he plays. If East has the king instead, you can make only one trick, because he plays last and will win your queen with the king, or play low under your ace.

Now we are going to look at some other finessing positions. In each case, remember you will always lead from the weaker side of the suit towards the stronger.

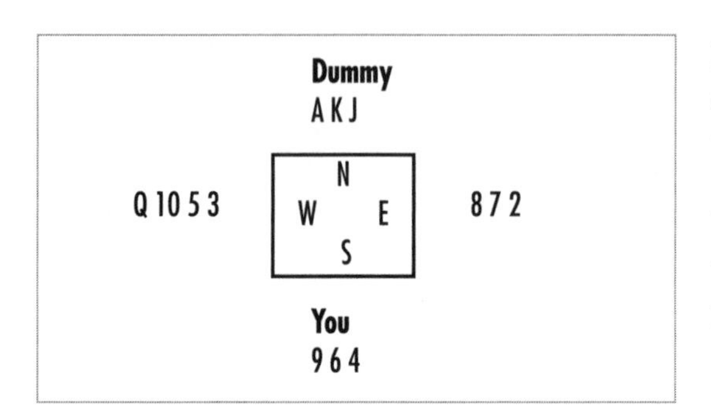

First, suppose you have the ace, king and jack, but are missing the queen. You can finesse in the same way. Let's look at an example, to the left.

You make the same play we have seen already. You lead low from your hand and play the jack unless West plays the queen. If he plays the queen, you play the ace or king.

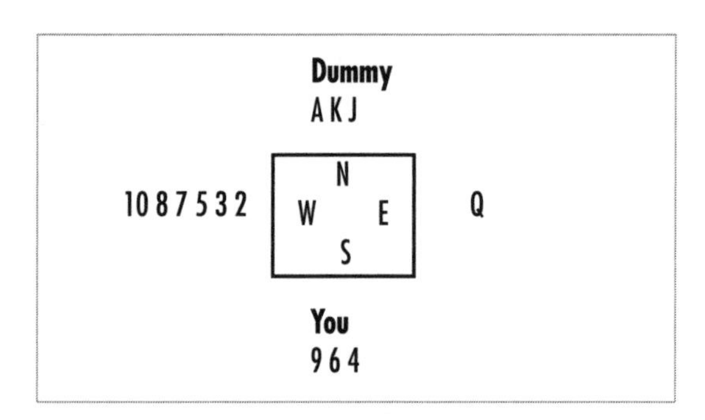

There is a small refinement possible here, too.

It doesn't hurt to play one of the top honors first in case the queen is singleton and falls under your high honor, as shown in the example above. If it doesn't work, you haven't lost anything. You can still return to your hand and finesse against the queen on the second round.

Try to work out how to make three tricks in the next example before you read the explanation.

The best way to play this combination is to play the king first (in case East has the singleton queen) and then play a small card towards the A-J in dummy. Playing the ace first won't work. You need the ace to take the queen if West plays it.

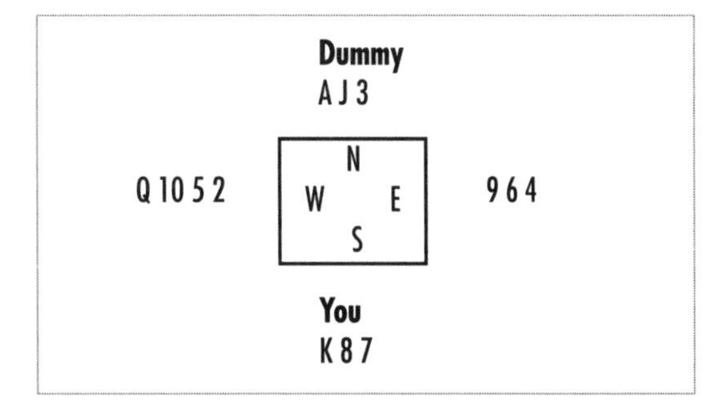

Now here is something a bit different. Look at this position.

Can you take a trick with this holding? Yes. If East has the ace, you can score your king — but you have to lead *from dummy* towards the king. If you lead a card from the South hand instead, you will not take any tricks in this suit. You need to lead from the weaker side of the suit *towards* the stronger side.

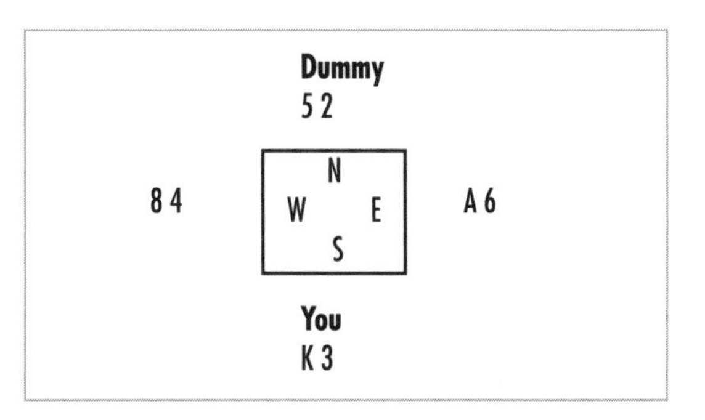

This is a similar position. If East has the king, you will lose one trick. Can you still take two tricks? Yes, you must lead a small card *towards* the queen. If East plays the king, you play low; if he plays low, you play the queen. This way, you are assured of two tricks. It works because you play after East does. Once again, you can refine your play by cashing the ace in dummy first in case West has the singleton king. Then you lead a small card from dummy towards the queen.

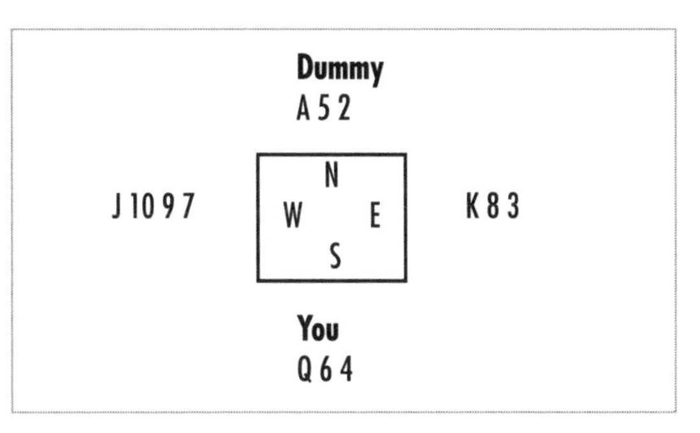

Did you think you could lead the queen towards the ace in dummy, hoping for this position (at the right)?

It doesn't work. If you lead the queen, then West can play the king. You win the ace, but now you've used both of your honors on a single trick. The jack and ten held by East will take the next two tricks in the suit.

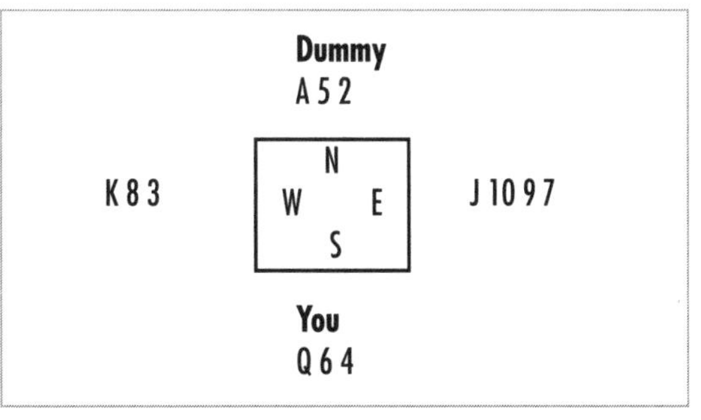

If you play a low card towards dummy instead of the queen, it still won't work. West plays low and you have to play dummy's ace; otherwise, East will win the jack. You can now lead low from dummy, but since West has the king, you will not be able to win the queen. Try this for yourself until you understand exactly how it works.

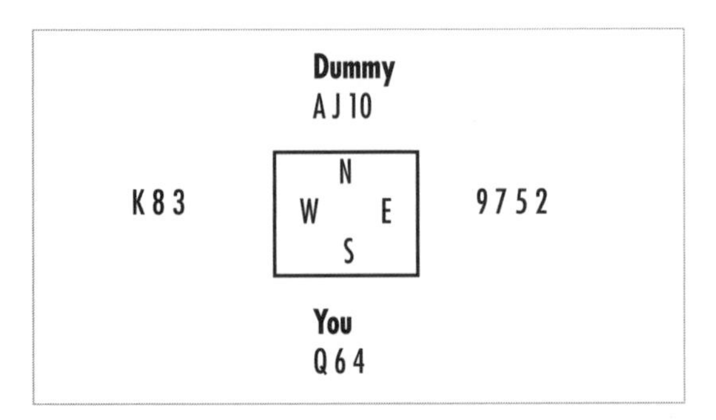

The situation is different (as shown here) if you have all those 'next-door neighbors' — the jack and the ten.

Now you can lead the queen; even if West plays the king, your jack and ten will be winners after you take the ace. If he does not play the king, the lead is still in your hand for another finesse.

Leading Partner's Suit

Now that we have both sides involved in the bidding, it is time to discuss another excellent opening lead. If your partner has bid a suit, you should lead partner's suit unless you have a strong reason to do something else. This is especially true if partner has overcalled. Remember, one of the two reasons to overcall is to ask for the lead of that suit. If partner has gone to all that trouble, then it is your job to oblige him. Among other benefits, this will help to keep your partner happy — always a plus. Use the same rules as usual to pick the actual card to lead: lead the top of a sequence or lead BOSTON (bottom of something and top of nothing). If you have a doubleton in partner's suit, always lead the top card even if it is an honor.

Deal 1 — Dealer South

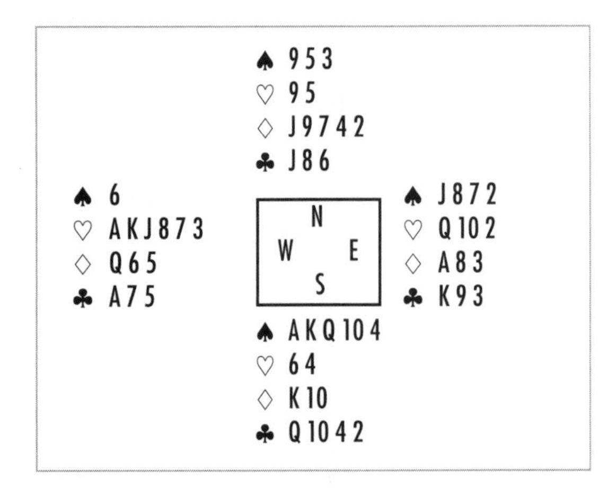

West	North	East	South
			1♠
2♡	pass	3♡	pass
4♡	all pass		

South opens the bidding with 1♠. West has 16 points and a good six-card suit, so he overcalls 2♡. With only 3 points, North passes. East has 10 points and three-card support, so he raises hearts one level. West has enough extra to bid game now. North leads the ♠9 (top of nothing) in his partner's suit.

South wins the first spade and continues with a second top spade. Declarer ruffs and counts his losers: one spade, no hearts, two diamonds and a club — one too many. His best chance is to try to set up his diamond queen as a trick. He hopes that South has the diamond king. First, declarer plays off two top hearts to remove the opponents' trumps. Then he plays the ♢A and leads the ♢3 towards the ♢Q. He expects South to have the ♢K most of the time (South opened the bidding, so he clearly has most of the missing high cards). As he hoped, South has the ♢K and declarer makes his contract.

Deal 2 — Dealer West

West	North	East	South
1♡	1NT	pass	2♡
pass	2♠	pass	3♠
pass	4♠	all pass	

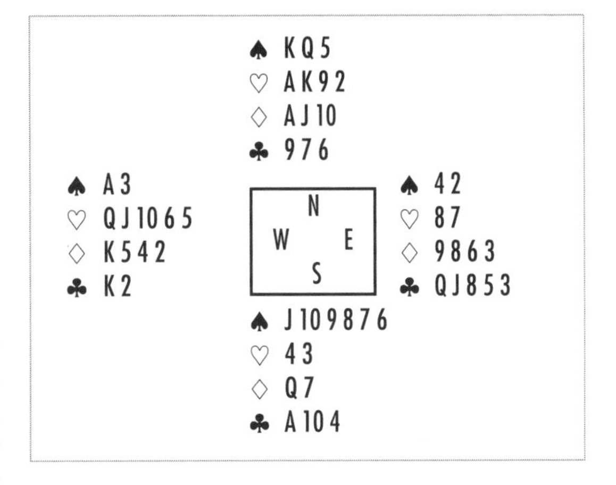

West opens the bidding with 1♡. North has 17 HCP, a balanced hand and a robust heart stopper, so he bids 1NT. East passes. South wants to play in spades. He has 7 HCP and a six-card suit and wants to invite to game. His first job is to get his partner, the notrump bidder, on play. He uses a Jacoby Transfer and bids 2♡. North bids 2♠. Now South does his second job — he lets North know he has invitational values by bidding 3♠. North has a maximum and bids 4♠.

East leads the ♡8, top of nothing in his partner's suit. West plays the ♡10 and declarer wins the ♡A. Now he counts his losers. This time, dummy is the long trump hand, so it works better to count losers from that hand's point of view. (This often happens after a transfer.) From South's point of view, there are two club losers, as well as a spade and a diamond. This is one too many. Fortunately, declarer can finesse against the diamond king and possibly avoid a loser in that suit. He may also be able to throw a loser on a diamond winner.

REMEMBER THIS!

When you have more trumps in dummy than in declarer's hand, it is best to count losers from the dummy hand's point of view.

Declarer starts out by drawing his opponents' trumps — he leads the ♠K. West wins and has many choices. Let's say West returns a heart. Declarer wins and plays another high trump. This removes all of the opponents' trumps. Now he ruffs a heart in dummy and is ready for his diamond finesse. Declarer should start by leading the ♢Q (always lead the honor to a finesse if your side has the next-door neighbors.) West plays the ♢K and declarer wins the ace. If West played a low card, then declarer would also follow low and the ♢Q would win the trick. Declarer can later throw a club loser away on a high diamond and will make eleven tricks.

Deal 3 — Dealer North

North: ♠ A5 ♡ A5 ◇ AK9765 ♣ 1042

West: ♠ KJ8432 ♡ J7 ◇ 104 ♣ A63

East: ♠ Q109 ♡ KQ1098 ◇ J2 ♣ KJ9

South: ♠ 76 ♡ 6432 ◇ Q83 ♣ Q875

West	North	East	South
	1◇	1♡	pass
1♠	pass	2♠	pass
3♠	all pass		

North has 15 HCP, but he does not have a balanced hand, so he opens 1◇. East overcalls 1♡ and South passes. West has 11 points, but no heart support; instead, he introduces his fine spade suit. The 1♠ bid is forcing, so West will get a chance to show his values later. With three-card support for spades, East bids 2♠. This does not show any extra points, as he is forced to bid when West bids a new suit. West makes a try for game, but East passes with his minimum hand.

North leads the ◇A and continues with the ◇K, which also takes a trick. At this point, let's suppose that North plays the ♠A and another spade, declarer winning in dummy. (If this does not happen, declarer will play spades early in the deal himself.) Declarer has already lost three tricks. He has two more possible losers, a heart and a club — one too many. However, he has a completely safe way to make nine tricks. Do you see it? He can now play hearts. After North takes the ♡A, declarer can enter dummy with a club and play winning hearts, discarding his club loser. He does not need to take the club finesse at all!

Deal 4 — Dealer East

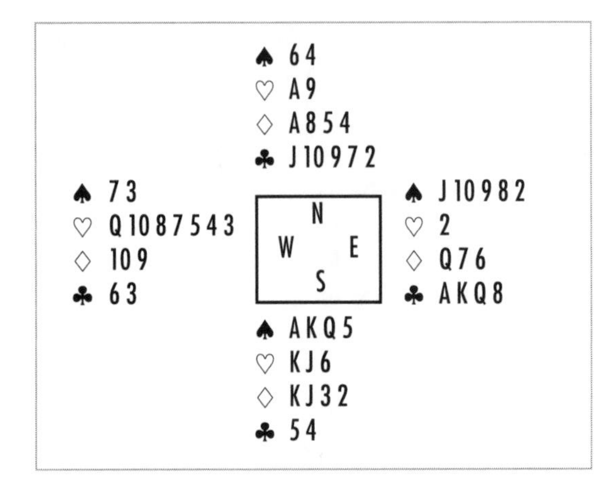

West	North	East	South
		1♠	1NT
pass	2NT	pass	3NT
all pass			

East opens 1♠. South has 17 HCP and spades very well stopped, so he bids 1NT. North invites to game with 2NT and South accepts.

West leads the ♠7, top of nothing in his partner's suit. Declarer counts his winners. He has seven winners: three in spades, two in hearts, two in diamonds and none in clubs. The most promising project suit is diamonds. He gets right to work on this suit. He cashes the ◇A and then finesses the ◇J. When that wins, he sees that the suit has divided 3-2 as he had hoped. He has four diamond tricks to bring his total to nine. If the diamond finesse had lost, he would have taken the heart finesse later. One of the finesses is bound to work, since East must have almost all of the high cards, because he opened the bidding.

CHAPTER**SUMMARY**

A An overcall is a bid of a new suit or notrump after an opponent has opened the bidding. It is used to suggest a lead and/or to compete and win the contract.

B In order to overcall in a new suit at the one-level, you need:
- at least 8 points and a good five-card suit (headed by two of the top three honors or three of the top five honors).
- 13 or more points if you have a weaker suit.

C If you have to overcall at the two-level, you need a good five-card or longer suit and at least 13 total points.

D With three-card support or more, responder to an overcall raises as follows:

8-11 points	Raise one level.
12-14 points	Raise two levels.
15+ points	Raise three levels.

E With 10+ points and a five-card suit, responder bids a new suit. This bid is forcing unless responder is a passed hand.

F With stoppers and a balanced hand with no fit for partner, responder may bid notrump:

8-11 HCP and one stopper	Cheapest notrump bid.
12-14 HCP and two stoppers	Jump in notrump.
15+ HCP and two stoppers	Bid 3NT.

G To overcall 1NT, you need a hand equivalent to an opening 1NT bid (15-17 HCP) and 1½ stoppers in the opponents' suit.
- Responses to a 1NT overcall are the same as to an opening bid of 1NT.

9 The Takeout Double

DID YOU KNOW?

In Ian Fleming's *Moonraker*, James Bond triumphs over the evil megalomaniac (and card cheat!) Hugo Drax by introducing a prepared hand into their high-stakes bridge game. It is in fact a variation of a famous deal from the days of whist, known as the Duke of Cumberland's hand. Despite holding only an ace and two queens between his hand and dummy, declarer cannot be prevented from making a grand slam!

WHAT YOU'RE GOING TO LEARN

In the previous chapter, we looked at two ways to compete in the bidding once the opponents have opened the auction. In this chapter, we will discuss the third major type of competitive action, the **takeout double**. This is used when you don't have a good suit of your own, but you have support for the unbid suits, or more rarely, when you have a hand that is too strong simply to overcall. We will look at the whole story: from the requirements for a takeout double and responder's actions to the doubler's rebid.

In the play section, we will discuss entries — cards that allows us to get to a hand so that we can take our winners in that hand. Sometimes an entry is in the suit that contains the winners and sometimes it is in another suit. Communication — switching the lead between declarer's hand and dummy or between the defenders — is one of the critical elements to consider in the play.

The Takeout Double

We mentioned early in this book that one of your options during the auction is to **double** your opponent's bid. If you double, it means that the stakes are raised: the opponents get more for making their contract and you will get more if they go down. When a player bids too much and arrives in a contract that he cannot make, an opponent who feels confident that his side can defeat the contract can say 'Double'. Saying 'Double' means 'I don't think you're going to make this.' Let's say that the opponents bid to 4♠ and your hand is:

♠ A Q J 10 ♡ A 4 ◇ A 4 2 ♣ J 10 9 8

You are certain that your opponents can't make this contract. You have three sure trump tricks, possibly four, and you have two aces that are also likely to take tricks. You say 'Double' to raise the stakes. This kind of double is called a penalty or business double. If your opponents bid 7NT and you are on lead with an ace, you can also say 'Double'. This, too, is a penalty double! You want to penalize your opponents for bidding too much.

However, how likely is it that you want to penalize your opponents right after they make an opening bid of 1♡? Not very. To defeat them at all, you will have to take more tricks than they do, and to make the risk of doubling worthwhile, you want to be confident of beating them by several tricks. Obviously, that situation isn't going to arise very often, if ever. Therefore, instead of using a double for penalty at a low level, we have another use for this call. We use this double as a request for partner to bid another suit. This kind of double is called a **takeout double**. We don't want to penalize the opponents; rather, we want partner to 'take out' the double by bidding another suit or notrump.

"Takeout Double"
A double of an opponent's bid that asks partner to choose one of the unbid suits.

We have, however, complicated our life a little by doing this. Now we have two types of doubles, takeout and penalty. How can we tell the difference? A takeout double has the following ingredients:

- The bidding is at a level below game (less than 3NT, 4♡, 4♠ etc.)
- The opponents have bid a suit (not notrump)
- It is the doubler's first opportunity to double
- The doubler's partner has not done anything except pass

If a double fits all of these requirements, then it is a takeout double.

Here are some examples of *takeout doubles*:

West	North	East	South
	Partner		*You*
1♡	dbl		

West	North	East	South
	Partner		*You*
1♡	pass	2♡	dbl

West	North	East	South
	Partner		*You*
pass	pass	1♡	dbl

Here are some examples of *penalty doubles*. These are not takeout doubles because they do not meet the requirements listed above.

West	North	East	South
	Partner		*You*
1♠	pass	3♠	pass
4♠	dbl		

West	North	East	South
	Partner		*You*
	1♣	1NT	dbl

West	North	East	South
	Partner		*You*
1NT	dbl		

In the first case, the opponents have bid game; doubles of game contracts or higher are not for takeout. In the second case, partner has already bid 1♣ and the opponents have bid notrump. In the third case, the opponents have bid notrump, not a suit.

What kind of hand should you have to make a takeout double?

You can make a takeout double with three types of hands.

First, let's look at a classic takeout double. Your right-hand opponent has opened the bidding with 1♡ and it is your turn to bid. Your hand is:

♠ K Q 3 2 ♡ 6 ◇ A K J 4 ♣ Q 9 3 2

You have a very nice hand, but you don't have any particularly good suit to overcall, nor can you bid 1NT. We use a takeout double to solve this problem. In order to make a takeout double in this situation you need:

- An opening bid (13 or more points)
- Adequate trump support (at least three cards) for all of the unbid suits

These hands are good examples of a classic takeout double over a 1♢ opening:

♠ A K Q 3 ♡ Q 10 9 8 ♢ 5 4 ♣ J 9 6
♠ A Q 7 ♡ A K 5 4 ♢ 6 ♣ J 9 8 7 6

These hands are not good takeout doubles of 1♢:

♠ A 3 ♡ Q 10 9 8 ♢ A 5 4 ♣ K 9 6 2
♠ A 9 8 7 ♡ Q 5 4 3 ♢ 4 ♣ Q 5 4 2

The first hand does not have support for spades. The second hand has the right distribution, but you do not have enough points. In each case, your hand is not suitable for any alternative action, so you have to pass.

The second type of hand that is suitable for a takeout double is one that is too strong to overcall — a hand with 18+ points and a good suit. Suppose your hand is:

♠ A K Q J 7 6 ♡ A K 4 ♢ K 7 ♣ Q 8

REMEMBER THIS! ☑

When you make a takeout double and bid a new suit, it shows a hand too good to overcall (18+ points).

Your right hand opponent opens 1♣. Your spade suit is good enough, but you are just too strong to overcall — with your 22 HCP, you need very little from partner to make 4♠! Instead, you double. Of course, this time, you are not really trying to get partner to pick a suit. You want to tell partner about your spade suit and also tell him that you have a great hand. Your plan is to bid spades over partner's response, whatever it is.

Let's say that partner bids 1♢ over your double. You now bid 1♠. If you did not have a huge hand, you would simply have overcalled 1♠ in the first place. Therefore, when you double and then bid a new suit, you are showing a hand too good to overcall.

The third type of hand that is suitable for a takeout double is a balanced hand that is too strong to overcall 1NT. It is easy to recognize this type of hand. You look at your hand and think, 'This is an excellent one notrump overcall.' The fly in the ointment is that you have 19 or more points — too many to overcall 1NT. In short:

- You have a balanced hand.
- You have at least one and a half stoppers in the opponents' suit.
- You have 19 or more points.
- Your plan is to double and then bid notrump over your partner's response.

Here is an example. Your hand is:

♠ A Q 10 ♡ K Q 9 ♢ A K 7 ♣ J 10 9 3

You hear 1♠ from the opponent on your right. You can't overcall 1NT, because your hand is just too strong for that bid — it promises 18 HCP at most. You start by doubling. Then when partner makes a bid, you rebid notrump at the minimum level.

LET'S TRY IT!

1. Your right-hand opponent has opened 1♢ and it's your turn. What do you bid with each of the following hands?

a) ♠ K J 10 9 ♡ A 5 4 2 ♢ 8 3 ♣ A J 10
b) ♠ K J 10 9 8 ♡ A 5 4 ♢ 8 ♣ A J 10 9
c) ♠ A 9 8 7 ♡ Q 9 8 7 ♢ 8 ♣ Q 9 8 7
d) ♠ A Q 2 ♡ K J 2 ♢ A Q J ♣ Q 10 3 2

2. Your right-hand opponent has opened 1♡. Your hand is:

♠ A K Q 9 8 ♡ A K 4 ♢ 8 ♣ A J 10 9

You decided to make a takeout double rather than overcall 1♠. Why?

Answers

1. a) Make a takeout double. You have an almost perfect hand for a takeout double. You have 13-15 points and good support for every other suit.
b) With a five-card major, it is best to overcall. Bid 1♠.
c) Pass. With fewer than 13 points, your hand is not good enough for a double
d) With 19 HCP, your hand is too strong to overcall 1NT. Double and bid notrump next.

2. Your hand is too strong to overcall (21 HCP). You plan to bid spades over partner's response.

Responding to a Takeout Double

REMEMBER THIS!

When partner makes a takeout double and there is no intervening bid, you *must* bid.

Takeout doubles are meant to be taken out. One thing is for sure: you must not pass a takeout double just because you have a bad hand or because you have no attractive suit to bid. You do not want the opponents to play in their doubled contact. Remember, partner can have a great hand and may even have a good suit of his own if he is very strong.

If there is an intervening bid, however, you are no longer under any obligation to bid with a weak hand. For example:

West	North	East	South
	Partner		*You*
1♢	dbl	2♢	?

Here, with 0-7 points, you should pass. If you bid, you promise 8 points or more. Partner will get another chance to bid if he has a big hand, and besides, the double has been 'cancelled' — the opponents are no longer playing in a doubled contract.

When partner doubles, he is asking you to do two things: to bid your best unbid suit and to show the strength of your hand. Your first job is to suggest a place to play by bidding your best suit (or bidding notrump if you have a suitable hand). Your second job is to show your strength either by bidding at a minimum level or by jumping or forcing to game.

Let's assume that there is no intervening bid after partner has doubled and you have 0-8 points. (Remember to count your distributional points.) Just bid your best suit at the cheapest possible level. For instance, if partner has doubled 1♢ and you have

♠ 9 8 7 ♡ 6 5 4 3 ♢ J 5 4 3 ♣ 3 2

bid 1♡. This bid does not promise any high cards at all. Even if your only long suit is the opponents' suit, you still have to bid something. For example if partner has doubled 1♢ and you have

♠ 9 8 7 ♡ 6 5 4 ♢ J 5 4 3 ♣ 4 3 2

you simply have to grit your teeth (mentally!) and bid 1♡ — your cheapest three-card suit. When your only long suit is the opponents' suit, make your cheapest bid in a three-card suit.

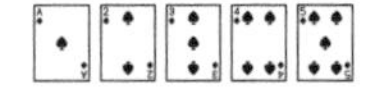

LET'S TRY IT!

The auction has started:

West	North	East	South
	Partner		*You*
1♣	dbl	pass	?

What do you bid on each of these hands?

a) ♠ 7 6 5 4 ♡ A K 2 ♢ 5 4 ♣ 10 8 7 6
b) ♠ 9 8 7 6 ♡ 3 2 ♢ 3 2 ♣ 9 8 7 6 5
c) ♠ 3 2 ♡ 10 9 8 7 6 ♢ 10 7 4 ♣ 4 3 2

Answers

1. **a)** Bid 1♠. It is your only unbid four-card suit.
   b) Bid 1♠. It doesn't matter that you have no high card points. You should still bid your longest suit. But with a choice between a minor and a major, pick the major every time — also, 1♠ keeps the contract lower than 2♣!
   c) Bid 1♡, your longest suit. That's all there is to it. With 0-8 points, bid your longest unbid suit.

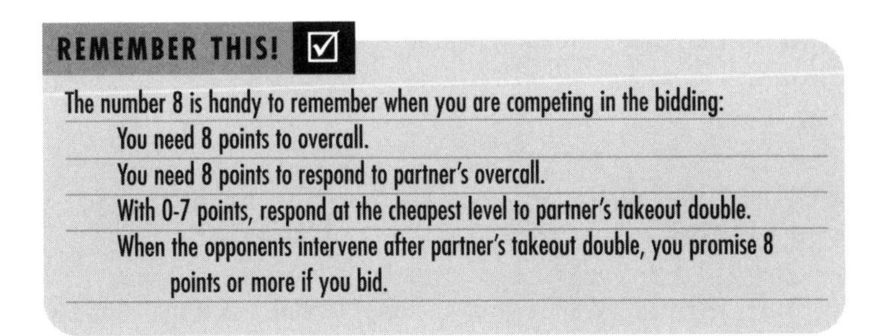
REMEMBER THIS!

The number 8 is handy to remember when you are competing in the bidding:
You need 8 points to overcall.
You need 8 points to respond to partner's overcall.
With 0-7 points, respond at the cheapest level to partner's takeout double.
When the opponents intervene after partner's takeout double, you promise 8 points or more if you bid.

If you have 9-11 points as responder to a takeout double, then you are in the invitational range. You know that partner has at least 13 points for the double, so game is possible if he has a little extra. Jump in your best suit to indicate that you have a hand in this range. Remember, that means bidding one level higher than necessary.

♠ K 6 5 4 ♡ A K 2 ◇ 5 4 ♣ 10 8 7 6

West	North	East	South
	Partner		*You*
1♣	dbl	pass	2♠

If you are lucky enough to have 12 points or more, you want to be in game. By adding your strength to partner's 13+, you know that your side is in the game range. If you have a five-card major suit, you can just jump to game, since partner's double promised you at least three cards in support. Failing that, you have to use a special bid to let partner know that you have a good hand. You bid the opponents' suit! Since it makes little sense that you would want to play in the opponents' suit, this bid is used to tell partner that you have 12 or more points and want to play in game. It is called a **cuebid**. A **cuebid** is a completely artificial bid: it doesn't say anything about your holding in the suit bid. It is safe to bid the opponents' suit after a takeout double, because partner knows you don't want to play in that suit. Your cuebid is forcing to game: partner must keep bidding until you reach a game contract.

West	North	East	South
	Partner		*You*
1♢	dbl	pass	?

♠ A K 5 4 ♡ Q J 7 2 ♢ 7 6 ♣ K 10 8

"Cuebid"

A bid of the opponents' suit. It does not show length in the suit bid. When used in response to a takeout double, it is forcing to game.

This hand is perfect for a cuebid of 2♢. Your double tells partner that you have enough for game. He will now bid his best suit and you can bid game once you have found a fit (in this case, probably one of the majors).

Bidding Notrump in Response to a Takeout Double

What if partner makes a takeout double and your hand is most suitable for play in notrump? If you have 9 HCP or more, no major suit to bid and have at least one stopper in the opponents' suit, you should bid notrump. For example:

♠ K 3 ♡ A J 10 ♢ Q 10 9 2 ♣ 9 8 7 5

West	North	East	South
	Partner		*You*
1♡	dbl	pass	?

You could bid one of your minor suits, but game in a minor is at the five-level. We strongly prefer playing in notrump or a major. This is a good hand on which to suggest playing in notrump. With 9 or 10 points, no major suit to bid and one stopper, bid 1NT.

To bid higher levels of notrump, you should have more than just one stopper. You should have at least 1½ stoppers. If you don't remember what a half stopper is, refer back to p. 135. However, this isn't an exact science — you might think of it as one sure stopper and another high card that may take a trick in the suit. With 11-12 HCP and 1½ stoppers in the opponents' suit, jump to 2NT. With 13 or more HCP and 1½ stoppers or better, bid 3NT.

Here are some examples of hands where you would bid notrump after a takeout double of 1♢ by your partner.

a) ♠ Q 10 2 ♡ 7 6 5 ♢ A Q 2 ♣ Q 10 9 2
b) ♠ A 10 2 ♡ 7 6 5 ♢ A Q 2 ♣ Q 10 9 2
c) ♠ K 10 2 ♡ Q 3 2 ♢ A Q 2 ♣ Q 10 9 2

On all three hands, you have 1½ diamond stoppers and a balanced hand.

On hand (a) you have 10 points, so bid 1NT.

On hand (b), with 12 HCP, bid 2NT.

On hand (c), with 13 HCP, bid 3NT.

Note that if you had a four-card major on any of these hands, you would be trying to find a fit there. When you bid notrump in response to partner's takeout double, you are stating that you do not have a four-card major.

Passing the Double

Earlier, we emphasized that you should not pass a double just because you have a bad hand and don't want to bid. However, it is right to pass in certain *rare* cases. When you pass, you are converting the double from a takeout double to a penalty double. Therefore, you must have a reason to believe that you are going to defeat the opponents' contract. You need to have length and strength in their suit. A rule of thumb for passing partner's takeout double is that you should have three trump tricks or more and a sure trick (like an ace) in a side suit.

For example:

West	North	East	South
	Partner		*You*
1♣	dbl	pass	?

You have:

♠ A 2 ♡ 9 ◇ K 5 4 3 ♣ Q J 10 9 8 7

You have a big surprise for the opponents and 1♣ doubled may be your best spot. With this hand, you can pass. Partner should lead a club if he has one: you have converted partner's takeout double to a penalty double.

Here is a summary of responses to a takeout double:

HCP	Bid
0-8 points	Bid your cheapest unbid suit — don't pass.
9-12	Jump in your best suit.
9-10 HCP	Bid 1NT with no major suit to bid and 1 stopper.
11-12 HCP	Bid 2NT with no major and at least 1½ stoppers.
13+	Cuebid to force to game or bid 3NT with no major suits and at least 1½ stoppers. With 13+ and a five-card major, jump to game in that major.
Very rarely, with length and strength in your opponents' suit and a desire to penalize them, you may pass.	

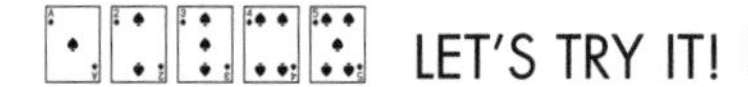

LET'S TRY IT!

The auction has started as follows:

West	North	East	South
	Partner		*You*
1♡	dbl	pass	?

What do you bid with each of the following hands?

a) ♠ J 8 7 ♡ A 10 9 2 ◇ Q J 3 ♣ Q 5 4
b) ♠ 10 9 8 7 ♡ A 2 ◇ 10 9 8 7 ♣ J 5 4
c) ♠ A Q 6 5 ♡ 6 5 ◇ K Q 9 8 ♣ K 3 2
d) ♠ A Q 6 5 ♡ 6 5 ◇ Q 9 8 4 ♣ Q 3 2
e) ♠ 4 3 2 ♡ Q 8 6 4 3 ◇ 7 2 ♣ 8 3 2
f) ♠ 5 ♡ Q J 10 8 7 6 ◇ A J 2 ♣ 4 3 2

Answers

1. a) Bid 1NT. You have a balanced hand and 10 HCP with a good stopper in the opponents' suit. Did you think about passing the double? Your hearts are not close to being good enough to pass!

b) Bid 1♠. You have 0-8 points, not enough to jump. Just bid your four-card major.

c) You have a super hand with 13-15 points, so you know you want to be in game. With only four spades, you should start with a cuebid, since 4♠ may not be the right contract. Bid 2♡; this is forcing to game.

d) You don't have quite enough to force to game. You should show partner you are close to that by jumping to 2♠.

e) This is the kind of hand where it's very tempting to pass, but you must not. You will almost never defeat 1♡ doubled with this hand. Do what partner is asking you to do — bid your best suit outside hearts. In this case, you bid 1♠. When your only long suit is the opponents' suit, make your cheapest bid in a three-card suit. It only hurts for a little while.

f) Pass. You have great hearts and enough values to expect to defeat the opponents in 1♡.

Doubler's Rebids

Let's suppose that you have started things off for your side by making a takeout double and partner has responded. It is your turn to bid again. Let's look at some auctions and decide what to do now.

West	North	East	South
	Partner		*You*
		1♣	dbl
pass	1♡	pass	?

Partner has made a minimum bid in a suit. Don't get too excited. Since you forced partner to bid, it is possible he has no points at all and he certainly doesn't have more than 8 points. With 13-15 points, you should pass. With 16-18 points, you can raise one level. In this case, you would bid 2♡. With a maximum, partner will bid on, and pass with a minimum. With 19-21, raise two levels to 3♠. Partner will know to bid game if he has 5 points or more. If you have 22 points or more, just bid game in the major.

Even if you are not crazy about the suit partner has bid, you should not bid a new suit over a minimum response unless you have 18 points or more. When you doubled, you made the decision that you were willing to play in any suit partner bid. For example, your hand is:

♠ A Q 9 8 ♡ K Q J 3 ◊ J 5 4 ♣ 7 6

West	North	East	South
	Partner		*You*
		1♣	dbl
pass	1◊	pass	?

What now? Unfortunately, partner bid your worst suit. Live with it. Pass, don't bid. This is a mistake that bridge players make all the time. Don't fall into this trap.

If partner jumps in a new suit over your takeout double, he is showing 9-11 points. It is now a matter of adding your points to partner's to decide if game is possible. For example:

West	North	East	South
	Partner		*You*
		1♣	dbl
pass	2♡	pass	?

Your hand is :

♠ A K 7 6 ♡ A J 8 7 ◊ Q 9 8 7 ♣ 5

You have a fine hand worth 16-18 dummy points. You know you have enough to bid game because partner has promised 9-11 points. Bid 4♡. If instead you had a hand with slightly fewer points:

♠ A Q 7 6 ♡ A 9 8 7 ◇ Q 9 8 7 ♣ 5

you could bid 3♡, asking partner to bid four with a maximum. See how it works?

If partner bids notrump over your takeout double, you can follow the same plan. For example, if you hold

♠ A K 7 6 ♡ A 9 8 7 ◇ A 9 8 7 ♣ 5

and the auction goes

West	North	East	South
	Partner		*You*
		1♣	dbl
pass	1NT	pass	?

you should bid 2NT. You have 15 HCP; if partner has a maximum, you have enough for game, so you invite. You already know that partner does not have a four-card major suit or he would have bid it in preference to bidding 1NT.

LET'S TRY IT!

1.

LHO	Partner	RHO	You
		1♣	dbl
pass	?		

♠ A 9 8 7 ♡ K Q 9 3 ◇ Q 4 3 ♣ K 2

What will you rebid in each case if partner bids the following, and RHO passes?

a) 1NT
b) 2NT
c) 1♠
d) 2♡

2.

LHO	Partner	RHO	You
		1◇	dbl
pass	1♠	pass	?

Your hand is:

♠ A J ♡ A K 10 ◇ K Q J 5 ♣ J 10 9 7

What do you bid now and why?

Answers

1. **a)** Bid 2NT. You have 14 HCP and partner has 9-11. If partner has a maximum, you have enough for game.
   b) Bid 3NT. Partner has 11 or 12 points, so your side has 25 or 26 HCP.
   c) Pass. Partner has 0-8 points. You don't have enough for game.
   d) Bid 3♡, inviting partner to bid game. Your hand is worth 15 in support of hearts. You have enough for game if partner has a maximum.

2. Bid 1NT. This was your plan when you doubled. You have 19 points and a balanced hand with good stoppers in hearts. You have the type of hand that could have overcalled 1NT, but you are just too strong.

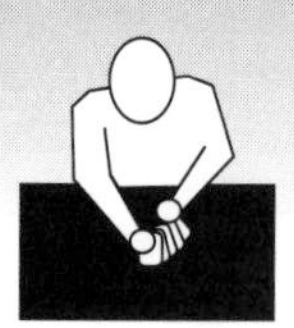

The Play of the Hand

Using Entries

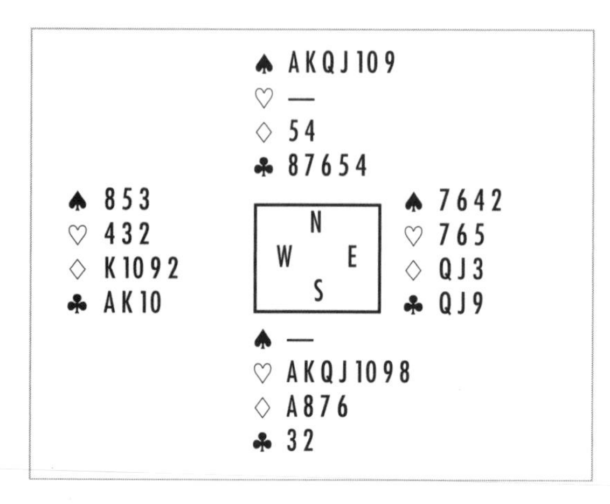

Lay out this deal.

Now, just for fun, let's assume that you are playing this deal from the South side in 4♡. West starts things off by playing three rounds of clubs, South trumping the third round. South counts his losers. He has three diamond losers and two club losers. That is two too many. He could plan to throw his diamond losers on the high spades in dummy, but there is a serious drawback to that: he has no way to get to dummy unless his opponents are helpful and lead spades for him. Eight tricks should be his limit.

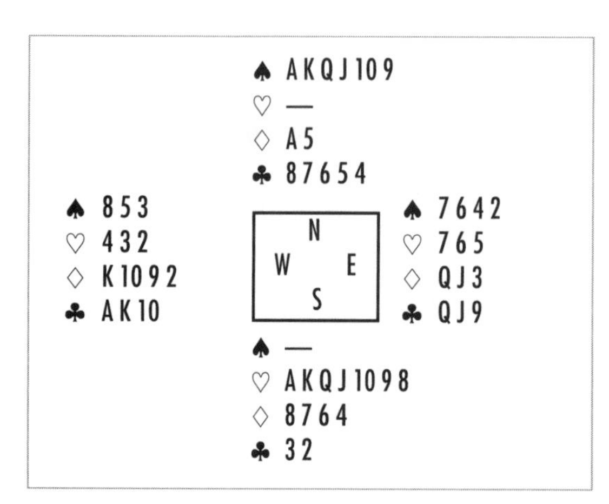

Now move the diamond ace and put it in dummy and give South the ◇4 instead. The deal now looks like this.

Can you make the contract now? Yes, you can get to dummy at some point with the ◇A and throw your diamond losers on the high spades. In fact, no matter what the defense does, you can actually make eleven tricks. The ◇A is an **entry**, a card that gives access to dummy so you can get to your winners.

As declarer, you want to conserve your entries and use them as needed. Let's look at another example.

> ***"Entry"***
> A winner that allows declarer or a defender to get from one hand to the other.

South is playing 3NT and West leads the ♢Q, top of his perfect sequence. South counts his winners. He has six winners: three hearts, two diamonds and a club. Spades looks like the best project suit. There is one problem: if South sets up spades, he needs an entry to dummy to enjoy the spade tricks. Therefore, he must win the first diamond in his hand to preserve his entry to dummy. At Trick 2, he immediately starts on the spade suit. He leads his ♠2. Let's say that West takes the ♠A and continues diamonds. South can now win this trick in dummy with the ♢A and take his spade winners.

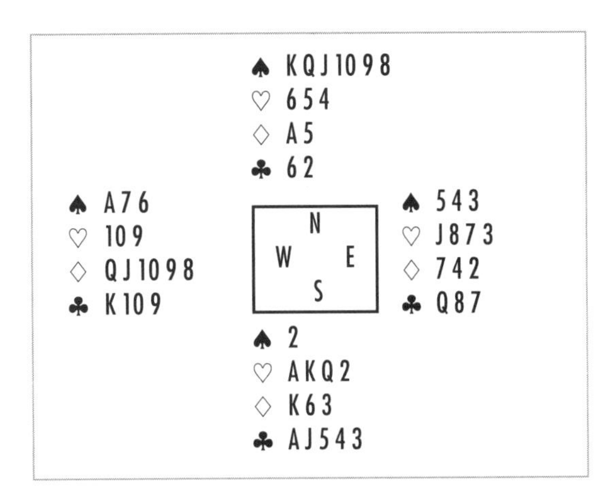

Deal 1 — Dealer South

West	North	East	South
			1♢
1♠	pass	1NT	all pass

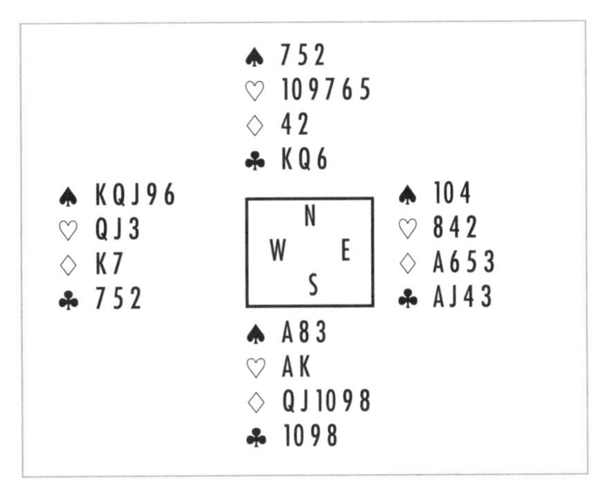

South opens the bidding with 1♢. He does not have quite enough to open 1NT. West has an opening bid and some support for the unbid suits; however, with a good five-card major, he should overcall 1♠ rather than make a takeout double. North passes. East does not have three-card spade support, but he does have a diamond stopper and a balanced hand — he bids 1NT. Since East can have at most 11 points, West knows his side does not have enough for game and he passes.

South leads the ♢Q, the top of a sequence from his longest suit. East has three top winners: the ♢A, the ♢K and the ♣A. Spades looks like a good project suit. If he can knock out the ♠A he can set up four spade winners — enough to make his contract. But notrump is a race. He has diamonds stopped twice so the defense will not be able to set up their diamond tricks before declarer can establish his spade tricks. There is a danger, however. Dummy has only one sure entry, the ♢K. It is important for declarer to preserve this entry until after spades are established.

Declarer therefore should win the first diamond in his hand with the ♢A, preserving dummy's entry. He now plays spades until South takes the ♠A. South should hold up twice to make things as hard as possible, but he must eventually win the ♠A. South will continue diamonds but declarer wins with dummy's ♢K and takes his seven tricks.

Deal 2 — Dealer West

North: ♠ K 8 2 ♡ A Q 5 ◇ Q 10 4 2 ♣ A 9 3

West: ♠ 10 9 6 ♡ J 2 ◇ A K J 7 3 ♣ K J 6

East: ♠ Q J 5 3 ♡ 6 4 3 ◇ 5 ♣ 10 8 5 4 2

South: ♠ A 7 4 ♡ K 10 9 8 7 ◇ 9 8 6 ♣ Q 7

West	North	East	South
1◇	1NT	pass	2◇[1]
pass	2♡	pass	2NT
pass	3♡	all pass	

1. Transfer to hearts.

West opens 1◇. With a balanced 15 count and a good diamond stopper, North overcalls 1NT. East passes. South bids exactly as he would have if North had opened 1NT — he transfers to hearts. North bids 2♡. Now, with a balanced hand, South invites to game by bidding 2NT. With three-card support, North prefers to play in hearts, but he does not have enough points to bid game.

East leads the ◇5, his partner's suit. West plays the top two diamonds and leads a third one. It is important that declarer play the ◇10 on this trick, not the ◇Q. Since East has no more, declarer knows the ◇10 will be the high diamond on the trick. East ruffs, but the ◇Q is preserved to take a later trick. Declarer will win whatever East leads back now and draw trumps. He will score five hearts, two spades, the ♣A and that precious ◇Q for nine tricks.

Deal 3 — Dealer North

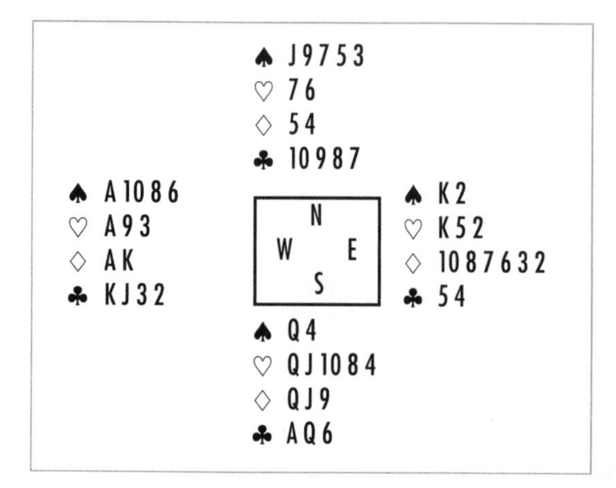

West	North	East	South
			1♡
dbl	pass	2◇	pass
2NT	pass	3NT	all pass

South opens 1♡ and West doubles (West is too strong to overcall 1NT). North passes and East makes a minimum bid of 2◇. West now bids 2NT, showing at least 18 HCP. With 6 HCP and a six-card suit, East can bid 3NT.

North leads the ♡7, top of nothing in his partner's suit. Declarer must win the ♡A in hand to preserve the ♡K as an entry to dummy for the diamond suit. He counts his winners. He has six winners: two in spades, two in hearts and two in diamonds. Diamonds is the obvious project suit. He plays the ◇A and ◇K, counting the opponents' diamonds. When everyone follows suit twice, he uses his spade entry to get to dummy to play another diamond. South wins and continues hearts. However, declarer is now able to win this heart in dummy and take his remaining diamond winners. After that, he can cash his ♠A as well. He takes five diamonds, two spades and two hearts to make his contract.

Deal 4 — Dealer East

West	North	East	South
		1♣	1♡
pass	2♡	pass	3♡
all pass			

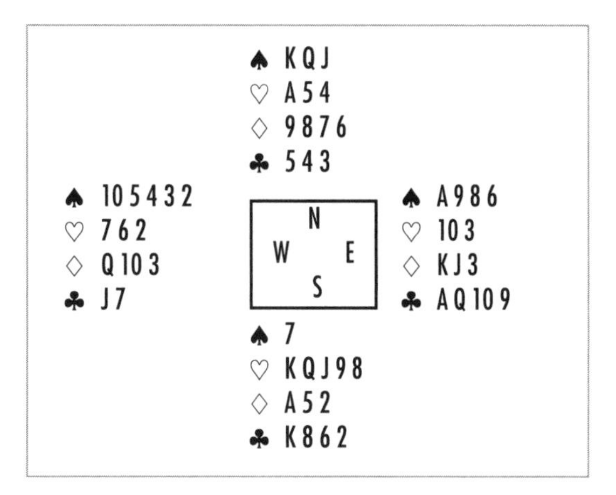

East opens 1♣ and South overcalls 1♡. With 10 points and three-card support, North raises South to 2♡. South has enough to want to be in game if his partner has a maximum; however, North has a minimum hand and so passes.

West leads the ♣J, the top of a doubleton in his partner's suit. East wins the ♣A and continues clubs, declarer's ♣K winning (if East switches to a diamond instead, declarer wins with the ◇A). Declarer has six losers: one spade, two diamonds and three clubs. He can throw two losers on the spades, but he has to be careful of his entries. His only entry to the good spades in dummy is the ♡A. He should therefore draw no more than two rounds of trumps, leaving the ♡A in dummy, before playing spades. East will win, but the defense has set up tricks in only one of the minors; declarer's losers in the other minor can now go on the spades, with the ♡A a vital entry.

CHAPTER**SUMMARY**

A Doubles are used both for penalty and for takeout. A takeout double follows these rules:

- The bidding is at a level below game.
- The opponents have bid a suit (not notrump).
- It is the player's first opportunity to double.
- The doubler's partner has not done anything but pass.

B A takeout double shows at least an opening bid and shows support for all of the unbid suits.

C You should also start with a double on a hand that meets the requirements to overcall in a suit or notrump, but is too strong (18+).

D Responder must not pass the double (unless there is an intervening bid), unless he expects to defeat the hand and has length and strength in the opponents' suit.

E Respond to a takeout double as follows:

With 0-8 points	Bid your best unbid suit at the cheapest level.
With 9-12	Jump in your best suit.
With 9-10 HCP, no major suit and 1 stopper	Bid 1NT.
With 11-12 HCP, no major and at least 1½ stoppers.	Bid 2NT.
With 13+, no major suits and at least 1½ stoppers	Cuebid to force to game or bid 3NT.
With 13+ and a five-card major	Jump to game in that major.

F Doubler with 13-15 points passes if partner has bid at the cheapest level. Over a jump response, doubler adds his points to partner's and may invite or bid game.

G An entry is a high card that allows declarer to move the lead from one hand to another. Make sure to use your entries wisely, so that you can reach your established tricks.

10 The Big Hand

DID YOU KNOW?

The origin of bridge is shrouded in mystery, although its precursors, such as whist and other trick-taking games that date from the 16th century, are obvious. The game arrived in London and New York in the early 1890s, and depending on which source you choose to believe came from India, Russia or Turkey. The earliest mentions are of a game called 'britsh' or 'biritch' in the mid-19th century.

WHAT YOU'RE GOING TO LEARN

On occasion, you are blessed with an exceptional collection of high cards. In this chapter, we are going to discuss how to bid those big hands. We will start by looking at some strong balanced hands, which are opened with 2NT or 3NT. Then we will move on to the remaining very strong hands, which start with an opening bid of 2♣, a trumpet call to announce to the table that you have a big hand.

We shall look at responder's options and how the auction proceeds to game or slam. To help make those slam decisions, we will discuss the world's most popular bidding convention, Blackwood. It is used to check for aces and kings on your way to slam.

When you are declarer in a suit contract, part of the planning process is deciding when to draw trumps. In the play section, we will discuss some considerations when making this choice.

Opening 2NT or 3NT

Up until now, we have looked at balanced hands in the 13-19 HCP range, which you open at the one-level, either opening 1NT or opening one of a suit and rebidding notrump. If you have a balanced hand with more points than this, you start at the two-level or higher.

With 20-21 HCP, you open the bidding 2NT. We know that it may seem risky to open at the two-level, but you have half of all the high cards in the deck. Even if partner has a poor hand, you will be able to make this contract most of the time.

If you happen to have a balanced hand with 25-27 HCP, then you have enough for game in your own hand and you can open the bidding with 3NT. In the next section, we will fill in the range from 22-24 HCP.

While these bids provide less space for exploration, they are specific enough that responder will have most of the information he needs to work out the best place to play. Once you have opened in notrump, partner has a very good idea about the nature of your hand. Therefore (just as when the opening bid is 1NT), responder is the captain of the auction. He will often just place the contract, but he may ask opener some questions on the way to making the final decision.

When the opening bidder starts with 2NT, responder goes through the same process as over 1NT. If he has no four-card or longer major suit, he decides what level of notrump is appropriate by adding his points to partner's points.

Recall that you need:

25 HCP for game in notrump.
33 HCP for a small slam.
37 HCP for a grand slam.

Assume that opener has started the auction with 2NT, showing 20-21 HCP. Let's first look at the point ranges where responder can simply make a final determination.

Points	Total for Your Side	Bid
0-3	20-24	pass
4-10	24-31	3NT
13-14	33-35	6NT
17+	37-40	7NT

On all of these hands, responder has enough information to place the contract. However, if he has 11 or 12 HCP, slam may be possible only if opener has a maximum 21. With a hand in this range, responder bids 4NT, inviting slam. Opener should bid 6NT with a maximum, but pass with a minimum. With 15 or 16 HCP, responder starts with 5NT. Responder knows that with at least 35 HCP between the two hands, his side has enough for a small slam. If partner has a maximum 21 HCP, his side might have enough for a grand slam! The 5NT bid is forcing. Opener cannot chicken out and pass, since his side has at least 35 HCP. This time, with a minimum, opener bids 6NT and with a maximum, he bids 7NT. Now we can add more rows to our table.

Points	Total for Your Side	Bid	Opener's Rebid
11-12	31-33	4NT	Pass or 6NT
15-16	35-37	5NT	6NT or 7NT

Here is an example:

Opener
♠ A K 5 — **21 HCP**
♡ K Q 10 3
♢ A Q 5
♣ Q J 9

N
W E
S

Responder
♠ 6 3 2 — **12 HCP**
♡ A J 2
♢ K J 6 2
♣ K 5 4

Opener	Responder
2NT	4NT
6NT	

Opener has a balanced 21 and opens the bidding with 2NT. Responder has 12 HCP and bids 4NT, inviting opener to bid 6NT with a maximum. Opener has enough to bid the slam.

Now let's look at hands where responder has at least one major suit. If responder has a four-card major suit and enough to bid on (which means at least 4 points if partner has opened 2NT), then he responds by using the Stayman convention, just as he would over 1NT. This time he bids 3♣ over 2NT. Opener uses a similar set of responses:

Opener	Responder
2NT	3♣
?	

3♢	no four-card major
3♡	4+ hearts (may also have four spades)
3♠	4+ spades

If responder has a major-suit fit, he bids to the appropriate level in the major. With no fit, he raises notrump. In both cases, he selects the appropriate level by adding his points to partner's (except that in a suit contract he can count distribution points as well as high card points).

Let's look at some examples where opener has started with 2NT. Responder has

a) ♠ K Q 5 4 ♡ Q J 5 4 ◇ J 5 4 ♣ 3 2
9 HCP (10 points if you find a major-suit fit)

b) ♠ K Q 5 4 ♡ Q J 5 4 ◇ K 5 4 ♣ 3 2
11 HCP (12 points if you find a major-suit fit)

c) ♠ A K 5 4 ♡ A J 5 4 ◇ A 5 4 ♣ 3 2
16 HCP (17 points if you find a major-suit fit)

On each of these hands, responder starts with 3♣. Let's suppose that this time partner responds 3♠. Once responder has found a fit, he can add a distribution point for the doubleton club.

Hand (a): Responder has enough for a small slam and no more. He simply bids 6♠.

Hand (b): Responder has enough to invite to slam; he bids 5♠, asking opener to bid 6♠ with a maximum and pass with a minimum.

Hand (c): Responder has enough to bid 7♠ once the spade fit is found.

What if opener had responded 3◇ (no major)? Then responder would bid 3NT with hand (a), 4NT with hand (b) — inviting slam — and 5NT with hand (c) — inviting grand slam. The whole thing works in exactly the same way as it does over a 1NT opening.

By this time, you can probably guess that with a five-card major, responder uses a Jacoby Transfer to ask opener to bid the major. After that, it works just the same way as over 1NT. After the transfer, with 0-3 points, responder passes and hopes that partner can manage nine tricks. With more than that, after transferring, he bids notrump at the appropriate level and gives partner a choice of contracts. With a six-card or longer major, responder uses a Jacoby Transfer and then bids the major at the appropriate level.

Responding to 3NT follows the exact same principles, but now 4♣ is Stayman and 4◇ and 4♡ are transfers.

LET'S TRY IT!

1. What do you open on each of the following hands?

a) ♠ A K 10 3 ♡ K Q 5 4 ◇ A 3 ♣ A 5 4
b) ♠ K Q 10 ♡ Q 10 9 ◇ K Q 6 5 4 ♣ A Q
c) ♠ 10 9 8 7 ♡ A K Q ◇ A K J ♣ A K Q
d) ♠ K Q 10 ♡ Q 10 9 ◇ K Q 6 5 4 ♣ A 4

2. Partner has opened the bidding 2NT. With each of the following hands, what is your response and what is your plan for your next bid (if any)?

a) ♠ K 10 9 8 7 6 ♡ 7 ◇ Q 10 3 2 ♣ 5 4
b) ♠ K Q 5 4 ♡ Q 8 7 6 ◇ 5 4 ♣ 10 3 2
c) ♠ A K 6 4 3 ♡ 9 8 7 ◇ Q 3 2 ♣ 5 4
d) ♠ A J 5 ◇ A Q 3 ♡ K 5 4 ♣ 9 8 7 6

Answers

1. a) Open 2NT. You have a balanced hand with 20 HCP.
b) Open 1◇. You have a balanced hand with 18 HCP. Open with 1◇ and jump in notrump next time.
c) Open 3NT. You have a balanced 26 HCP. (We had to count it twice to make sure!)
d) Open 1NT. You have a balanced hand in the 15-17 HCP range.

2. a) Use a Jacoby Transfer and bid 3♡. After partner bids 3♠, you plan to bid 4♠. Your hand is good enough for game in spades, but not for slam.
b) Bid 3♣, Stayman. If you have a 4-4 major fit, you prefer to play in a major. You have 7 HCP, enough for game, but not slam. If partner bids a major, you will raise him to four of that major. If partner bids 3◇, showing no majors, you plan to bid 3NT.
c) Bid 3♡, Jacoby Transfer. After partner bids 3♠, you plan to bid 3NT. You are giving partner a choice between game in spades or notrump. With three or more spades, partner will bid 4♠; with only two spades, partner will pass 3NT. You have 9 HCP, enough for game, but not enough for slam.
d) You have a balanced hand with 14 HCP. Your side has enough for a contract at the six-level. With no majors and a balanced hand, just bid 6NT.

The Opening 2♣ Bid

Sometimes you are dealt a hand that is so strong that you are afraid to open it at the one-level because partner might pass when you could make game. For example, you hold:

♠ A K Q J 9 8 ♡ A 3 ◇ A Q J 10 ♣ 4

This hand totals 21 HCP and climbs up to at least 23 points when you count distribution. In fact, you expect to have a good chance of making game in spades even if your partner has no high card points at all. For example, if partner's hand is

♠ 3 2 ♡ 5 4 3 ◇ 5 4 3 2 ♣ 5 4 3 2

you are likely to make ten tricks with spades as trumps, and his hand can't get much worse than that. Unfortunately, if you open 1♠, there is no way that partner is going to bid on that hand, so you must use a special opening bid of 2♣ to announce that you have a really big hand. This is an artificial bid in the sense that it doesn't say anything about clubs at all. It is the only opening bid that partner cannot pass, even if, as in the example above, he has no card above a five!

Opening 2♣ with a Balanced Hand

Let's look at balanced strong hands first. We use 2♣ as the opening bid for strong balanced hands that do not fit in the ranges for an opening 2NT or 3NT. Those are hands that meet all of the notrump requirements and have either 22-24 HCP or 28+ HCP.

With 22-24, you open 2♣ and then rebid 2NT.

With 28+, you open 2♣ and then rebid 3NT.

Once responder hears your rebid, the bidding continues along the same lines as if you had opened 2NT or 3NT.

We can now create a complete chart for opening balanced hands.

HCP	Opening Bid	Rebid by opener
13-14	one of a suit	notrump at lowest level
15-17	1NT	
18-19	one of a suit	jump in notrump
20-21	2NT	
22-24	2♣	2NT
25-27	3NT	
28+	2♣	3NT

Notice that unless you have 25 HCP or more, it is possible that your rebid will not take you any higher than 2NT.

Opening 2♣ with an Unbalanced Hand

What are the requirements to open 2♣ with an unbalanced hand? The key factor is not just high cards, but the trick-taking potential of the hand. Holding

♠ A K Q J 9 8 ♡ A 3 ◇ A Q J 10 ♣ 4

(the hand at the beginning of this section), opener has an excellent six-card suit. Even opposite a weak hand with no particular fit, he has a good chance to make game. Therefore, the longer and stronger your primary suit, the fewer points you need. Here are the requirements to open 2♣ on an unbalanced hand:

25+ points (including distribution) and a good five-card suit
23+ points and a good six-card suit or two five-card suits
21+ points and a seven-card suit

Let's look at a few examples.

a) ♠ A K Q J 7 ♡ K Q J 9 8 ◇ A J 7 ♣ —
b) ♠ A K 10 8 6 5 4 ♡ A K J ◇ K Q ♣ 5
c) ♠ A K J 10 5 ♡ A K Q ◇ A K 9 2 ♣ 5

All of these hands should be opened 2♣.

Hand (a) contains 21 HCP and two five-card suits. Hands like this can take a lot of tricks (we call that **playing strength**). You should open 2♣ and then bid the higher-ranking of your two five-card suits. If partner has a fit for one of your suits, you don't need him to have any high cards at all to make game. One way to test this is to imagine the sample dreadful hand we used above opposite your hand and see how you might fare in a game contract.

♠ 3 2 ♡ 5 4 3 ◇ 5 4 3 2 ♣ 5 4 3 2

By the way, you don't need to wait for a hand that will make game opposite a 0-point hand before you venture an opening bid of 2♣; you should count on partner for either some sort of fit or approximately 3 HCP.

Hands (b) and (c) have a lot of playing strength. On each, you should open 2♣ and rebid 2♠.

Finally, let's look at one other hand with a lot of playing strength:

♠ — ♡ A K Q 9 8 7 6 5 4 ◇ 5 4 3 ♣ 2

This hand will take nine tricks in hearts without any help from partner. However, it does not meet the qualifications for an opening 2♣ bid, because it contains only 9 HCP (and 13-14 total points). We shall see how to manage hands like this in the next chapter.

Responding to 2♣

When your partner opens 2♣, you cannot pass even if you have 0 points. His hand is unlimited and he is quite likely to be able to make a game opposite a very poor hand.

That is why he opened 2♣ in the first place. Most of the time, you are going to respond with 2♢. This is an artificial bid, just as 2♣ is. It does not say anything about your strength or your distribution at all. The point of bidding 2♢ is that it gives partner room to tell you exactly what type of hand he has. Technically this bid is called a **waiting bid**: you are waiting to hear more from partner before you start to describe your hand. If opener now rebids notrump, you become captain and are well positioned to determine the best place to play the deal. If he rebids a suit, you know that he has a strong hand with at least a good five-card suit.

After a 2♣ opening, the plan is to keep bidding until you reach at least game and possibly slam. There is only one exception. If partner opens 2♣ and then rebids 2NT, showing 22-24 HCP, responder can pass if his hand is not good enough for game. With a hand such as this

♠ 5 4 ♡ 10 9 8 7 6 5 ♢ 4 3 2 ♣ 3 2

you will not reach game.

The auction would go:

Partner	You
2♣[1]	2♢[2]
2NT[3]	3♢[4]
3♡[5]	pass[6]

1. I have a great hand.
2. Waiting.
3. I have 22-24 HCP balanced.
4. Transfer. Please bid 3♡.
5. Okay.
6. This may not make, but it should be better than notrump.

In all other cases, your side is forced to game. You keep bidding until you find the best place to play. Is there any way to tell opener that you have a really terrible hand and want to put the brakes on after he rebids a suit? You start off the same way by bidding 2♢ as a waiting bid. Then, if you have support for partner's major suit, just bid game in that suit. You are forced to game anyway and this suggests to partner that you have no interest in bidding slam. Without support for partner's suit, you bid your cheapest minor. This is also artificial. It is a bid that simply says, 'I have a terrible hand — be very careful, partner'.

Sometimes you have an excellent suit of your own and a good hand. If you have 8 HCP or more as responder, then you know that game is a snap. Your side certainly has more than 26 points and slam is highly possible. With a very good five-card or longer suit, bid it rather than making a 2♢ waiting bid. With three-card support, opener will raise your suit. Otherwise, he will (as he originally planned) bid notrump or reveal his own suit by bidding it.

When you open the bidding 2♣, if partner makes a positive response by bidding a new suit, you should be considering the possibility of slam, especially if you have a fit. Even if partner makes a waiting bid slam is still a possibility; remember, responder is unlimited. However, proceed with caution if partner bids the cheapest minor, a real negative.

REMEMBER THIS! 

You *must* bid over an opening 2♣ bid. A 2♢ response is a waiting bid allowing partner to describe his hand further. With at least 8 HCP and a very good five-card or longer suit bid your suit instead.

Let's look at a sample auction featuring a strong 2♣ opening bid:

♠ A K J 10 5	♠ Q 7 6 3
♡ A K Q	♡ 5 4
♢ A K Q 2	♢ 10 4 3
♣ 5	♣ Q 8 4 3

Opener	Responder
2♣	2♢
2♠	4♠
6♠	

On this hand, responder jumps to 4♠ on the second round. He has good spades, but few high cards, and no aces, kings, voids or singletons. However, opener's hand is so huge that it is worth bidding slam anyway once he knows responder has some spade support.

LET'S TRY IT!

1. What do you open on each of the following hands?

a) ♠ A K Q 2 ♡ K J 9 ◇ A Q J ♣ K 5 4
b) ♠ A K J 9 8 7 ♡ A 5 ◇ A 5 ♣ K Q J
c) ♠ A Q J 10 9 5 4 ♡ A 5 4 ♣ 6 ◇ A 5

2. Partner has opened 2♣. What do you respond on each of these hands?

a) ♠ A J 5 ♡ 10 9 8 7 6 3 ◇ 4 2 ♣ 5 4
b) ♠ A K Q 5 4 ♡ 5 4 3 2 ◇ 4 2 ♣ 10 2
c) ♠ A K 5 4 ♡ Q 5 4 3 ◇ 3 2 ♣ 9 3 2

Answers

1. a) Open 2♣. You have a balanced hand and plan to rebid 2NT. With 23 HCP, you have too many points to open 2NT.

b) Open 2♣. With 24 points and a good six-card suit, you have enough to start with 2♣ and bid spades at your next turn.

c) Open 1♠. You have a nice hand, but only 18 points. The hand is not strong enough to open 2♣.

2. a) Bid 2◇, waiting. With a weak hand and a poor suit, wait and see what partner can tell you.

b) Bid 2♠. You have enough for a positive response and you have a good five-card suit to bid.

c) Bid 2◇, waiting. You have a good hand, but you do not have a good five-card suit. You will support partner or try to find a major-suit fit next round.

Using Blackwood

We have talked about bidding slams, but as yet we haven't provided you with much in the way of tools for doing it. We are going to remedy that now by introducing what we believe is the most popular bridge convention ever: Blackwood. Almost all bridge players throughout the world play some version of the Blackwood convention. Like Jacoby Transfers, the Blackwood convention was named after the man who invented it, in this case an American, Easley Blackwood. Blackwood was an expert bridge player, a syndicated bridge columnist, teacher, author and administrator. While his convention is now played the world over, when he first wrote about it in 1933, he had some trouble getting the article published!

The Blackwood convention is very popular because it is easy to use and solves an important problem. When you are deciding whether to go to slam, you often know that you have 33 points, but you also may be missing two aces (your 33 HCP may include some distribution points). The opponents might be able to take the first two tricks before you even get going towards twelve for your side! Blackwood allows your partnership to make sure that you are not missing the aces and kings you need for a slam.

So how does it work? Very simply: after the trump suit is agreed, a bid of 4NT asks partner how many aces he has. The responses are just as straightforward:

5♣	0 (or 4) aces — it's usually not hard to figure out which!
5♢	1 ace
5♡	2 aces
5♠	3 aces

After the first response, a subsequent bid of 5NT (used to check for grand slam) confirms that your side holds all four aces and asks about kings. The responses are similar:

6♣	0 (or 4) kings
6♢	1 king
6♡	2 kings
6♠	3 kings

The key point to remember is that in order to use this convention, you must have agreed clearly on a trump suit. In auctions like these:

Partner	You
1NT	4NT

or

Partner	You
1♡	2♣
2♠	3♣
3NT	4NT

the 4NT bid is not Blackwood, because you have not agreed on a trump suit; in fact, notrump is the likely contract. In each of these two cases, you are simply inviting partner to bid 6NT.

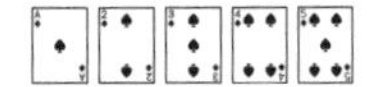

LET'S TRY IT!

1. The auction has been

Partner	You
1♠	3♠
4NT[1]	

1. Blackwood.

What do you bid now on the following hands?

a) ♠ A 9 8 7 ♡ A 5 4 3 ◇ K 10 3 ♣ 6 5
b) ♠ K J 8 7 ♡ K J 8 7 ◇ K 10 3 ♣ 6 5

2. Your hand is

♠ A K Q 10 9 8 ♡ K Q J ◇ A K Q ♣ 6

The auction has been:

You	Partner
2♣	2◇
2♠	3♠
?	

What do you bid now and what do you plan to do after that?

Answers

1. a) Bid 5♡. This shows two aces.
b) Bid 5♣. This shows 0 (or 4) aces. Partner will know that you cannot have four aces, since you made a limit raise showing 10-12 points.

2. Bid 4NT (Blackwood). Since partner has a spade fit, you are sure that you can make eleven tricks in spades. Even though partner has 0-7 points, he could still have one ace. If he has either of the missing aces, you can make slam. If partner responds 5◇, showing one ace, then you plan to bid 6♠. If he shows no aces, then you will play in 5♠.

The Play of the Hand

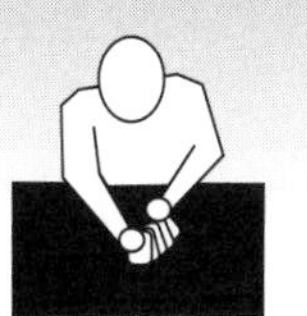

Drawing Trumps

We have looked at different aspects of declarer play in previous chapters. When dummy comes down, the first thing that you do in a suit contract is count your losers. If you have too many losers, you make a plan to dispose of them. Part of your plan is to decide whether you should draw trumps right away or if you need to do something else first.

Sometimes you may need to keep some trumps around for a while. We're going to show you some examples where this is the case and you should try playing each of them through for yourself.

Against your 4♠ contract, the opponents start off with four rounds of clubs and you trump the last one. You need to take the rest of the tricks. You can trump your two diamond losers in dummy, but you must hold off on drawing trumps until you have done so.

Sometimes you need to set up winners in a side suit in order to dispose of a loser, but playing trumps first here would give the opponents time to set up their own winner.

Dummy
♠ A 10 9
♡ 8 7 6 5 4
◇ 3
♣ 6 5 4 3

N / W E / S

Declarer
♠ K Q J 8 7
♡ A K
◇ A 5 4
♣ 9 7 2

Here you are declarer in 4♠. The opponents start with the ◇Q and you win with the ◇A. The danger is that you will lose a trick in each suit. You need to get rid of your diamond loser before the opponents can set up their high diamond, so you must play clubs before drawing trumps. After the opponents win the ♣A, they continue diamonds. You must now play two more rounds of clubs, discarding your diamond loser, before finally playing trumps.

A third reason to delay drawing trumps is if you need to use a high trump in the dummy as an entry to established winners.

Dummy
♠ 10 6 3
♡ K Q
◇ 8 7 3 2
♣ K Q J 2

N / W E / S

Declarer
♠ K Q J 8 7 4
♡ 7 4
◇ A K 4
♣ 7 6

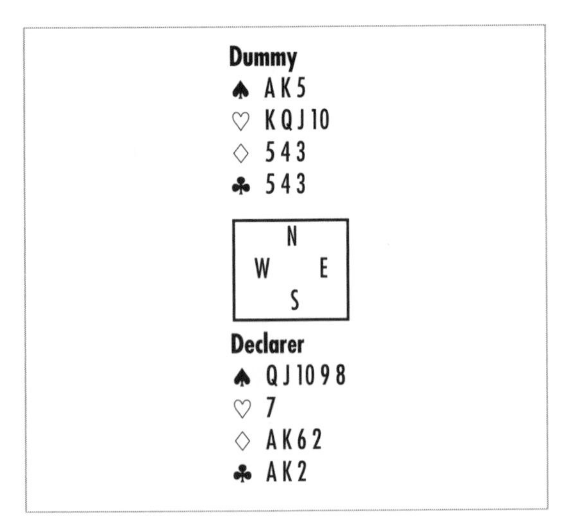

You are playing 6♠ and the opponents start with the ◇Q. You must play hearts before drawing all the trumps, because you will need a high trump in dummy as an entry to the hearts. In this example, you can draw two rounds of trumps first, as long as you keep at least one high trump in the dummy.

In general, we suggest that you make a plan first and then ask yourself the question, 'Is it safe to draw trumps or will that ruin my plan?' If you can draw trumps safely, then do so; you wouldn't want the opponents to ruin your day by trumping your winners.

Deal 1 — Dealer South

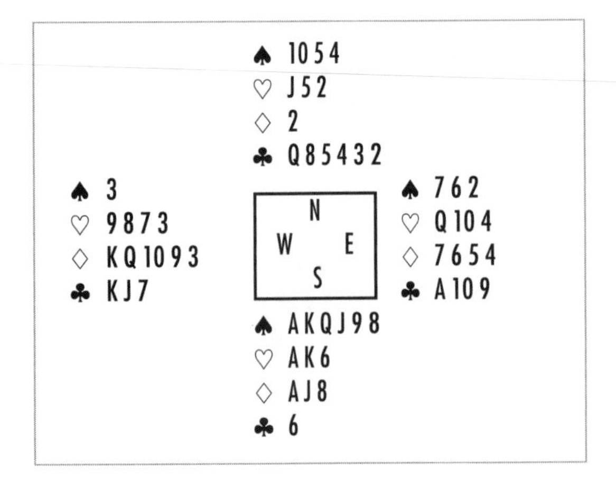

West	North	East	South
			2♣
pass	2◇	pass	2♠
pass	4♠	all pass	

With 24 points and a good six-card suit, South opens the bidding with 2♣. North responds 2◇, waiting. When South shows his spade suit, North simply raises to game with his weak hand. West starts off with the ◇K, top of a broken sequence, and South wins with the ◇A in his hand.

Declarer has four losers: a heart, two diamonds and a club. If he draws all of the trumps right away, he will have no way to make the contract. Instead, he trumps a diamond in dummy immediately, reducing his losers to three. Actually, declarer can now make an overtrick by playing a trump (or a heart) to his hand and then ruffing his last diamond in the dummy. After crossing back to his hand with a heart, he finally draws the opponents' trumps.

Deal 2 — Dealer West

West	North	East	South
2NT	pass	3♣	pass
3♡	pass	4♡	all pass

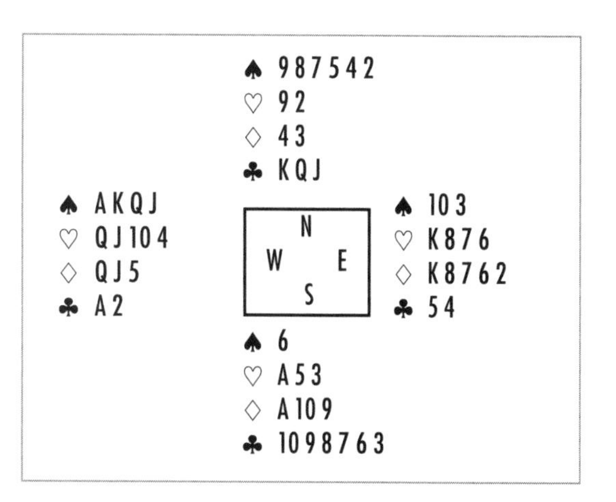

With a balanced 20 HCP, West opens 2NT. With 6 HCP, East has enough for game, so he uses Stayman to find out if West has four hearts. When West shows his hearts, East raises to game.

North leads the ♣K, the top of his sequence. Declarer counts his losers: he has a heart loser, a diamond loser and a club, perfect. He also notices that by immediately playing his top spades, he can discard his club loser. However, it would be a mistake to do so at this point. It is true that if the spades break 4-3, declarer will be able to discard the club loser from dummy, but the risk is too great. In fact, on this deal, declarer will fail in his contract if he follows this plan. South will ruff the second spade and the defense will be able to take a club and the two red aces for down one. Instead, declarer should immediately set out to draw trumps. He should lead high trumps until South wins the ♡A. When declarer regains the lead, he draws any remaining trumps and finally leads a high diamond, forcing out the ◇A.

Deal 3 — Dealer North

West	North	East	South
	2NT	pass	3♣
pass	3♠	pass	4♠
all pass			

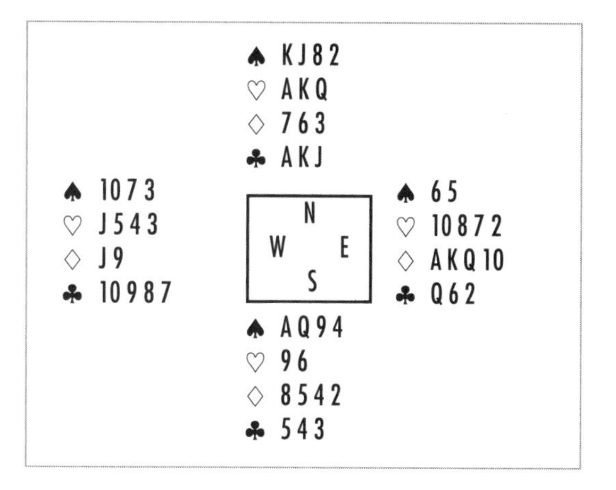

With 21 HCP and a balanced hand, North opens the bidding with 2NT. South uses Stayman to check for spades and raises North's 3♠ response to game.

East leads the ◇A and continues with the ◇K and ◇Q as declarer follows. Declarer wins whatever the defense returns at Trick 4. Declarer, who has already lost three tricks and cannot afford another loser, also has a potential club loser. He has no need to try the club finesse, however, since he can throw the club loser in dummy on a high heart and then ruff a club. Since he plans to ruff only one club, he should draw trumps first. Declarer therefore starts off with three rounds of trumps and then plays his top hearts. After throwing a club from dummy, he trumps the ♣J and makes his contract.

Deal 4 — Dealer East

	North	
	♠ J873 ♡ A5 ♢ 98762 ♣ Q2	
West ♠ 64 ♡ 732 ♢ 103 ♣ A97654	N W E S	**East** ♠ A2 ♡ KQJ1098 ♢ AKQ ♣ KJ
	♠ KQ1095 ♡ 64 ♢ J54 ♣ 1083	
	South	

West	North	East	South
		2♣	pass
2♢	pass	2♡	pass
3♡	pass	4NT	pass
5♢	pass	6♡	all pass

East opens 2♣ with 25 points and a good six-card suit. West bids 2♢ and East rebids 2♡, showing his excellent heart suit. When West raises hearts, East can see that slam is possible if his partner can provide just a little bit of help. East uses Blackwood to find out if West has any aces. When West shows him one ace, he bids the small slam. South leads the ♠K, top of his sequence.

Declarer wins the ♠A. He has two losers, a spade and a trump. He can discard a spade from dummy by playing his top diamonds, but he must do this right away. If he lets North have the ♡A first, then North will be able to play another spade to South's ♠Q.

Declarer therefore plays three rounds of diamonds right away, throwing a spade from dummy. He can then trump a spade in dummy and only now does he lead a trump, forcing out North's ♡A. Declarer wins the return and draws trumps, making his slam.

CHAPTER SUMMARY

A With a balanced hand and 20-21 HCP, open 2NT.

B With 25-27 HCP, open 3NT.

- Responses are similar to those over 1NT. Responder adds his points to partner's range to determine the level.

C With very strong hands, open 2♣.

- Strong balanced hands:
  - ❍ with 22-24 HCP, rebid 2NT; with 28 or more, rebid 3NT.
- Strong unbalanced hands:
  - ❍ 25+ points and a good five-card suit.
  - ❍ 23+ points and a good six-card suit or two five-card suits.
  - ❍ 21+ points and a seven-card suit.

D Responder to 2♣ bids

- 2♢ (waiting) except when he has 8 HCP or more and a good five-card suit.

E All rebids by opener are forcing to game, except for 2NT, which can be passed. Responder may also use a Jacoby Transfer and pass the response.

F On the second round, with a really terrible hand, responder should either raise opener's suit to game (if he has a fit) or bid the cheapest minor as an artificial second negative.

G Use the Blackwood convention, 4NT, to check for aces and kings on the way to slam when a trump suit has been agreed:
The responses are:

5♣	0 or 4 aces
5♢	1 ace
5♡	2 aces
5♠	3 aces

H When playing a trump contract, decide as part of the planning process if you can afford to draw trumps immediately or must defer drawing trumps because of other priorities.

11 Preemptive Bidding

DID YOU KNOW?

Joseph B. Elwell, a regular partner of Harold S. Vanderbilt, was one of the great players and writers in the early days of bridge. Today it is suspected that many of his books were actually written by his wife, Helen, who was probably the stronger player of the two. On July 11, 1920, he was discovered by his housekeeper, dying of a gunshot wound in his New York townhouse. The murder was never solved in real life, but *The Benson Murder Mystery*, a Philo Vance novel by mystery writer S.S. van Dine, is based on the facts of the case, and offers an ingenious possible answer to the riddle.

WHAT YOU'RE GOING TO LEARN

Most of the time when you bid, you have a reasonable number of high cards in your hand. Whether you are opening the bidding, overcalling or responding to bids other than a forcing bid of 2♣, you have a minimum number of points. There are, however, some occasions where you can and should bid with a long suit and a weak hand. In this chapter, we will discuss bidding with this type of hand. We will start with the rationale for bidding and then discuss the bids available to you. We will also look at how responder bids when his partner has opened with a weak hand.

In the play section, we will spend some time in the defenders' shoes looking at how to plan the defense and some of the strategies you can use to defeat declarer.

Opening with a Preemptive Bid

Normally, when you open the bidding, you have at least 13 points. Some bids, like 1NT, promise even more. However, just because you have a very weak hand does not mean that you can't ever bid. Suppose your hand is:

♠ K Q J 10 9 8 7 ♡ 3 ◇ J 10 7 6 ♣ 2

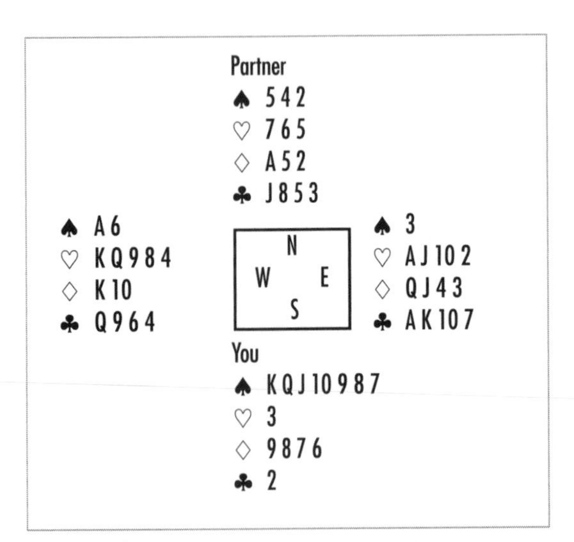

If spades are trumps, you can be sure to take at least six tricks; in fact, you might even be able to take seven tricks if you can establish a diamond trick. Of course, partner might be able to provide some help too. Hands like this have **playing strength**, meaning they can take a lot of tricks. Hands with few high cards can have playing strength, but they need to include a good quality long suit. Why would you open this type of hand? While you can take a lot of tricks if spades are trumps, you may not be able to take many tricks on defense against another suit, so it's in your best interest to have your side declaring. Let's look at an example deal (left).

First, look just at your hand and your partner's hand. Count your losers. You have one in spades, one in hearts, three in diamonds and one in clubs, for six losers. You can trump one of your diamond losers in dummy, holding your losers to five. In other words, you can take eight tricks if spades are trumps. Now look at the opponents' hands. Imagine you are West and you are playing the hand in hearts. You can take twelve tricks on the layout shown. Deals like this, with lots of distribution and good fits, allow both sides to make a lot of tricks if they get to pick trumps. Clearly, on the example deal, your opponents should be able to outbid you and select the trump suit. Your goal is to disrupt their auction and make it as hard as possible for them to get to the right contract — in this case, 6♡. Now, since you have so much distribution, you *can* afford to get into the auction. Even if the opponents were to double you in three or four spades, the penalty would not make up for their missed slam bonus.

> ***"Preemptive Bid"***
>
> A bid designed to use up space in the auction and to make it difficult for the opponents to bid effectively. A preemptive opening bid such as 3♠ is made with a weak hand and a long strong suit.

All opening suit bids at the two-level, three-level and four-level (with the exception of 2♣) are reserved for weak hands. These bids are called **preemptive bids** (often referred to as 'preempts'). They allow you to get into the auction before your opponents, which both uses up a lot of the bidding space and makes it harder for the enemy to find their optimal contract, even if they have most of the high cards.

Opening Weak Two-Bids

One of the most common preemptive opening bids is the **weak two-bid**. As the name implies, this is an opening suit bid at the two-level made on a weak hand with a good suit.

Since 2♣ is the opening bid reserved for strong hands, we can't use it for a preempt, but 2♢, 2♡ and 2♠ are available and we use them for this purpose. To make a weak two-bid, you need a quality suit exactly six cards in length. By 'quality suit', we mean it should contain two of the top three honors or three of the top five honors. You should have 6-10 HCP and less than an opening bid when you add distribution. If your hand is better than this, you can open it at the one-level. Also, you should not have a side four-card or longer major. (You don't want to lose the chance to find a major-suit fit if your side has one.)

Let's look at some examples of hands that qualify as weak two-bids:

♠ Q J 10 8 5 4 ♡ A 2 ♢ 10 7 5 4 ♣ 5

Open this hand with 2♠. You have 7 HCP and a six-card spade suit headed by three of the top five honors.

♠ 7 6 ♡ A K 8 5 4 3 ♢ 7 6 ♣ Q 3 2

This hand can be opened 2♡. You have 9 HCP and the six-card heart suit is headed by two of the top three honors.

♠ K 3 2 ♡ 5 4 ♢ K Q 10 4 3 2 ♣ 3 2

This hand should be opened 2♢. It is worth 10 points and the six-card diamond suit has two of the top three honors.

Here are some hands that should *not* be opened with a weak two-bid:

♠ A Q 10 8 5 4 2 ♡ 5 2 ♢ 10 7 5 ♣ 5

Here you have a seven-card suit (we will see how to bid this hand in the next section).

♠ 7 6 ♡ A 9 8 5 4 3 ♢ 10 3 2 ♣ A 2

Your heart suit is not good enough for a weak-two opening. Pass.

♠ Q 3 2 ♡ 5 4 ♢ 3 2 ♣ K Q 10 4 3 2

This would be an appropriate hand, but unfortunately we do not have a weak two-bid available in clubs. If you open this hand 2♣, you are going to give partner a big surprise, since he will expect a really strong hand! Again, you should pass.

♠ A Q J 7 6 5 ♡ J 8 5 2 ◇ 10 7 ♣ 4

Here you have a side four-card heart suit, so you must pass.

♠ A Q J 5 4 3 ♡ 2 ◇ K 10 7 5 ♣ 5 3

Here you have 10 HCP and your spades are suitable, but when you count distribution (and use the rule of 20), you have enough to open the bidding. Open this hand 1♠.

There are a number of advantages to opening a weak two-bid. First, like all preemptive bids, it makes life more difficult for the opponents by forcing them to start bidding at a higher level — sometimes they may not get into the auction at all! Second, it tells partner a lot about your hand and helps your side find your own best contract. Third, if you end up defending, your bid suggests a good lead for partner.

REMEMBER THIS! ☑

To open a weak two-bid you should have:

- 6-10 HCP and less than an opening bid even with distribution.
- Exactly six cards in spades, hearts or diamonds.
- Two of the top three honors or three of the top five honors in your six-card suit.
- No side four-card major suit.

Responding to Weak Two-Bids

Raising Opener's Suit

When partner opens with a weak two-bid, you have a number of choices. Your first consideration is whether you have a fit with your partner. With a fit, even with a weak hand, you want to raise partner's suit — actually, especially with a weak hand! You want to cooperate with partner and use up even more bidding space, since you have the safety of your trump fit.

With three trumps and a weakish hand, raise to the three-level. This bid is not invitational, but is simply designed to make things even harder for the opponents. Opener *must* pass. Here is an example. Your hand is:

♠ Q 9 8 ♡ A 6 5 ◇ 7 6 5 4 2 ♣ 5 2

West	North	East	South
	Partner		*You*
	2♠	pass	3♠

If partner opens 2♠, you can raise him to the three-level, since you have three-card support for spades. Now if your opponents want to enter the bidding, they have to start looking for their trump suit at the four-level. Partner will pass your 3♠ bid.

With a weak hand and four trumps, you can have a lot of fun. Jump to the four-level to make life really difficult for your opponents!

♠ Q 9 8 2 ♡ A 6 ◇ 7 6 5 4 2 ♣ 5 2

West	North	East	South
	Partner		*You*
	2♠	pass	4♠

When you raise to four of a major, you have an added advantage. If you had trump support and a good hand, you would be making the same bid expecting to make your contract. So your opponents can't be sure whether you are continuing the preempt or whether you have a good hand. For example, you would also bid 4♠ with this hand over partner's 2♠ opening:

♠ Q 9 8 ♡ A K 6 5 ◇ A 6 5 4 2 ♣ 5

West	North	East	South
	Partner		*You*
	2♠	pass	4♠

You would be very happy to see the opponents get into the auction at the five-level when you have a hand this good! You would have a very good chance of defeating them.

Passing

Since partner has on average about 8 HCP, you need at least a good opening bid to have any expectation of making game. The worse your fit with partner, the better your own hand needs to be in order to make a bid, since almost all of partner's high cards are going to be in his own suit. With a singleton or void in partner's suit, you should consider passing, even if you have 15 HCP; your partner cannot have more than 10 HCP, so you are unlikely to miss game. Here are two hands on which you should pass an opening bid of 2♠:

♠ 5 ♡ K Q 5 4 3 2 ◇ 9 8 7 6 ♣ 3 2

You have a nice weak two-bid of your own, but partner got there first. You do not have a fit with partner and you should pass. There is no evidence that you will actually do better in hearts than in spades. It may simply be a case of jumping out of the frying pan and into the fire. As you will see shortly, if you bid a new suit, partner will expect you to have at least 13 points.

♠ 2 ♡ A K 9 8 ◇ A J 10 9 ♣ J 10 9 5

Here you have a good hand and may well make 2♠ even though you don't have a fit. However, without a fit for partner, you do not have enough to bid. If the opponents enter the auction, you have a good chance of defeating their contract, so pass for now.

Bidding a New Suit

If you do not have trump support for partner, but you have a good hand with a good five-card suit of your own, you can bid your suit. However, with a singleton or void in partner's suit, you must have a hand worth 16 points or more. You are making a bid in a new suit with an expectation of reaching game and you are hoping to find a better place to play the hand. A new suit by responder is always forcing, so partner must bid again. With a three-card fit for you, the opening weak-two bidder will raise your suit. Failing that, he will bid a side suit if he has one. With no other bid available, he will just rebid his original suit. You can now decide the best place to play the hand. Here is an example:

Partner	You
♠ Q 5 4	♠ A K 10 8 5
♡ K Q 7 6 5 4	♡ 3
◇ 4	◇ A J 2
♣ J 8 7	♣ K Q 4 2
2♡	2♠
3♠	4♠

Even though you have a singleton in partner's suit, you have 17 HCP — enough to justify a bid in a new suit. When you bid 2♠, you are pleased to hear partner raise and you can go on to game.

Asking for More Information

There is one more choice available when partner opens a weak two-bid. You can use a special bid to ask him for more information: bid 2NT to ask opener if he has a **feature** — an ace or king in a side suit. (This particular convention doesn't have a name.) If partner has a high card in one of your long suits, you may be able to take a lot of tricks. Conversely, if he has a high card in one of your short suits, it probably won't help you very much. Let's see how this works in practice. Suppose this is your hand:

♠ J 5 4 ♡ K Q 5 3 ♢ 5 ♣ A Q 5 4 3

Partner opens 2♠. You have a spade fit, but the critical factor is whether partner can help you in hearts or clubs. This hand is suitable for a 2NT response. Partner will show you any side card he has by bidding that suit or will rebid 3♠ without one. For example:

Partner	You
♠ K Q 9 6 3 2	♠ J 5 4
♡ A 6 4	♡ K Q 5 3
♢ 9 8 7	♢ 5
♣ 7	♣ A Q 5 4 3
2♠	2NT
3♡	4♠[1]

1. Now that you know partner has the ♡A, your hand has improved.

Let's give partner a different hand:

Partner	You
♠ K Q 9 6 5 4	♠ J 5 4
♡ 9 8	♡ K Q 5 3
♢ K 6	♢ 5
♣ 7 3 2	♣ A Q 5 4 3
2♠	2NT
3♢	3♠

Here your hand has not improved after partner's bid of 3♢. Partner's diamond honor is not helpful at all and even 3♠ will be no picnic. You were really searching for a heart or club honor.

Summary

If partner opens a weak two-bid:

- With a weak hand and three trumps, raise to the three-level.
- With a weak hand and four trumps, raise to the four-level.
- With a good hand and at least three trumps, raise a major to game.
- With a good hand, no fit for partner's major and a good five-card suit of your own, bid your own suit.
- With a fit for partner's minor, you can still bid a good five-card major of your own.
- With an invitational hand and a trump fit, you can use the 2NT response to find out whether partner has a useful feature (the ace or king in a side suit).

LET'S TRY IT!

1. You are dealer. What do you bid with each of the following hands?

a) ♠ K 10 7 6 ♡ K Q 8 7 6 3 ◇ 5 4 ♣ 4
b) ♠ K 2 ♡ K Q 8 7 6 3 ◇ 5 4 3 2 ♣ 4
c) ♠ A 2 ♡ 6 4 3 ◇ A Q J 9 8 7 ♣ 3 2

2. Partner opens the bidding with 2♡ and the next player passes. What do you respond with each of the following hands?

a) ♠ K J 5 4 3 ♡ A 5 4 ◇ K Q J 7 ♣ 3
b) ♠ 3 2 ♡ 10 9 8 7 ◇ K 10 4 3 2 ♣ 5 3
c) ♠ A 10 7 ♡ J 3 2 ◇ 10 9 8 7 2 ♣ 3 2
d) ♠ A K J 10 4 ♡ 4 ◇ A Q 10 9 ♣ Q 3 2
e) ♠ A Q 7 6 ♡ J 3 2 ◇ K Q 6 5 ♣ 3 2

Answers

1. a) Pass. Don't open 2♡ with a side four-card spade suit.
b) Open 2♡.
c) Open 1◇. With a hand worth 13 points, you are too good to open 2◇.

2. a) Bid 4♡. You expect to make it.
b) Bid 4♡. You don't expect to make this one, but you want to continue to preempt the opponents (take away their bidding space). You don't have much defense at all. Let them start guessing at the five-level!
c) Bid 3♡. You have a weak hand and with three trumps you can further disrupt the opponents' auction. Opener must pass this bid.
d) Bid 2♠. You have an excellent hand, but not much of a heart fit. Perhaps partner has three spades.
e) Bid 2NT. If partner shows a feature in spades or diamonds, bid 4♡. Otherwise, retreat to 3♡ and keep your fingers crossed.

Opening at the Three-Level or Higher

The longer your suit, the more tricks you can take with that suit as trumps and the higher you can safely bid. With a quality seven-card suit in a hand worth less than an opening bid, with most of your high cards in your long suit, you can open at the three-level. With an eight-card suit, open at the four-level. Remember, you do not expect to make your contract unless partner has a very good hand for you. A preempt is primarily a destructive bid. Your goal is to prevent the opponents from reaching their own best contract. However, don't forget that the opponents can double you. If you go down four or five tricks doubled, it will cost a lot of points, especially if you are vulnerable. The key to avoiding a big penalty is having a high quality suit. The best preemptive hands have most of their high cards in the long suit where they will produce some tricks. Here is an example of a good hand for an opening bid of 3♠ when you are vulnerable:

♠ A K J 9 7 6 5 ♡ 8 7 6 ◊ 4 3 ♣ 5

A good yardstick to use is the Rule of 2 and 3 — when you open a preempt not vulnerable, you should expect to go down three tricks even if partner has no help for you; vulnerable, you should expect to go down two tricks. This means that if the opponents double you, the penalty will be no more than 500 points, which is not serious if they can make a game.

If you want to start out with a simpler way to decide whether to preempt, you can boil it down to this: with a good quality six-card suit, you can open at the two-level; with a good seven-card suit, you can open at the three-level; and with a good eight-card suit, you can open at the four-level. Just remember that if you are vulnerable, the penalty for going down is greater, so you should tend to have a better suit.

These two hands could both be opened at the three-level:

♠ K Q J 5 4 3 2 ♡ 5 4 ◊ 10 9 8 7 ♣ —
♠ 4 ♡ 3 ◊ J 10 9 8 ♣ K J 10 8 7 6 2

On this next hand, you can open at the four-level:

♠ A K J 10 9 8 7 6 ♡ 3 ◊ 5 4 3 ♣ 2

How about this next hand — is it suitable for a preemptive opening?

♠ 10 9 6 5 4 3 2 ♡ A 9 4 ◊ K 5 ♣ 3

We would never open a preempt on this hand! The spade suit is too weak and your high cards are in the other suits, where they will be more use on defense than in a spade contract. Suppose we change the hand around, though:

♠ A K 10 9 4 3 2 ♡ 9 4 3 ◊ 5 4 ♣ 3

Now you could open 3♠. You expect to make six spade tricks, for down three not vulnerable. You are following the Rule of 2 and 3. Notice that with the previous hand, you could not really count six tricks. When your high cards are not in your long suit, the hand is defensive rather than offensive in nature.

REMEMBER THIS! ☑

When opening a high-level preempt, you need a seven-card suit to open at the three-level and an eight-card suit to open at the four-level. The Rule of 2 and 3 is also useful: not vulnerable, you should be within three tricks of making your contract; vulnerable, you should be within two tricks of making your contract.

Responding to Higher-Level Preempts

When partner opens at the three-level, you will often just pass. Remember, partner does not have a particularly good hand.

If you have some support for partner and some potential tricks for him, you can raise his major-suit preempt to game. For example, suppose you have:

♠ 7 6 ♡ A K 7 4 ◇ A J 4 3 2 ♣ A 2

You can raise 3♠ to 4♠. Partner should be able to make about six tricks by himself. You have four probable tricks in aces and kings along with a couple of trumps to help him out.

You may introduce your own suit on occasion, but you need to have a good hand and a high-quality six-card suit. Remember, partner is less likely to have a fit for your suit when he has seven or eight cards in his own suit. If partner opens 3♡, what do you respond with this hand?

♠ A K Q 8 7 2 ♡ 3 2 ◇ A K 9 5 ♣ 3

Bid 3♠ over 3♡. You hope that partner has a fit with you in spades. If he doesn't, you are willing to try 4♡.

LET'S TRY IT!

1. You are the dealer on each of these hands. What do you do?
a) ♠ A K J 10 9 8 7 2 ♡ 5 4 ◇ 5 3 2 ♣ —
b) ♠ Q 10 8 6 5 4 3 ♡ 2 ◇ 9 8 7 ♣ 3 2
c) ♠ 3 ♡ 4 2 ◇ Q J 10 ♣ K Q J 8 6 4 3

2. You are dealer on each of these hands. What do you do?
a) ♠ 7 ♡ K Q J 9 8 7 6 ◇ 6 5 ♣ 7 6 3
b) ♠ A K Q 10 9 8 7 ♡ A 3 2 ◇ 5 4 ♣ 2
c) ♠ 3 ♡ A Q J 10 6 5 4 3 ♡ 5 4 ♣ 3 2

3. Partner has opened 3♡. What do you do on this hand?

♠ A 3 ♡ K 10 3 ◇ A K 9 8 6 ♣ 7 6 3

Answers

1. **a)** Open 4♠. You have eight tricks, all of them spades. (This is consistent with the Rule of 2 and 3.)
   b) Pass. You have a weak suit and you cannot count on making enough tricks to warrant opening 3♠.
   c) Open 3♣. You have a good seven-card suit.

2. **a)** Open 3♡. You have an excellent seven-card suit.
   b) Open 1♠, not 3♠ or 4♠. You have 13 HCP and a hand worth 16 total points. This is too much to preempt — you might miss game or even a slam.
   c) Open 4♡. This time you have a good eight-card suit, enough for a four-level preempt.

3. Bid 4♡. Partner should be able to make about six tricks and you can add four more to them, since the ♡K will be a great help to partner and is worth a trick. Expect partner to make game.

Preemptive Jump Overcalls

Even if the opponents have opened the bidding, you can still preempt. It is a bit less effective, since the opponents have already had a chance to open communications, but you can still disrupt their auction. A **jump overcall** is an overcall in a suit made one level higher than necessary. So over an opening bid of 1♡, a bid of 2♠ is a jump overcall; over 1♢, 3♣ is a jump overcall.

"Jump Overcall"
An overcall in a suit made one level higher than necessary.

Many years ago, bridge players generally used a jump overcall to show a hand that was stronger than a normal overcall. However, the hands for this type of bid rarely occurred, and now most people use the bid to show a preemptive hand. When you make a preemptive jump overcall at the two-level, your hand should look like a weak-two bid (with a good six-card suit). Similarly, a hand for a preemptive jump overcall at the three-level should look like an opening bid at the three-level; it will include a seven-card suit. So if your opponent opens 1♢ and you bid 2♡, you should have:

- A good six-card suit with two of the top three honors or three of the top five honors
- 6-10 HCP
- Less than an opening bid

If the opponents open 1♡ and you bid 3♢, you should have:

- A decent seven-card suit
- Less than an opening bid

You respond to a preemptive jump overcall in the same way that you would respond to an opening bid at the same level.

LET'S TRY IT!

1. You have

♠ 6 ♡ K Q J 10 6 2 ◇ 9 8 7 2 ♣ 4 3

Your right-hand opponent has opened the bidding with 1◇.

a) What do you do?
b) What would you do if he had opened 1♠ instead?

2. The bidding has gone:

West	North	East	South
	Partner		*You*
1◇	2♡	pass	?

What do you bid with each of the following hands?

a) ♠ 4 ♡ 10 9 8 ◇ K Q 5 4 ♣ J 9 8 7 3
b) ♠ 8 7 ♡ Q 9 8 7 ◇ 4 3 ♣ K Q J 3 2

Answers

1. a) Over 1◇, bid 2♡. With a good six-card suit and 6 HCP, your hand meets the requirements for a preemptive jump overcall at the two-level.
b) Over 1♠, you should pass. You do not have a hand suitable to bid at the three-level: you need to have a seven-card suit. Likewise, you cannot bid 2♡: remember that for a non-jump overcall at the two-level you need an opening bid.

2. a) Bid 3♡. With three-card support for partner and a weak hand, raise his preempt. This will make it harder for the opponents to find their best spot.
b) Bid 4♡. With four-card support, raise to game. You do not have a good enough hand to expect to make it, but the opponents are likely to be able to make something their way. It is better for you to take a small minus than to let the opponents bid and make a game or slam.

The Play of the Hand

Defending—The Opening Lead

In the play sections of this book, we have spent most of the time talking about contracts from declarer's perspective. Now it is time to look at the play from the defenders' point of view. Perhaps the most important decision that the defense needs to make is the opening lead. A surprisingly large number of contracts are won or lost based on its selection. Let's review some good choices of lead, more or less in order of preference.

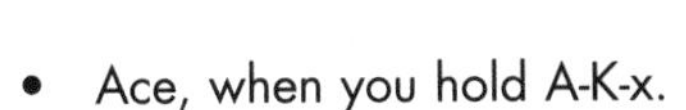

- Ace, when you hold A-K-x.
- Partner's suit, if partner has opened or overcalled a suit.
- Top of an honor sequence.
- A singleton or a doubleton if you also have some trumps.
- Fourth highest of a suit headed by an honor.
- Top of nothing.

The Opponents' Auction

Apart from your own hand (and partner's bids, if any), you have one other source of information to help you to decide what to lead — the opponents' auction. Let's look at an example. Your hand is:

♠ 3 2 ♡ K Q J ◇ K Q J ♣ 8 7 6 5 2

The opponents have arrived at 4♠. Which of your kings should you lead? Actually, you can't answer that question properly without knowing the opponents' bidding. Suppose this was their auction:

West	North	East	South
			You
1♡	pass	1♠	pass
2♠	pass	3♡	pass
3♠	pass	4♠	all pass

On this auction, the king of diamonds is the obvious lead. The opponents have two good suits: hearts and spades. You want to set up your diamond tricks before they can set up the heart suit — if you lead hearts, you will be helping them! Remember, you can use what the opponents are saying to each other in the auction to your advantage.

Signaling

> ***"Attitude Signal"***
> When partner leads a high card in a suit, the spot card you play tells partner whether or not you like the suit. A high spot card says you like the suit and a low spot card says you don't.

Another important aspect of defense is signaling. Signaling is a way for the defenders to communicate with each other. Since it is illegal to do that by talking or making faces or hand gestures, the defenders have to use their cards to tell each other about their hands. There are many aspects to signaling and most of them are beyond the scope of this book. We are going to introduce you to one kind of signal. It is called an **attitude signal**. When partner leads a high card, you want to tell him how you feel about the suit. Use a high spot card to say you like the suit and a low spot card to say you don't. Think of a high spot card as a smile and a low spot card as a frown.

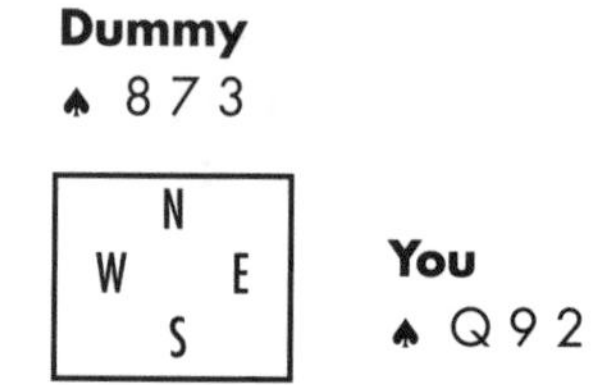

Here is the spade holding for you and dummy when your partner, West, leads the ♠A, promising the ♠K as well. How do you feel about spades? You like them! You want partner to play the ♠K, and if that wins the trick, a third spade to your queen. So you tell partner by playing a high spot card, here the ♠9. Partner will read this as a smile and continue spades.

However, if this is the situation instead:

You have no reason to want partner to play more spades and you should (in a bridge sense only!) frown by playing the ♠2. Partner will realize that you want him to try another suit.

Let's look at an example of this in a full deal.

North	South
	1♠
3♠	4♠
all pass	

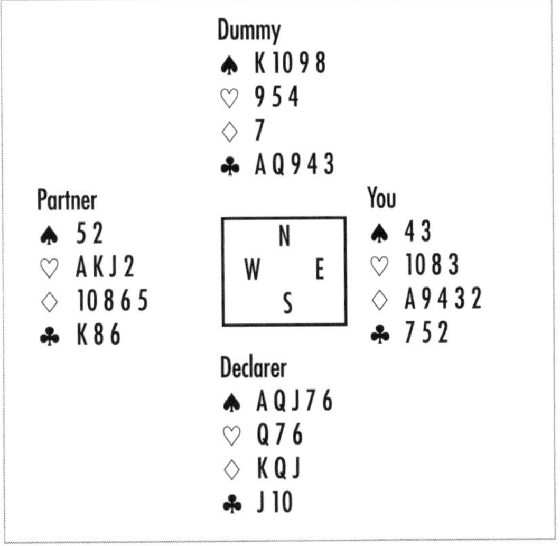

Partner leads the ♡A. You do not have any help for partner in hearts, so you play the ♡3, your lowest heart (a frown). Now partner knows that you do not have the ♡Q and he will not continue hearts — low means 'No!' Partner can see by looking at the dummy that there are no tricks coming for your side in clubs, so he should try a diamond. You will gain the lead with the ♢A and can now lead a heart through declarer's ♡Q. Partner will be able to take tricks with the ♡K and ♡J in addition to the ♡A and you will defeat the contract.

If partner plays the ♡K at Trick 2, the ♡Q becomes a trick for declarer and the game will be made.

However, suppose this is the layout instead (right).

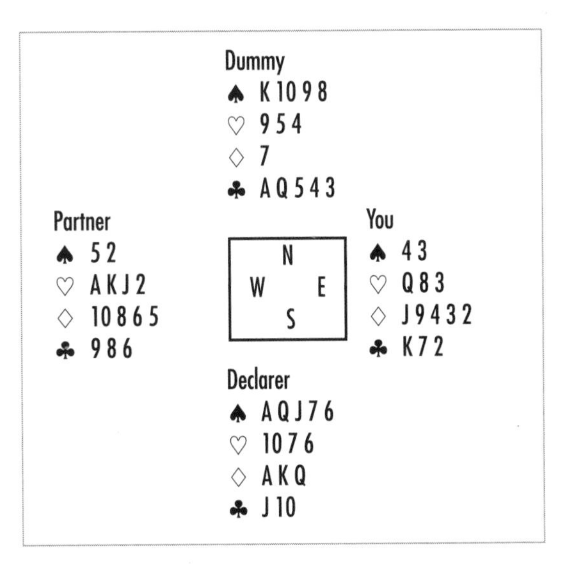

This time when partner leads the ♡A, you should play the ♡8 (a smile). Now if partner continues hearts, you will take three heart tricks and eventually make your ♣K. You will beat the contract. If partner plays a different suit at Trick 2, declarer will make his contract, since he will be able to discard dummy's remaining hearts on the high diamonds. By playing the ♡8 at Trick 1, you help partner to find the right defense.

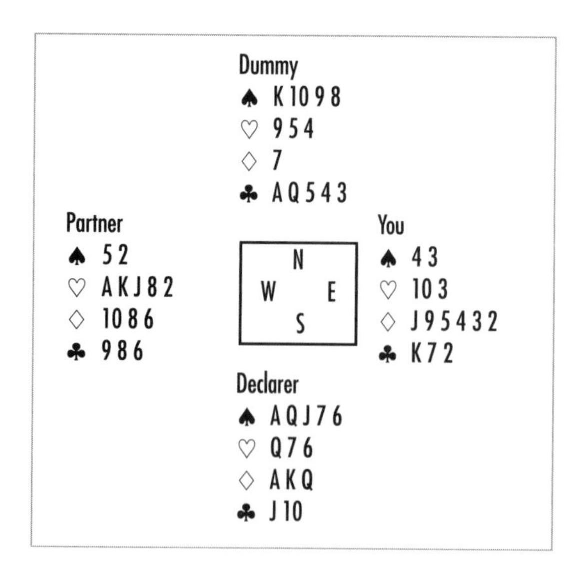

Let's look at one more very important example. Suppose this is the deal (left).

When partner leads the ♡A, you suspect that he has the ♡K as well. You want him to play three rounds of hearts so that you can trump the third round. Give partner a (bridge) smile and play the ♡10 on his ace. When partner plays the ♡K, you play the ♡3, which makes it clear that you like hearts, since your first heart was a high one. Now partner will know to play a third heart. In fact, this is the only way to defeat this contract, since if partner does not play hearts, declarer can discard dummy's hearts on his own high diamonds.

Deal 1 — Dealer South

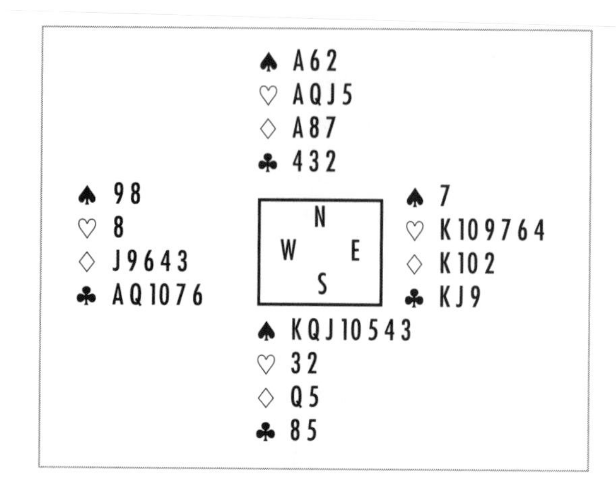

Neither side vulnerable.

West	North	East	South
			3♠
pass	4♠	all pass	

With an excellent seven-card suit, South opens 3♠. His hand satisfies the Rule of 2 and 3 not vulnerable. West passes and North has enough to raise to 4♠ with a reasonable expectation of making the contract. West leads his singleton heart.

Declarer counts his losers. He has two club losers, a diamond loser and a heart loser. One too many. He could finesse in hearts and hope that West has the ♡K. Even if it loses, he will be able to throw his diamond loser away on the ♡J. There is one problem with this plan. If West has led a singleton heart, East will win the king and return a heart for West to trump. The defense can take two top clubs and then East can lead a third heart for West to trump — down two.

Declarer must resist the temptation of the heart finesse and instead win the ♡A at Trick 1. He can then draw trumps and give up a heart to East's ♡K. After that, he can throw a diamond on the ♡J and make his contract. This line of play gives up the chance of an overtrick if West has led from the ♡K, but more importantly, it guarantees making the contract.

Deal 2 — Dealer West

East-West vulnerable.

West	North	East	South
1♠	3♢	3♡	pass
4♡	all pass		

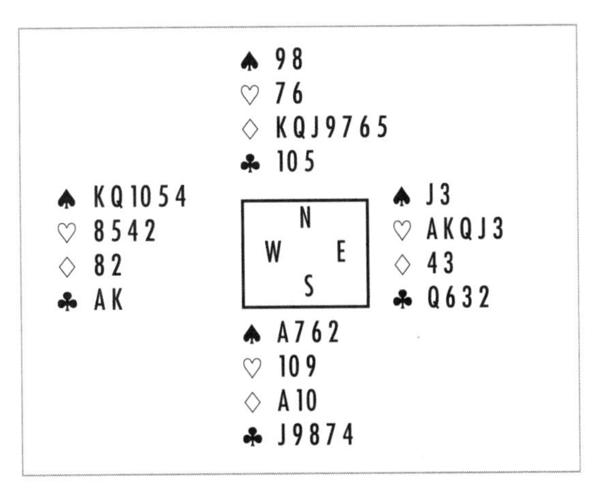

West opens the bidding with 1♠. North has a good seven-card suit and six tricks — enough for a preemptive jump overcall at the three-level at this vulnerability. Next, with a full opening bid, East can introduce his good heart suit. This bid is forcing. With four trumps for his partner, West raises to 4♡. North's bid helps South to find the best lead of the ♢A. North 'smiles' by playing the ♢9 and South continues with another diamond.

Declarer counts his losers. He has the two diamond losers and the ♠A to lose as well. His plan is to lead trumps as soon as possible and then force out the ♠A to set up his spade winners. If North plays a third round of diamonds at Trick 3, declarer has to be careful to trump it with a high heart. North is almost certain to have seven diamonds and declarer cannot afford to have South overruff the third diamond with the ♡10 or the ♡9.

Deal 3 — Dealer North

Both vulnerable.

West	North	East	South
	2♡	pass	2NT
pass	3♢	pass	4♡
all pass			

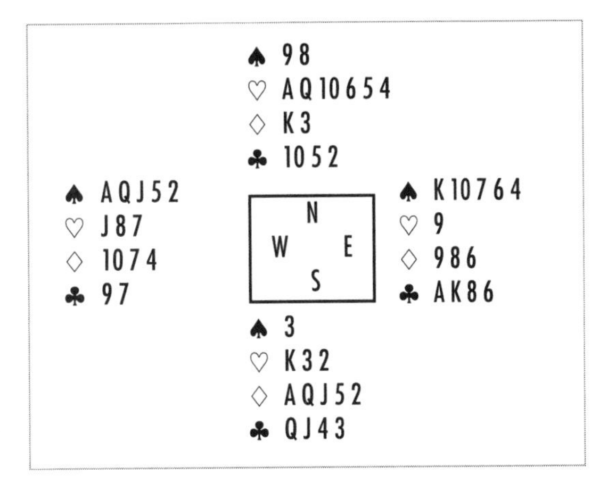

North opens with a weak two-bid in hearts. East passes and South considers whether he has enough to raise North to game in hearts. Feeling unsure, he decides to find out more by bidding 2NT. When North shows the ♢K, South likes the prospects a lot better and bids 4♡.

East starts off with the ♣A and when West plays the encouraging ♣9, he continues with two more rounds of clubs, West trumping. West will cash the ♠A and defeat the contract.

Even though the contract did not make, South did not make a mistake by bidding 4♡. First, 4♡ has just three top losers (without the ruff) and will make a lot of the time. Second, as it turns out, East-West can make nine tricks in spades, so even if North-South go down one, it is better than letting East-West play and make 3♠.

The defense did very well here by selecting the right lead and using an attitude signal to find the club ruff.

Deal 4 — Dealer East

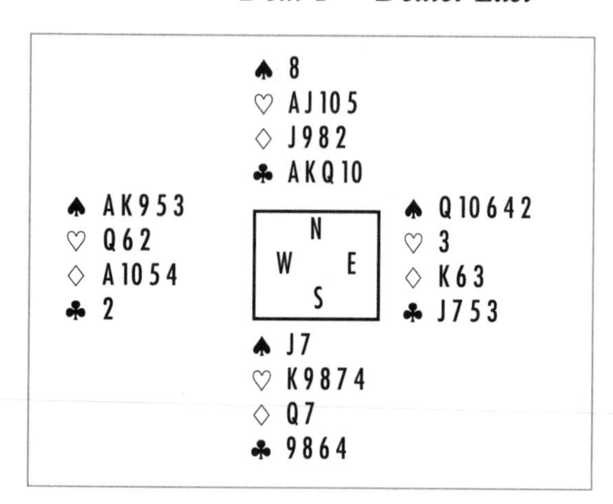

Neither vulnerable.

West	North	East	South
		pass	pass
1♠	dbl	4♠	all pass

After East and South both pass, West opens the hand 1♠. North has an excellent hand with support for all of the unbid suits and makes a takeout double. With five-card trump support for his partner, East leaps all the way to 4♠, a preemptive game raise. South just doesn't have enough to bid 5♡.

North starts off with the ♣A and South discourages with the ♣4. North may choose to play the ♣K next anyway, since he has the ♣Q as well, making it a fairly safe continuation. Declarer will trump the ♣K. Now he stops to count his losers. He has three heart losers, two diamond losers and a club loser. He can trump two heart losers in dummy. If trumps divide 2-1, he will also have enough trumps in dummy for his diamond loser if diamonds don't break. Declarer starts off with the ♠A and when the trumps split, he is sure of his contract. He draws the remaining trump and eventually ruffs one diamond loser and two heart losers in dummy.

CHAPTER**SUMMARY**

A A weak two-bid is an opening bid of 2♢, 2♡, or 2♠, which shows
- 6-10 HCP (and no more than 12 total points).
- a good six-card suit.
- no side four-card major.

B Responses to a weak two-bid are:
- Raise to the three-level with three trumps and a weak hand (for play).
- Raise to the four-level on any hand with four trumps.
- Bid 2NT to find out if partner has a feature in another suit (ace or king).
- Bid a new suit with a good hand and a good five-card suit.

C With a seven-card suit, open at the three-level.

D With an eight-card suit and 6-10 total points, open at the four-level.

E Use the Rule of 2 and 3, which says you should expect to go down two tricks vulnerable and three tricks not vulnerable. Responses:
- Pass.
- Bid game if you have enough tricks in aces and kings.
- With a very good hand and a good suit of your own, you can bid that suit (it is forcing below game).

F A preemptive jump overcall at the two-level can be made on a hand similar to a weak-two bid; a preemptive jump overcall at the three-level can be made on a hand similar to a three-level preempt.

G Use an attitude signal on defense when partner leads a high card:
- A high spot card means you like the suit.
- A low spot card means you can't help partner in that suit. Low means 'No!'

Appendix

Rubber Bridge Scoring

We	They
860	210
500	
150	30
40	60
70	
	120
100	

The traditional method of scoring at bridge is as follows.

A scoresheet is used like the one shown here. The left hand side of the sheet is used to enter the scores for the "We" side (the one doing the scoring) and all scores for the "They" side are entered on the right hand side. Your goal in rubber bridge is to make two games before the opponents do. The dark horizontal line is important because it is used to separate overtricks, bonuses and penalties from points that count towards making game.

The only points that go "below the line" are the trick scores for contracts bid and made. All other points are scored above the line. The same values are used for trick scores and penalties as in all bridge scoring. Thus if you bid 2♠ and make nine tricks you score 60 below the line (for 2♠) and 30 above the line (for the overtrick). And if you defeat a contract of 4♠ three tricks not vulnerable you get 150 above the line.

There is one bonus score peculiar to rubber bridge: **honors.** In a suit contract, any player holding four of the top five honors in trumps is given 100 points; holding all five top honors (ace through ten) is worth 150 points. In notrump, any player holding all four aces is awarded 150 for honors.

The first side to accumulate 100 points below the line has won the first game and become vulnerable. This can be done in one deal or a series of deals. A line is drawn on the sheet as shown to indicate that a new game is starting at nil-nil and any new trick scores are entered below the new line.

The first side to score up two games has won the rubber and gets a bonus: 500 for winning the rubber 2-1, and 700 for winning it 2-0. This replaces the game and partscore bonuses that you receive in other forms of scoring. For example, you do not get an extra 50 points for making a partscore. However, the usual bonus is still awarded if you bid and make a slam.

At the end of the rubber, all the points for each side are added together, both above and below the line, and the winner is the side with the higher total – which may not be the side which won the rubber!

Where do you go from here?

Okay, so now you can play bridge — at least, you can play well enough to have fun with your friends. But bridge is a game that you never stop learning, however good you get to be. Here are a few ways that you can expand your bridge horizons and sample more of the fascinating world that is just opening up for you.

Read more books

(You knew we were going to say that!) Thousands of books have been written about bridge. Here's a very short list of titles that you may find helpful in expanding your bridge knowledge:

25 Ways to Take More Tricks as Declarer (Barbara Seagram / David Bird)
The basic ideas of declarer play explained for newcomers to the game

25 Ways to be a Better Defender (Barbara Seagram / David Bird)
The basic ideas of defense explained for newcomers to the game

25 Ways to Compete in the Bidding (Barbara Seagram / Marc Smith)
Better competitive bidding makes you a tougher opponent

25 Bridge Conventions You Should Know (Barbara Seagram / Marc Smith)
The best-selling bridge book since Charles Goren was writing in the 1950s — add these popular and handy gadgets to your bidding arsenal

Modern Bridge Defense (Eddie Kantar)
A comprehensive basic book on defense by one of the game's best players and writers (also available as interactive software)

The Pocket Guide to Bridge (Barbara Seagram / Ray Lee)
A neat carry-along ready reference for basic bidding

All these titles should be available at most good bookstores. You can also find them at bridge supply houses such as Baron Barclay (1-800-274-2221) in the USA.

Barbara Seagram's **Cheat Sheet** is another invaluable aid for new players. It is available from bridge supply houses and also directly from the author (www.barbaraseagram.com). It is a detailed summary of standard bidding that you can keep in your lap and refer to while you play.

A great way to practice your declarer play is with Fred Gitelman's *Bridge Master 2000* software — but make sure you get the Beginner edition!

Find a bridge club and/or take lessons

There is almost certainly a bridge club in the area where you live. If you live in a large city, there may be several. A bridge club runs duplicate games, and often there will be separate events for novice players. Most clubs will help you find a partner if you show up on your own. To find a bridge club in North America, check the listings on the American Contract Bridge League web site (www.acbl.org). Many bridge clubs also offer lessons at various levels, which is another good way to improve your game. You can also look for a local teacher through the American Bridge Teachers' Association (www.abtahome.com).

Play more bridge

The best way to get more out of this wonderful game is to play more of it. Play in your own home with friends, or summon up your courage and head out to a local bridge club — you'll soon meet lots of people who share your passion. If you really get into the game, you may want to try a local tournament — again, these will often feature events restricted to newcomers, so you don't have to play against the sharks!

And today, you can even play bridge online. There are a number of bridge-playing Internet sites, but the most popular is Bridge Base Online (www.bridgebase.com/online), in part because it's absolutely free. Just download the software (also free) and you'll quickly find yourself in a world-wide bridge club. Sit down at a table, pick up a hand, and start playing — it's as simple as that. The site keeps detailed records of all the hands and results, so you can look at what other people did on the same cards and see how you might improve. Play at any time of the day or night, for as short or long a time as you want. Players indicate their level, so you can easily find a group playing at the same standard as yourself. Have fun and make new bridge friends from all over the world. BBO also offers shows that feature world championships and other top competitions, with expert commentary. Log in any time and watch the very best that bridge has to offer.

Finally...

It's entirely possible that we have done a terrible thing to you by helping you learn to play bridge. Like many others before you, you may have taken the first steps along the road to a lifelong addiction. If that is so, we make no apology. You're going to have a great time, so enjoy it.

Happy bridging!

GLOSSARY OF **TERMS**

Adequate Trump Support
Three cards including an honor in partner's suit (or any three if partner is known to have at least a five-card suit).

Artificial Bid
A bid that does not mean what it says; a convention.

Attitude Signal
When partner leads a suit, the spot card you play tells partner whether or not you like the suit. A high spot card says you like the suit and a low spot card says you don't.

Auction
A bidding process in which each side bids for the contract.

Balanced Hand
A hand with even distribution and no short suits — at most one doubleton.

Blackwood
A conventional bid of 4NT once a trump suit has been agreed, to ask for aces in a slam auction.

Book
The first six tricks taken by declarer. These tricks have no value in the scoring.

Broken Sequence
An imperfect sequence, featuring a gap between the second and third cards. Examples: KQ10, Q J9.

Captain
When one player has made a limited bid showing an exact point range, his partner becomes 'captain' of the auction and can take charge of the bidding.

Chicago Scoring
A popular way to play bridge, where vulnerability rotates around the table, and bonuses are awarded for making partscore, game or slam.

Contract
The final bid of the auction. It identifies the trump suit (if any) and the number of tricks above book that must be taken by the partnership that won the auction.

Convention
A bid with a specific agreed-upon artificial meaning. It may not say anything about the suit bid.

Cuebid
A bid of the opponents' suit. It does not show length in the suit bid. When used in response to a takeout double, it is forcing to game.

Deal
The distribution of fifty-two cards dealt around the table to all four players.

Dealer
The player who distributes the cards at the start of a deal. Dealer always starts the auction, by bidding or passing.

Declarer
The player who first named the final denomination (suit or notrump) for the side that won the auction. Declarer decides what to play to each trick from both his hand and dummy.

Defenders
The opening leader and his partner, whose goal it is to prevent declarer from taking all of the tricks he needs to make his contract.

Discard
If a player has no cards in the suit led, then he can 'discard', which is to play any card he chooses.

Double
A bid of 'double' raises the stakes: the opponents get more for making their contract and you will get more if they go down. Often a special meaning is assigned to a double (see **Takeout Double**).

Drawing Trumps
The act of leading high trumps to remove the opponents trumps. Some people call it 'pulling' trumps or 'getting the kiddies off the street'.

Dummy
Declarer's partner's hand, which is laid face up on the table after the opening lead.

Dummy Points
A way of evaluating your hand when you have a fit for partner's suit (and thus your hand will be dummy), placing high value on your short suits.

Entry
A winner that allows declarer or a defender to get from one hand to the other.

Excellent Trump Support
Four-card support for partner's suit.

Finesse
A method of making tricks by leading towards your high cards; this can enable you to win a trick even when you are missing a top honor.

Following Suit
Playing a card of the suit led to the trick (if you have one). The rules of bridge require you to follow suit, if you can do so.

Forcing
A forcing bid is one that partner may not pass. A bid may be forcing for this turn only, or may be forcing until a game contract is reached.

Game
A contract that is worth at least 100 points: 3NT, 4♡, 4♠, 5♣ and 5◇ are all game contracts.

Go Down
Fail to make your contract.

Grand Slam
A bid of seven of anything (7♣, 7◇, 7♡, 7♠ or 7NT); a contract to take all of the tricks.

Hand
The thirteen cards a bridge player is dealt.

Hold-Up
A strategy of refusing to win a trick with a high honor, saving the winner for a later trick.

Honor
Any card above the ten in a suit.

Honors
At rubber bridge, a bonus scored for holding four or five of the top trumps in one hand, or all four aces at notrump.

Jacoby Transfer
In response to an opening 1NT bid, a bid of 2◇ asks partner to bid 2♡; a bid of 2♡ asks partner to bid 2♠. This promises at least five cards in the transfer suit. A similar convention can be used in other notrump auctions, such as when responding to an opening 2NT bid.

Jump Overcall
An overcall in a suit made one level higher than necessary.

Jump Shift
A jump bid in a new suit. When responder makes a jump shift at his first bid, it shows 19+ points and is game-forcing.

Lead
The person who plays the first card to a trick is said to lead to the trick.

Limit Raise
A raise to three of a suit in response to an opening bid in the same suit. It shows 10-12 points and excellent trump support.

Limited Bid
A bid that shows a specific point range.

Major Suits
The two higher-ranking suits: hearts (second from top) and spades (top).

Minor Suits
The two lower-ranking suits: clubs (lowest) and diamonds (second from bottom).

Not Forcing
A bid which partner may pass if he wants to.

Not Vulnerable
When not vulnerable, a pair scores smaller bonuses for game, small and grand slams, and suffers lower penalties for going down than they would if vulnerable.

Notrump
The highest denomination. Notrump contracts are played without a trump suit.

Opening Lead
The very first card played in a deal, by declarer's left-hand opponent.

Opening Leader
The person on declarer's left, who starts the play by leading to the first trick.

Overcall
A bid of a new suit or notrump after an opponent has opened the bidding.

Overtricks
Tricks that the declaring side takes over and above the contract requirements.

Partscore
A contract worth less than 100 points.

Playing Strength
The trick-taking potential of a hand, as opposed to the high-card strength.

Preemptive Bid
A bid designed to use up space in the auction and to make it difficult for the opponents to bid effectively. A preemptive opening bid such as 3♠ is made with a weak hand and a long strong suit.

Preference
A bid that chooses between two suits partner has bid.

Raise
A higher bid in partner's suit.

Responder
The partner of the player who opens the bidding.

Rubber Bridge
A form of bridge in which your objective is to make two games (called 'winning the rubber') before the opponents do.

Ruff, Ruffing
See *Trumping.*

Single Raise
A raise of partner's bid by one level (e.g. bidding 2♠ in response to 1♠), which shows that you have a fit for partner's suit.

Slam
A contract at the six- or seven-level.

Small Slam
A bid of six of anything (6♣, 6♢, 6♡, 6♠ or 6NT); a contract to take twelve tricks.

Stayman
A conventional response in clubs that asks an opening notrump bidder whether he holds a four-card major (e.g. a 2♣ response to 1NT).

Stopper
A likely winner in a suit that will prevent the opponents from taking lots of tricks in the suit right away.

Takeout Double
A double of an opponent's bid that asks partner to choose one of the unbid suits.

Transfer
A conventional bid that asks partner to bid a suit, instead of doing so yourself. A common example is a **Jacoby Transfer**.

Trick
During the play, each player in turn, going clockwise, places a card face up on the table until four cards have been played.

Trump Suit
The suit decided (through the bidding) to be worth more than the other suits; a card played in the trump suit will beat any card played in an ordinary suit.

Trumping (also called 'Ruffing')
Playing a trump when a different suit has been led. This can be done if you cannot follow suit.

Undertricks
Tricks by which the declaring side falls short of making its contract.

Unlimited Bid
A bid whose upper range is as yet unknown. An unlimited bid is always forcing.

Vulnerable
When vulnerable, a pair gets bigger bonuses for game, small and grand slams, and suffers larger penalties for going down.

Waiting Bid
This type of bid gives partner room to tell you exactly what type of hand he has — you are waiting to hear more from partner before you start to describe your hand.

Weak Two-Bid
An opening suit bid at the two-level made on a weak hand with a good suit.

Winner
A trick that you can take without giving up the lead.